CREATIVE
HOMEOWNER®

WALLS, WALKS & PATIOS

CREATIVE HOMEOWNER®, Upper Saddle River, New Jersey

CREATIVE HOMEOWNER®

COPYRIGHT © 1997
CREATIVE HOMEOWNER®
A Division of Federal Marketing Corp.
Upper Saddle River, NJ

Editorial Director: Timothy O. Bakke
Art Director: Annie Jeon

Editors: Jeff Day, David Schiff
Copy Editor: Candice Levy, Ph.D.
Editorial Assistant: Georgette Blau

Graphic Designers: Melisa DelSordo
                   Heidi Garner
                   John Larimer
Illustrators: Ron Carboni
              Craig Franklin
              Paul M. Schumm

Cover Design: Annie Jeon
Cover Photo: Jessie Walker
Photo Researcher: Georgette Blau

Manufactured in the United States of America

Current Printing (last digit)
10 9 8 7 6 5

Walls, Walks & Patios
Library of Congress Catalog Card Number: 97-68497
ISBN: 1-880029-97-9

CREATIVE HOMEOWNER®
A Division of Federal Marketing Corp.
24 Park Way, Upper Saddle River, NJ 07458
Web site: www.creativehomeowner.com

Photo Credits

Title page: Catriona Tudor Erler, Vienna, VA
p.6: Crandall & Crandall, Dana Point, CA
p.7: Photo Network/Gay Bumgarner, Photographer, Tustin, CA
p.13: ALD Photography, Glen Rock, NJ
p.14: H. Armstrong Roberts, New York, NY
p.15: James M. Mejuto, Ossining, NY
p.19 (top l): James M. Mejuto, Ossining, NY
p.19 (top r): Omni-Photo Communications, Inc., New York, NY
p.21 (bot. l): Light Sources Stock/Paul Rocheleau, Photographer, Richmond, MA
p.21 (bot. r): Photo Network, Tustin, CA
p.22: H. Armstrong Roberts, New York, NY
p.33: Karen Bussolini, South Kent, CT
p.34 (top): Crandall & Crandall, Dana Point, CA
p.34 (mid.): John Schwartz, New York, NY
p.34 (bot.): James M. Mejuto, Ossining, NY
p.35 (top): Melabee M Miller, Hillside, NJ
P.35 (mid.): Southern Forest Products Association, Kenner, LA
p.35 (bot.): Southern Forest Products Association, Kenner, LA
p.36: Terry Wild Studio, Williamsport, PA
p.52: Paul M. Schumm/Creative Homeowner Press
p.57: Crandall & Crandall, Dana Point, CA
p.71: Steve Skjold, St. Paul, MN
p.86: Crandall & Crandall, Dana Point, CA
p.97: Steve Skjold, St. Paul, MN
p.98 (top l): Mark Turner, Bellingham, WA
p.98 (top r): Karen Bussolini, South Kent, CT
p.98 (bot.): Jerry Pavia, Bonners Ferry, ID
p.99 (top): H. Armstrong Roberts/Camerique, New York, NY
p.99 (bot. l): Bobbi Lane, Los Angeles, CA
p.99 (bot. mid.): Crandall & Crandall, Dana Point, CA
p.99 (bot. r): Crandall & Crandall, Dana Point, CA
p.100: (top l & r): Karen Bussolini, South Kent, CT
p.100: (bot.): Eric Roth, Boston, MA
p.101: Saxon Holt, Boyes Hot Springs, CA
p.107: Mark Turner, Bellingham, WA
p.115: Catriona Tudor Erler, Vienna, VA
p.130: Nancy Hill, Mt. Kisco, NY
p.148: Crandall & Crandall, Dana Point, CA
p.163: Photo Network/Gay Bumgarner, Tustin, CA
p.164 (top): Crandall & Crandall, Dana Point, CA
p.164 (bot.): Melabee M Miller, Hillside, NJ
p.165: H. Armstrong Roberts, New York, NY
p.166 (top): Nancy Hill, Mt. Kisco, NY
p.166 (bot.): Melabee M Miller, Hillside, NJ
p.167 (top): Karen Bussolini, South Kent, CT
p.167 (bot.): Melabee M Miller, Hillside, NJ
p.168 (top and bot. l): Karen Bussolini, South Kent, CT
p.168 (bot. r): Crandall & Crandall, Dana Point, CA
p.169: H. Armstrong Roberts/Camerique, New York, NY
p.175: Portland Cement Association, Portland, OR
p.182: Catriona Tudor Erler, Vienna, VA
Back cover (top): Paul M. Schumm/Creative Homeowner Press
Back cover (bot. l): H. Armstrong Roberts/Camerique, New York, NY
Back cover (bot. r): Crandall & Crandall, Dana Point, CA

Though all the designs and methods in this book have been reviewed for safety, it is not possible to overstate the importance of using the safest construction methods possible. What follows are reminders; some do's and don'ts of basic carpentry. They are not substitutes for your own common sense.

- *Always* use caution, care, and good judgment when following the procedures described in this book.

- *Always* be sure that the electrical setup is safe; be sure that no circuit is overloaded and that all power tools and electrical outlets are properly grounded. Do not use power tools in wet locations.

- *Always* read container labels on paints, solvents, and other products; provide ventilation, and observe all other warnings.

- *Always* read the manufacturer's instructions for using a tool, especially the warnings.

- *Always* use hold-downs and push sticks whenever possible when working on a table saw. Avoid working short pieces if you can.

- *Always* remove the key from any drill chuck (portable or press) before starting the drill.

- *Always* pay deliberate attention to how a tool works so that you can avoid being injured.

- *Always* know the limitations of your tools. Do not try to force them to do what they were not designed to do.

- *Always* make sure that any adjustment is locked before proceeding. For example, always check the rip fence on a table saw or the bevel adjustment on a portable saw before starting to work.

- *Always* clamp small pieces firmly to a bench or other work surface when using a power tool on them.

- *Always* wear the appropriate rubber or work gloves when handling chemicals, moving or stacking lumber, or doing heavy construction.

- *Always* wear a disposable face mask when you create dust by sawing or sanding. Use a special filtering respirator when working with toxic substances and solvents.

- *Always* wear eye protection, especially when using power tools or striking metal on metal or concrete; a chip can fly off, for example, when chiseling concrete.

- *Always* be aware that there is seldom enough time for your body's reflexes to save you from injury from a power tool in a dangerous situation; everything happens too fast. Be alert!

- *Always* keep your hands away from the business ends of blades, cutters, and bits.

- *Always* hold a circular saw firmly, usually with both hands so that you know where they are.

- *Always* use a drill with an auxiliary handle to control the torque when large-size bits are used.

- *Always* check your local building codes when planning new construction. The codes are intended to protect public safety and should be observed to the letter.

- *Never* work with power tools when you are tired or under the influence of alcohol or drugs.

- *Never* cut tiny pieces of wood or pipe using a power saw. Cut small pieces off larger pieces.

- *Never* change a saw blade or a drill or router bit unless the power cord is unplugged. Do not depend on the switch being off; you might accidentally hit it.

- *Never* work in insufficient lighting.

- *Never* work while wearing loose clothing, hanging hair, open cuffs, or jewelry.

- *Never* work with dull tools. Have them sharpened, or learn how to sharpen them yourself.

- *Never* use a power tool on a workpiece—large or small—that is not firmly supported.

- *Never* saw a workpiece that spans a large distance between horses without close support on each side of the cut; the piece can bend, closing on and jamming the blade, causing saw kickback.

- *Never* support a workpiece from underneath with your leg or other part of your body when sawing.

- *Never* carry sharp or pointed tools, such as utility knives, awls, or chisels, in your pocket. If you want to carry such tools, use a special-purpose tool belt with leather pockets and holders.

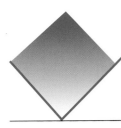

CONTENTS

INTRODUCTION

Walls, walks, and patios can turn an outdoor area into a living space. A brick, stone, or block wall adds character and privacy. A patio links your house and yard, providing outdoor living, eating, cooking, and entertainment space. Walks connect the focal points of your yard, both physically and visually.

While you can build any of these projects by itself, it pays to think about how each will affect your yard and how each affects the other. How do you balance the different parts of your design? How do you use the terrain to your advantage? How can you make a site appealing? The design section that makes up the first two chapters of this book shows you how professional landscape designers think about such questions. In simple language, these chapters help you design the projects you'll build. They show you how to get your ideas onto paper, and more importantly, from paper into your yard.

A section on walls, a section on walks, and one on patios follow the design section. The first chapters of each section have the easiest projects; the later chapters have the more advanced projects. Each chapter begins with the technical information you'll need—how high you can build, what type of stone you'll need, and so on. The second part of each chapter is projects. If you're just getting your feet wet, choose projects in the front of the chapter. If you're ready to take on some serious building, look in the back of the chapter. No matter which you choose, simple, thorough directions will get you from the store to the finished project.

Think seriously about how much effort you want to put into a project. A mortared retaining wall can be a major undertaking. If you're looking for something you can do in a weekend or two, consider a mortarless wall made of interlocking landscape blocks.

Or maybe you'd like to build a garden path. Thumb through the section on walks and pick one that matches your needs and ambitions. Stepping stones or a gravel walk may give you both the look and the service you need, while a more durable mortared stone path requires an entire sidewalk underneath it for support. If you would like something in between, consider brick placed on a sand bed. The excavation required may not be any more than that required for a gravel path. And brick over a sand bed is durable—so durable that it once was used to make streets.

Patios, too, come in a variety of shapes and materials. A mortared brick patio looks elegant but involves a lot of work—you'll need to pour a concrete pad to support it. But a patio made of prefabricated landscape pavers requires nothing more than sand and gravel underneath. There's no mortar required, so you can take your time, cutting and fitting as you go.

Somewhere between is the utilitarian concrete slab. You have options here, too. You can excavate, set the forms, and learn concrete finishing as you go, or you can simply build the forms and have a mason do the concrete work.

Given the wide variety of materials and techniques, you're bound to find a method that will be fun and still create the look you want. As you're trying to decide on the best approach for your project, be sure to talk with sales staff at materials yards, hardware stores, and home improvement centers. Find out what the favorite local stone is or which bricks will withstand the local weather. Local codes, customs, and availability may make certain materials and techniques affordable in one area and cost prohibitive in another.

A final note: The materials you're likely to use for walls, walks, and patios are heavier than they are for almost any other project. Take it easy on your car: Rent a truck or have the material delivered. Take it easy on your back, too. Lift with your knees, and have help around for the really big part of the job.

PLANNING AND DESIGN

PRINCIPLES OF SITE DESIGNING AND PLANNING

A good site design, like a hearty homemade soup, is a rich blend of ingredients and flavors. These elements are a mixture of technical considerations (originating from the constraints and opportunities of your site and budget) and creative possibilities (originating from within you and influenced by your particular needs). One of the most exciting challenges to every design is that each site is unique and brings with it a unique set of opportunities.

Site design and planning complete your yard. A well-designed site extends your house beyond the walls and helps to bring your daily life into contact with the outdoors. The benefits to you can be substantial and rewarding. By taking the time to understand a few basic principles about designing a site, you will be able to create an outdoor area that is more comfortable and relaxing; more private and secure; warmer in the winter and cooler in the summer; and, well, just more pleasant and satisfying to you, your family, and your friends.

WHAT DO YOU WANT YOUR SITE TO OFFER?

In many ways, the concept of site design goes back a long time. The Romans called it *genius loci*—spirit of place. A place affects all of our senses by providing a combination of sights, sounds, smells, textures, and temperatures. A place is memorable; we can return to it again and again in our minds whenever we want. We all have special places that we hold dear. A good site design can and should provide a memorable experience for all who visit that particular place. Essentially, there are two factors for you to consider as you begin the design process:

■ Identifying. This is the process of recognizing the unique combination of elements that your site has to offer. These could be such things as special views and vistas; natural features such as trees, rocks, or streams; or even historical artifacts or events that occurred there in the past. Any and all of these will add up to the unique spirit of your particular location. Spend some time getting acquainted with your landscape and noting these special features. Every site has something to tell you—you just need to listen to what it has to say.

■ Intensifying. Once you feel that you understand the special qualities and elements of your site, think of ways in which these features can be preserved and, better yet, enhanced through the placement of such things as walks, walls, patios, and vegetation.

Working with your surroundings. If your site is in a historic district or in an architecturally distinct region of the country—New England or the Southwest come to mind— your design will fit into these contexts if you make an effort to work with the prevailing materials, colors, and architectural elements. This doesn't necessarily mean copying or mimicking every little detail you can find in your neighborhood. There's still plenty of latitude here to design your personal interpretation of what you think makes your region or neighborhood unique. Of course, the choice of whether or not you want to fit into or stand out from your surroundings is entirely up to you. In fact, with so many of today's newer houses looking pretty much like duplicates of every other house in the neighborhood, this is the perfect opportunity to express your personal values and tastes.

Of the site versus to the site. Another concept related to location is the idea of "of the site versus to the site." A design that is considered of the site appears to grow or spring directly from what is already a part of the site, as if the new design were always meant to be there or as if the new design simply grew naturally from the inherent features of that site. Frank Lloyd Wright, the famous

American architect, liked to call this "organic design." On the other hand, a design that is considered to be to the site can be thought of as something imported or brought to the site from somewhere else, something like a New England Cape Cod house in the middle of the Sonora Desert. Although most professional site designers prefer the former approach, that doesn't mean you can't incorporate something like a Japanese Zen rock and sand garden into your design if you wish. It simply means being sensitive and not trying to force something onto the site that seems unnatural or incongruous. As with much of site design (particularly drainage!), the best advice is to work with the site and not against it.

Formal Versus Informal

As you start the design process, consider whether you want a highly formal layout; a more relaxed, informal layout; or some combination of both. Consider the size and shape of your lot, the style of the house itself, and your own lifestyle needs and preferences. Formal site layouts are usually symmetric and uniform, whereas informal site layouts are typically asymmetric with irregular or naturally flowing shapes. Feel free to mix formal and informal layouts in your overall design; some of the most satisfying site plans have aspects of both. By combining these two approaches in close proximity, each will enhance and strengthen the other through their obvious contrasts. For example, you might try a formal patio layout integrated into a system of informal, curvilinear walks, walls, and planting areas (or just the opposite).

But remember that informal doesn't mean random or chaotic, neither of which is satisfying in the long run. An underlying sense of balance is just as important to informal layouts as it is to formal layouts. Base a curving walk or wall on circles, radii, and tangents, not just careless squiggles across your site.

Positive and negative spaces. Site designers often talk about creating positive and negative spaces. This is a simple yet extremely important aspect of designing a good site. Positive space refers to well-defined

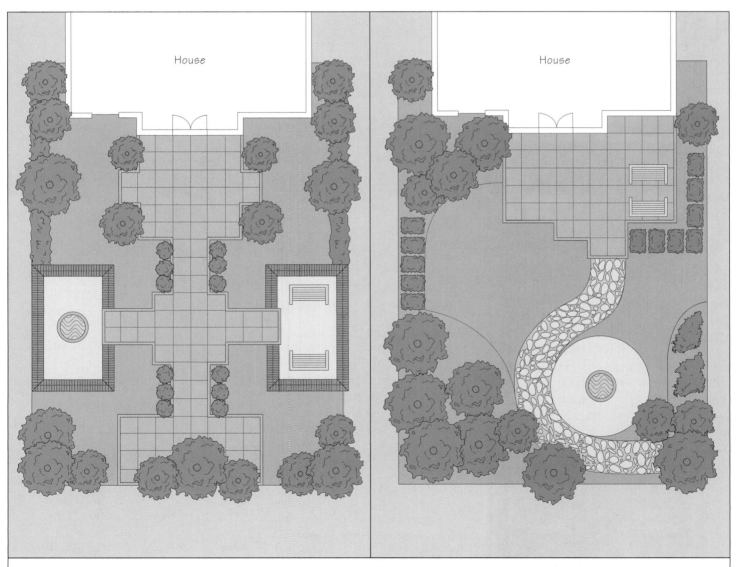

Formal versus informal. A symmetrical layout (left) tends to be more formal, while an asymmetrical plan (right) is casual. If you choose an asymmetrical plan, don't let it become random: Mix formal and informal design elements.

Positive and negative spaces. A positive space (top) provides a sense of enclosure and comfort. A negative space (bottom) is open and undefined.

and enclosed spaces, while negative space refers to poorly defined spaces and/or spaces with little or no sense of enclosure. Think of trying to drink out of a good solid coffee mug versus a sieve or of keeping your valuables in a good solid safe versus a paper bag. Positive spaces, with well-defined borders and edges—walls or walkways, for example—help to gather and contain as well as define spaces. They have a feeling of reaching around and embracing you. Negative spaces, on the other hand, tend to leak and flow out and away from you. As human beings we tend to find negative or shapeless spaces much less satisfying than well-defined, positive spaces.

Enclosure. The best site designs provide varying degrees of enclosure. A good way to think of enclosure is in terms of shelter—how much we

Enclosure. Walls, walks, fences, and plantings can extend from the house to provide enclosure and turn a negative space into a positive one.

are protected from the elements and how much the enclosure provides a sense of privacy and intimacy. A sense of enclosure or positive space is really very simple to achieve, but it certainly does not mean an airtight box! After all, we want to be outdoors to enjoy a free, open feeling. A low wall along the edge of a planting area or along the side of a walk—even the edge of a patio with one or more low planters—is all we need to provide a satisfying degree of enclosure.

A sense of security. Perhaps you remember how pleasant and secure it felt to sit on the front porch of your grandparents' house in the summertime, or perhaps you have another special place that gave you a feeling of security. Ever wish you could recreate that feeling? Well, you can. The people who study these types of things tell us that humans have a natural tendency to seek slightly elevated and sheltered places and to avoid open, exposed places whenever possible. The slight elevation allows

us to see farther in all directions, and the semi-open shelter provides us with a sense of security and allows us to watch and participate in the passing world. Whether it's in your front yard or backyard, you can

create this sense of security simply by elevating your patio slightly above the surrounding grade, providing a sense of enclosure with a few low walls and planters, and perhaps adding an overhead trellis or patio roof to provide shade and rain protection. Voilà! Time to make some lemonade.

Outdoor scale. A quick note about outdoor scale versus indoor scale. No rocket science here, folks. Outdoor spaces need to be scaled up from the typical dimensions used for rooms inside. If you are using an average-size room inside your house to get a feel for the size of your new patio, add a few extra feet to the dimensions, if possible. What seems like a perfectly adequate space inside can feel uncomfortably cramped and small when it is outside. And you thought we weren't going to give you a good reason for making that new patio just a little bit larger.

Forcing perspective. Here are a couple of neat tricks to use when working with small spaces. The perceived size of a space can be increased by slightly narrowing the far end of the area in relation to the width of the end nearest the viewer. This is called forced perspective. Our eyes trick our brains into thinking that the space is longer than it really is.

A sense of security. An elevated spot gives you a better view and a feeling of safety.

Forcing perspective. To make a short space seem longer, make the far end of the view narrower.

This type of perspective can be reinforced by placing larger or taller trees or shrubs in the foreground and then placing smaller, shorter trees or shrubs toward the far end of the space.

Varying texture. The other neat trick is to use fine and coarse textures to increase (or decrease) your perception of spatial depth. Think about standing on a small mountaintop and looking out into the distance. We can see every leaf on the trees and shrubs near us. Then as we look farther out into the distance, the leaves begin to blur until we can no longer perceive individual leaves or even individual trees. By varying the textures of the vegetation and/or the wall surfaces in small spaces from coarse at the near end to finely textured at the far end, you can trick your eyes into thinking that the space is larger than it really is. The reverse is also true (just in case you want to make a large space look smaller).

Other Considerations

Here are a few additional points to consider as you attempt to find the right site for your project.

Shrubs are coarser than brick walls.

Trees are coarser than shrubs.

Varying texture. Putting coarse textures in the foreground and finer textures in the background makes the background seem farther away. If you reverse the order, objects in the background appear closer.

Site repair. Instead of picking the nicest spot in your backyard to locate your new patio or other site improvements, choose an area that could stand some enhancement or repair; use this opportunity to fix up the neglected area.

Maintenance. It goes without saying that maintenance is an important consideration, especially outdoors. Once your new patio and walks are constructed, it's time to take care of them. Obviously, it pays to select durable and easily cleaned materials, but keep in mind that your design can also create headaches when it comes to cleaning, raking, sweeping, shoveling snow, etc. Odd angles and tight corners might increase your cleaning tasks. If you live in snow country, ask yourself where you will pile the snow from your walks and patio, and plan accordingly.

Life-cycle costs. Over the long run, the cheapest materials may turn out to be the most expensive if they need to be replaced or repaired often. For example, if you have 100 square feet of a material that costs $3.00 per square foot and it needs to be totally replaced every five years, the annual replacement cost will be $60.00 (100 square feet x $3.00 = $300.00 divided by 5 years). On the other hand, if you pick a material that costs $4.50 per square foot and it needs to be replaced every ten years, the annual replacement cost will only be $45.00 (100 square feet x $4.50 = $450.00 divided by 10 years). Balance initial costs with long-term replacement and maintenance costs when designing a project.

A QUICK COURSE IN SITE DESIGN

To get to the point where you can put your ideas onto a site drawing, you will first have to understand some basic techniques and terms involved in designing your site. Then you will have to know how to organize all this information.

Basic Design Techniques

These basic design techniques are more or less common to all design professions including artists. They can be used to help you create your new site design both in two dimensions (your plan concept) and in three dimensions (how it will look when actually built).

Balance. This is the process of arranging various site elements so that they are resolved and balanced. Think of a fulcrum or teeter-totter as

Balance. You can visually balance large, dark objects such as a group of conifer trees with an object such as a gazebo that has more color or texture.

you attempt to balance the elements. A visually heavy or larger object can be balanced by a lighter or smaller object in the site if the smaller object is darker in color value, is unusually or irregularly shaped, has a contrasting texture, or is more elaborately detailed. All of these strategies will help to draw attention to the smaller object and thereby visually balance it with the larger object. For example, let's say you have a large clump of conifer trees on one side of your yard. To visually balance the trees you might plant smaller, more colorful ornamental trees on the other side of the yard, or you might use a man-made object such as a decorative fountain or a gazebo.

Harmony. Harmony can be achieved by selecting and using elements that share a common trait or characteristic. By using elements that are similar in size, shape, color, material, texture, or detail, you can create a cohesive

The steps, walls, and garden in this yard all use stone as a common element, a technique designers call harmony.

feeling and relation among the various elements on the site. An example of this might be a brick patio that is bordered by a brick planter near a brick walkway leading to a brick-lined garden area. In this case, the various elements are made of a common material. Another example might be using a common shape, such as a square. Imagine having a square concrete patio scored in a square (or diamond) pattern with a square table, square chairs, and a square-checkered tablecloth. Nothing too difficult here, and the results can be extremely pleasing and harmonious.

Unity and variety. While both balance and harmony are used to achieve unity, too much unity can be, well, boring. That's where variety and contrast come in handy. By varying size, shape, color, material, texture, and detail, you can introduce a note of interest or a focal point into the total composition. For instance, placing a round wooden planter onto the square-patterned patio discussed earlier will provide a pleasing contrast of both shape and material. The contrasting object (the round wooden planter) will

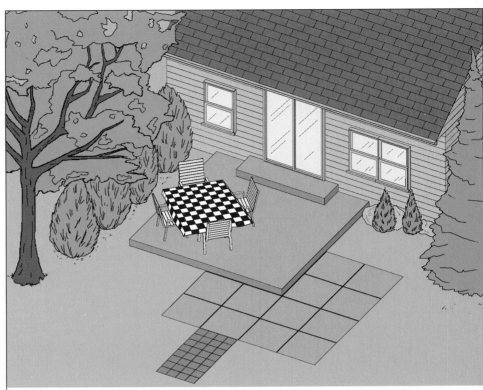

Harmony. Similar materials and repetition of similar shapes give a design visual harmony.

draw attention to itself and provide a degree of visual relief and interest to the total setting. This is the right time and place to add your individual touch, including a bit of whimsy or humor if that feels right. However, too much variety can be worse than too much unity and result in a confusing, chaotic jumble. When introducing variety into your plan layout, it's probably better to lean toward the conservative side.

The use of brick throughout this design unifies it. The round planter on the edge of the rectangular steps and patio creates variety.

Unity and variety. Too much harmony can be boring, and too much variety results in chaos. Mix the two to create a balanced look.

The dark, contrasting pavement in this walk punctuates and ties the walk together, giving the design what landscape architects call rhythm.

Rhythm. No, this isn't a dance class. In design terms, rhythm—or the spacing of elements relative to similar elements—can create another type of unity in a composition. Rhythm helps to establish a visually satisfying progression or sequence to a site design. For example, on a walkway, you can establish a regular rhythm if you place a band of decorative brick at 4-foot intervals. This acts as both a control joint and as a source of visual rhythm. Or as another example, you can place pilasters or half-columns along a brick or masonry wall at regular intervals, say every 8 feet. This again acts as a structural element and sets up a regular visual rhythm. On the other hand, a song composed of only one sequence of notes is boring. You can avoid visual boredom by varying such things as the interval, color, size, shape, texture, or material of the elements you use to create your sequence. Another fun way to introduce an interesting visual rhythm is to create subsets of elements between the evenly spaced

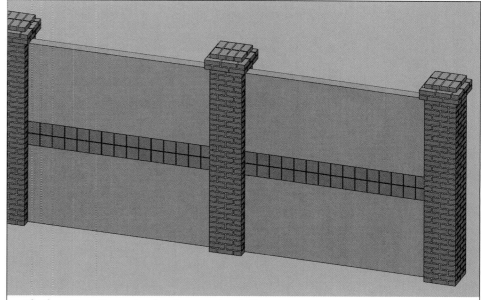

Rhythm. Repeating a visual pattern creates rhythm.

elements. For instance, between the regularly spaced pilasters of the brick or masonry wall in the example above you could place a series of colorful glazed tiles with their own rhythmic sequence.

Emphasis. This one is a lot like unity and variety and assumes that within your site some of the elements have more significance or importance than the rest and that these special elements should be somehow emphasized. This is probably starting to sound familiar to you by now, but we can give a special element its due emphasis by making it larger; by giving it a different shape (round versus square); by using a singular color,

Emphasis. Isolating an object with a unique size or shape helps emphasize its presence in your landscape.

texture, or material; by shifting or rotating its orientation; by centering it within a circle or at the end of a walkway; or literally by highlighting it at night with floodlights or accent lights. But like unity and variety, if you emphasize everything then nothing is really emphasized and you end up with a chaotic, visually confusing site design. Use this one with caution.

Simplicity. Just because simplicity is the last item on the list doesn't mean it's the least important. In fact, it's probably the most important of all—and you thought this was going to be complicated! Ironically, simplicity is also one of the hardest things to achieve in any design concept. That's because when you realize how many design tools and elements you have to work with, you have a natural tendency to want to use all of them. Remember trying to mix every color in your new watercolor set together just to see what that color would look like? Remember the results? In virtually every case, the most elegant and satisfying site designs are those that begin and end with simplicity as their guiding design principle. The Zen rock gardens of Japan are perhaps the best example of this way of designing—so much is said with so little effort. And that's probably because so much is left to our own individual interpretations. Subtlety and simplicity are good words to remember.

Dividing Your Design into Specific Parts

There is more to a design, however, than the actual physical parts and conceptual places of any given site. To help you arrive at your overall plan, you will have to juggle the following design elements.

Centers. Centers are gathering areas where people come together for a common purpose. We are typically drawn to centers because of their location or placement on the site and their sense of importance within the design. On a larger scale, some examples of centers might be the town square in a traditional New England village or even Rockefeller Center in New York.

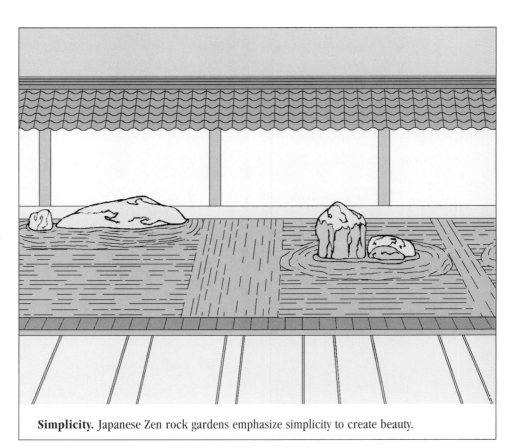

Simplicity. Japanese Zen rock gardens emphasize simplicity to create beauty.

Centers. The new patio will become a center of your landscape, no matter where it is located. Arrange it so that people can interact comfortably.

For our purposes, the obvious example of a center is the patio you are about to design. What are some of the social activities you intend to accommodate in your new patio?

Edges. Edges can be thought of as the linear boundaries between distinctly different areas. Edges can take many forms: natural features such as streams and rows of shrubs or man-

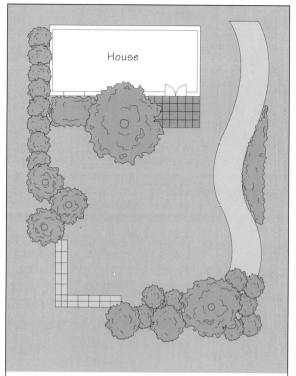

Edges. Edges can be natural or manmade. Use them to define the boundaries between areas of your yard.

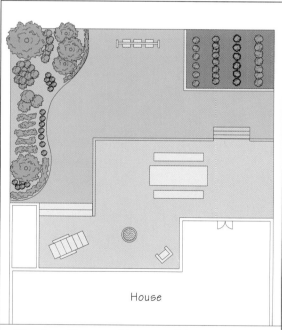

Districts. The central location of this patio breaks the yard into three distinct districts.

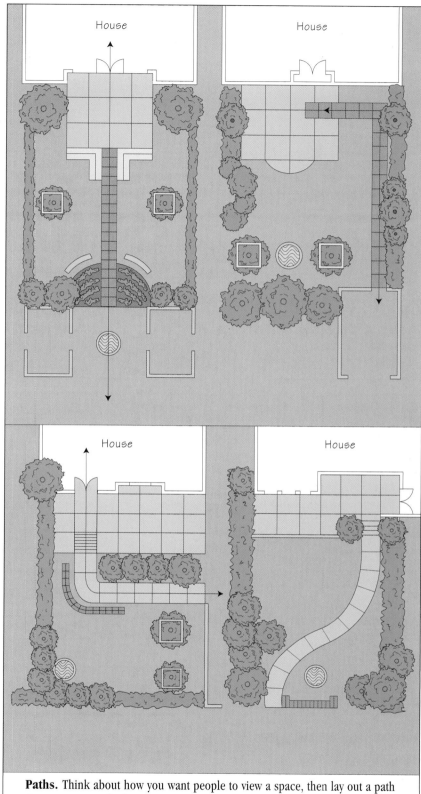

Paths. Think about how you want people to view a space, then lay out a path that meets your needs.

made elements such as fences and, more important, walls. Low walls, such as the ones illustrated in this book provide very effective edges between, for example, planting beds and lawns and can help to give these areas a crisp definition that is much more aesthetically pleasing than unclear, poorly defined boundaries.

Districts. Districts can also be thought of as areas, zones, or fields. For our purposes, examples of districts might include lawn areas, flower beds, play areas, gardens, and especially patios.

Paths. Paths are the obvious complements to the areas of your site, sometimes called outdoor rooms. Paths or, better yet, walks connect the outdoor rooms of your site together and make them usable and accessible and therefore deserve a high degree of thought and consideration on your part.

Nodes. Nodes are basically the same as centers, except that they are more closely associated with walks. You might also think of them as intersections or crossroads. Since intersections are typically busy places when there is a lot of traffic, consider enlarging the major nodes or intersections of your site plan to accommodate passing room or the occasional impromptu conversation.

How to Organize the Parts of Your Site Design

So how are you going to organize all the elements of your site? That's where the use of one or more ordering systems can help make sense of it all. These are the planning tools we can use to gather and arrange the physical places of your site into a cohesive, unified whole instead of a haphazard assortment of unrelated spaces. Keep in mind, though, that using an ordering system doesn't exclude variety, spontaneity, and points of emphasis within your plan. Also, you might consider using more than one ordering system, depending on which element or place you're designing. For example, a grid system might work best when you are laying out the walls for a lawn and garden area; then you might switch to a symmetrical layout for the patio and to an axial layout for the walks. Impress your friends and neighbors, not to mention your family. Let's see what's in the planning toolbox.

Axes. An axis is an imaginary yet powerful line. You can arrange your outdoor rooms or the lineal elements such as walks and walls on either side of an axis to achieve a sense of balance. An axis will end either in a panoramic view or with a symmetrical vertical element such as a statue, fountain, or arbor. Walks and sight lines are good places to use an axial layout.

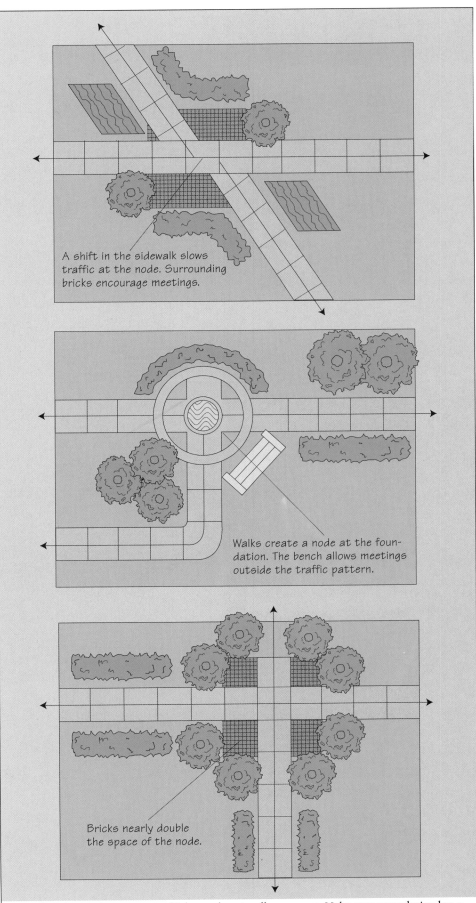

A shift in the sidewalk slows traffic at the node. Surrounding bricks encourage meetings.

Walks create a node at the foundation. The bench allows meetings outside the traffic pattern.

Bricks nearly double the space of the node.

Nodes. A node is an area at which people naturally converge. Make sure your design has a little extra space to accommodate the people who will meet there.

The light colored stone in this brick walk forms an axis along which other parts of this design are balanced.

This formal garden is laid out in a diamond grid. Smaller grids can be used to lay out the elements in your yard.

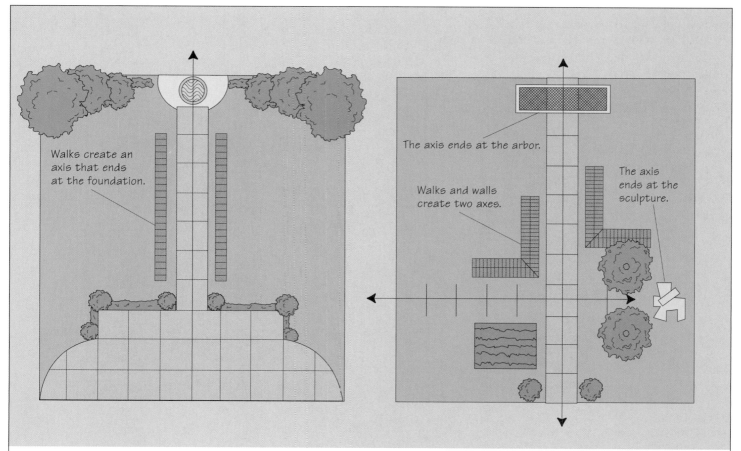

Walks create an axis that ends at the foundation.

The axis ends at the arbor.

Walks and walls create two axes.

The axis ends at the sculpture.

Axes. Walks and walls create axes within the yard. Organize elements around them. Make sure each axis is anchored by a visual element such as a fountain, arbor, or sculpture.

Grids. Grids can be useful in site design. For example, you might think of your yard as a nine-square grid. The illustration shows how you might overlay this grid on your site to organize such elements as patios, play areas, gardens and a gazebo. In arranging elements in your grid, consider such factors as traffic patterns, views, and the path of the sun over the yard.

Hierarchy. This is where we rank spaces and elements by order of importance. Every site plan will have certain spaces that are more important than others. Think of it this way: Normally, the living room is a far more important space than the utility room. You put your best furnishings and carpets and the most money into the living room—not the utility room. Of course, your priorities are up to you, but it's a good bet that your new patio is probably going to be the most important space you are planning. You can give your important spaces the amount of attention they deserve by making them larger than the other spaces, by giving them an unusual or unique shape (for example, a round space within a square grid), or by locating the space in a prominent position such as the center of your site or at the end of an axis.

In the example shown, the patio is given prominence by its shape, size, and central location. The gazebo also is prominent because it is located on an axis with the patio.

Datum. A datum is a reference point, or more accurately, a reference line or plane. An axis is a datum in that it gives elements on either side of it a common line of reference. Walls make good datum lines. Their presence and continuity often help emphasize unique elements. For example, a fence could act as a datum to emphasize plantings of various shapes. Interestingly enough, grids also make good datum lines, as when we overlay a variety of differently shaped objects on a regular pattern. The grid holds everything together in a cohesive composition.

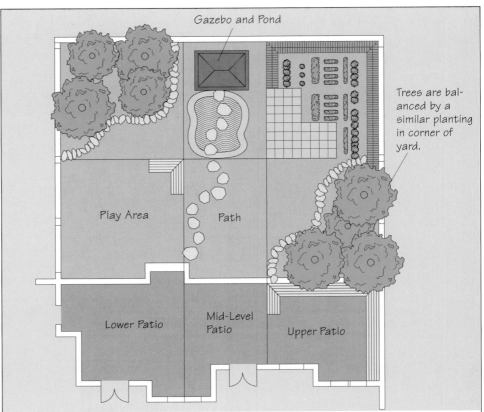

Grids. Dividing your yard into grids can help you think of ways to organize elements of the landscape. Notice that the center of this grid is composed of rectangles that are smaller than the squares to the left and right.

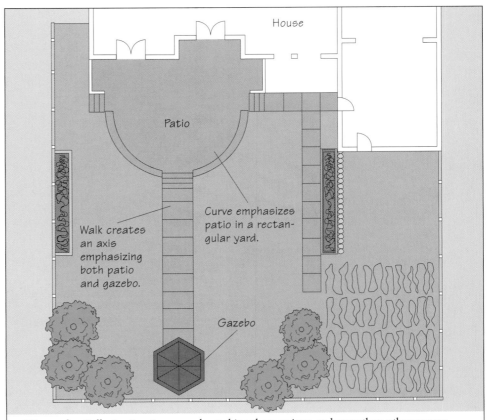

Hierarchy. Call attention to spaces by making them unique or larger than other spaces. Changing the size, shape, or order of an element changes its importance in the design.

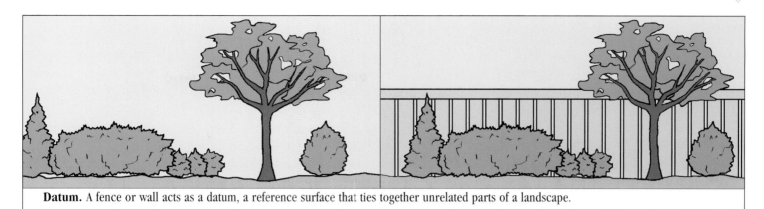

Datum. A fence or wall acts as a datum, a reference surface that ties together unrelated parts of a landscape.

Basic geometry. Geometric shapes are always fun to use when designing just about anything, especially site plans. The basic geometric shapes are the circle, square, and triangle. With these shapes, combined with our other ordering systems, you can design just about everything that comes along. Interesting geometric variations include overlapping the basic shapes to form a third shape (or space) and creating spiral or pinwheel compositions. All of these geometric systems can be combined, overlapped, rotated, and shifted relative to each other and themselves for added variety and complexity. In your yard the geometric elements might be a triangular trellis, rectangular patios and round shrubs.

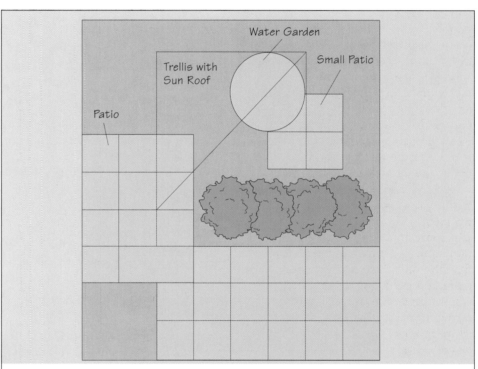

Basic geometry. Squares, triangles, circles, and combined geometric shapes can all help unify the elements in your yard. This yard is organized by overlapping a circle, a triangle, and several squares.

The combination of geometric shapes in these steps makes them a focal point of the garden.

This formal park is organized around a single geometric shape, the rectangle.

WORKING WITH THE LAND

Before you can actually apply design principles, you must understand the landscape of your site and where to place the things on it. Such things as the soil, drainage patterns, and grading are extremely important for your final design. After all, even the most beautiful patio won't be very pleasant to use if it's under several inches of water. The most carefully laid out walks won't function if they're a river of mud, and the retaining wall you're thinking of putting in won't serve its purpose very well if it cracks or falls over.

SOILS

Soils have three main properties that we are interested in: the bearing (structural) capacity, the drainage characteristics, and the fertility (ability to support plant life). Soils are divided into two major classifications, depending on the size of the soil particles. There are coarse-grained soils, such as gravel and sand, and fine-grained soils, such as clays and silts. For both structural and drainage purposes, the coarse-grained soils are preferable. As you can imagine, coarse-grained soils will support more weight and will drain much better than fine-grained soils. Soils such as clays and stilts, besides having poor structural and drainage capacities, also

The terrain determines what you can and can't do with your yard. New projects need to work with the slope of the land, the existing drainage, and possible erosion problems, among other things.

have a tendency to shrink and swell as they become saturated with ground water and then dry out. This can cause major problems such as cracking and excessive settling of walks, patios, and footings. If you suspect that the soil on your site has these characteristics, you should remove it to a suitable depth and replace it with coarser soil. Almost every county in the United States has a County Soil Conservation Service, which will provide countywide soil surveys, indicating the predominant soil types in your area. Another source for this information is your local plant nursery, which will have a general knowledge of soil types in your community.

How Soils Are Layered

Most soils have distinct profiles, or horizontal layers, roughly divided into organic topsoils (the top layer), nonorganic subsoils (in the middle), and rock-bearing (bedrock) soils at the bottom. Topsoils, with their varying mixtures of organic materials composed of decaying vegetation, are not suitable for structural purposes and must be removed or excavated from the areas where you plan to construct your walks, walls, and patios. Usually this is not a problem since most topsoil layers are relatively shallow (6 to 12 inches deep) and will be removed

in the course of excavating for your new construction. However, if you do encounter highly organic soils below your planned excavation depths, these soils must be removed and replaced with suitable fill dirt.

Regardless of the soil type found at the bottom of your footing, walkway, or patio excavations, you must compact it before you begin construction. Failure to do so will increase the risk that your new structure will settle and crack. Compaction helps to remove the air pockets between the soil particles and to provide a stable base or platform on which to build. Most equipment rental companies have plate compactors for this purpose, and they're relatively easy to use.

Shallow constructions, such as walks and patios, require a layer of gravel, 4 to 6 inches thick, that will act as a drainage base underneath the actual concrete. This drainage base helps to prevent water from collecting or ponding beneath these shallow constructions.

DRAINAGE

Unless you happen to live on a rock in the middle of the Mojave Desert, you probably already know where the low spots on your site are. You know, those miniature bogs and swamps where the water tends to collect after every good rain. Note and record these places, as well as the existing natural drainage patterns, on your site plan. Here is your opportunity to correct any annoying drainage problems. The best advice is to identify and work with the natural drainage paths whenever possible. These existing paths have generally reached a state of equilibrium with the surrounding terrain. Altering, blocking, or interfering with these natural paths requires extra labor and materials—and can be disastrous if not done properly.

Drainage Systems

Site drainage involves the collection of rainwater and snow runoff, the channeling of this water, and the disposal of the excess water. There

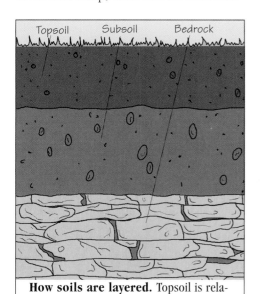

How soils are layered. Topsoil is relatively unstable and should be removed from underneath walls, walks, and patios.

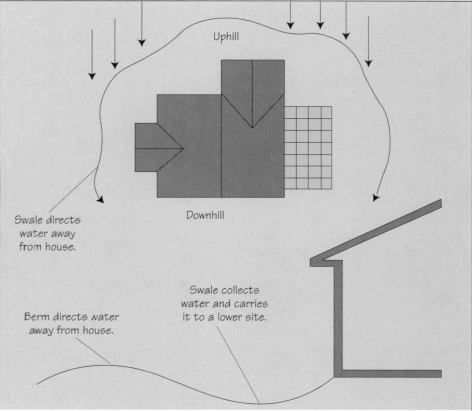

Drainage systems. A shallow depression, called a swale, is the simplest way to direct water away from a site. Berms direct runoff away from important sites.

Determining a Slope for Directing Water Away from Your Site

Water must be directed away from your house (on all sides) and away from your new patio, walkways, and walls. The idea is to get the runoff to flow around these areas rather than through them. The minimum recommended slope away from these locations is 1 percent—roughly a ⅛-inch drop for every 12 inches of horizontal run. The preferred minimum slope is 2 to 3 percent for planted areas. The maximum recommended slope is 10 percent, which is equal to a 1¼-inch drop per 12 inches of run. The maximum recommended slope for use areas, such as play areas, planting beds, lawn areas, is 5 percent—a ⅝-inch drop per 12 inches of run. Any swales over 3 percent and any sloping areas over 33 percent must be planted immediately with grass or groundcover to help prevent erosion.

To determine the percentage of your existing or proposed slopes simply divide the vertical distance or drop by the horizontal distance (run). For example, a slope that drops 2 feet in 25 feet of run would be equal to an 8 percent slope (2 divided by 25 = 0.08, or 8 percent).

Paved areas such as patios and walks must also be sloped to shed rainwater and runoff. The minimum recommended slope for paved areas is 0.5 to 1 percent. The preferred slope is 2 percent, which is equal to a ¼-inch drop for every 12 inches of horizontal run. If you design a 15-foot-wide patio and place it next to the house, for example, the top edge should be next to the house, and 3¾ inches should be above the bottom edge. To ensure that your concrete walkways and steps also drain properly, apply the same 2 percent slope to them as well.

An additional measure you'll want to consider is to raise or elevate your patio and walkways above the surrounding nonpaved areas as much as possible. Besides ensuring good drainage, this approach usually requires less excavating—a nice little bonus

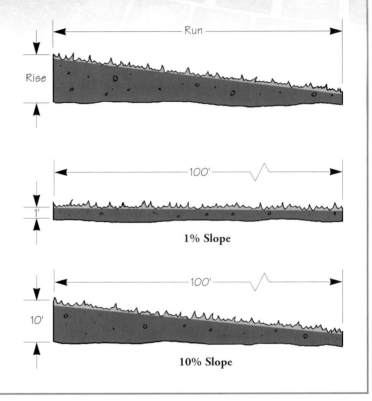

1% Slope

10% Slope

are two primary kinds of systems: surface drain systems and subsurface drain systems, such as area drains, catch basins, trench drains, dry wells, and drain tiles. Due to the expense and work involved, use subsurface systems only as a last resort.

Surface drain systems basically consist of shallow drainage ditches, called swales, and built-up mounds that direct runoff, called berms. After you have identified where runoff enters your site, the next step is to decide where to channel this water. Generally, you'll want to direct it to an existing storm sewer located in the street. You'll try to channel this water with swales, berms, and retaining walls. If for any reason it is impossible to run storm water to the street system, a substitute location must be chosen (and, no, not in your neighbor's yard). The new drainage

pattern should not cause damage to or increase runoff directed at surrounding properties.

Grading Your Site

Site grading involves reshaping and recontouring the earth, which is a fancy way of saying "moving a lot of dirt around." Try to work with the existing contours whenever possible to minimize time and expenses. The grading operation consists of two basic operations: cutting and filling. A cut involves removing dirt (that is, cutting into a hillside), and a fill

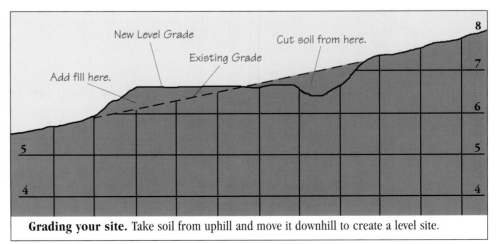

Grading your site. Take soil from uphill and move it downhill to create a level site.

involves adding dirt to the original grade. To avoid having to move excess dirt to or from your site, try to roughly balance the amount of dirt you wish to cut with the amount you wish to fill.

Choosing the right slope. Site grading accomplishes two things. The first is functional and involves creating relatively flat areas and walks. The second enhances the aesthetic and sensory qualities of the site. Remember that a completely flat area can be just as undesirable as an excessively steep slope. Water will inevitably collect and remain in a flat area. For this reason, provide a slight slope to play areas, patios, and other areas of use. What we are really trying to do is to find a balance between creating relatively flat areas and avoiding water incursion and ponding. Recommended maximum and minimum slopes for different site functions are shown in the chart at right. Note that a 0 percent slope is never recommended.

Erosion Control

The most common areas of erosion are unprotected slopes and excessively steep slopes. A slope with a rise greater than 1 foot over a run of 3 feet is likely to erode. If you plan to have large and/or steeply sloped areas of bare ground exposed for any length of time, protect these areas with either some kind of mulch, such as loose straw, thin mats of straw, or coconut fibers held between lightweight plastic netting. These coverings interrupt the force of raindrops and slow down the water that seeps through, collects into rivulets, and runs downhill. Otherwise, that unexpected summer downpour could send a river of mud into the yard or, worse, into your house.

When planning your new site, consider adding retaining walls or terracing to reduce the steepness of existing slopes. When you have finished with the construction, replant any sloping areas immediately with grasses or low groundcovers to stabilize these areas and decrease the risk of property-damaging runoff. A quick fix for replanting large areas is hydroseeding, which covers the ground with a combination of organic mulches, grass seeds, and fertilizers in one application.

Area	Function	Recommended Slope Max.	Min.
Walkways Approaches and Entrances		5%	0.5%
Patios		2%	1%
Lawn Area and Playgrounds		4%	0.5%
Swales		10%	1%
Grassed Banks		25% Maximum	
Planted Banks (unmowed vines or groundcover)		50% Maximum	

Choosing the right slope. The desired slope varies depending on the use of the land.

Formula for Determining the Grade of Your Site

This simple formula will help you determine existing grades or set new ones:

$$D = G \times L$$

D equals the vertical drop in feet, G equals the existing or desired grade as a decimal percentage (that is, 2 percent will be expressed as 0.02), and L equals the horizontal distance (length), also expressed in feet.

Let's look at an example: Say you want to slope an area to a 1 percent grade and this area is 25 feet long. Plug 0.01 (for G, the desired grade) and 25 (for L, the length in feet) into the formula:

$$D = G \times L$$
$$D = 0.01 \times 25$$
$$D = 0.25 \text{ feet (which translates into 3 inches)}$$

This means that the low end of your space will be 3 inches below the high end.

This formula can also be rearranged to solve for existing or desired grades (G = $\frac{D}{L}$) and for existing or desired lengths (L = $\frac{D}{G}$).

CREATING A COMFORTABLE CLIMATE FOR YOUR PATIO

A properly designed site can literally extend the comfortable temperature ranges experienced outdoors by several weeks or more. That means a more comfortable patio and back-yard beginning earlier in the spring and lasting later into the fall. The two variables you want to work with are temperature and humidity. The two natural modifiers with which you have to balance these variables are the sun and the wind. As temperatures and humidity begin to rise we want to introduce more wind and reduce or block the amount of direct sunlight. Conversely, as the temperatures and humidity begin to fall below your comfort zone, you want to allow more sunlight into the site and reduce or block the amount of wind entering the site. If all this sounds simple and obvious, that's because it is.

How to Make a Site Cooler or Warmer

One way to block the high summer and afternoon sun is to plant decidu-ous trees to the south and west of your house and patio. Manmade structures that block the sun include overhead pergolas covered with deciduous vines; and strategically placed screen walls to block the hot afternoon sun.

For admitting the sun and blocking cold winds, try to think in terms of creating sun pockets. These are spaces, such as patios, that are open to the south and surrounded by screens, dense vegetation, or walls, one of which is typically the side of your house. Inside these sun pockets the still air is warmed by the sun. This reflected heat can be as much as 10 degrees warmer than outside these spaces.

Breezes. Strategies for admitting cooling winds in the summer include locating your patio so it is directly in the path of the summer wind. Locate

How to make a site cooler or warmer. Trees and sun screens will block the sun and help keep a site cooler.

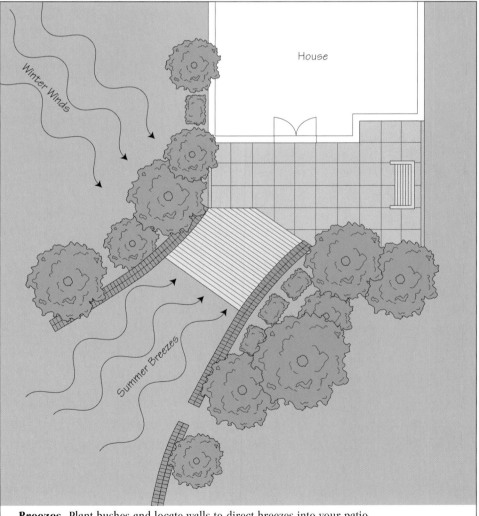

Breezes. Plant bushes and locate walls to direct breezes into your patio.

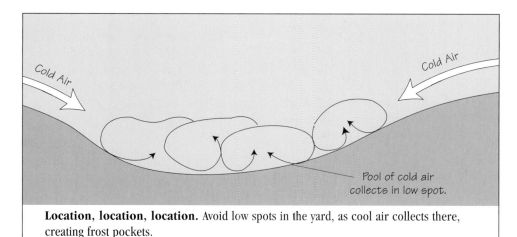

Location, location, location. Avoid low spots in the yard, as cool air collects there, creating frost pockets.

walls and vegetation so that summer winds are directed and channeled into the patio. An added bonus is that your indoor spaces will probably benefit as well: A deciduous tree or overhead pergola that shades your patio will also prevent sunlight from directly entering the house. And if that row of bushes or that freestanding wall you're about to build is located correctly, it can channel cooling breezes into your patio and house during the summer and then act as a buffer against the cold winds of winter—in most locations in the United States, summer and winter winds come from entirely different directions.

Location, location, location. If you live in the temperate or cooler regions of the country, the most important overall strategy for locating your patio is to place it to the south, southeast, or southwest side of your house. Here it will receive sun for most of the day, absorb the warming rays, and continue to radiate them back well into the evening. In southern climates, locate your patio to the east or northeast side(s) of the house so the sun will warm it early in the day when temperatures are relatively cool. In the late afternoon when it's overly warm, the patio will be shady. If you live on sloping or uneven terrain, place your patio on high ground because cold, heavy air collects, much like water, and runs down slopes and into valleys and low spots. A patio located in one of these pockets, called a frost pocket, will be much cooler throughout the year.

WALKS

Walks connect or link the areas of your site and make them accessible and useful. Beyond solving just the functional aspects of moving around, you can also design walks so that they are pleasant and provide a sense of enjoyment and delight. There are two approaches you can take when placing walks: You can locate certain areas of your site first and then connect them with your walks, or you can lay out your walks first and then locate the other areas.

As you begin to lay out your walks, consider the following design goals:

■ Try to achieve a balance between functionality and aesthetics, between effort and safety, and between initial installation costs and future maintenance and replacement costs.

■ Design walks to be compatible with the existing scale, materials, and character of your house and neighborhood.

■ Design your walks so that they reinforce and intensify the spirit of your site.

■ Be continually aware of the need to provide safe, effortless, barrier-free routes to all parts of your site.

■ If you're designing in the spring or summer, keep fall and winter in mind.

■ Think in terms of a sequence of spaces, spots such as seating areas and views, as you progress along your walks. To achieve this, think more of designing a scenic route with lots of little rest stops and roadside attractions (like the seating areas) along the way

versus designing a freeway or highway (we all know what they look like).

■ Always think in terms of clarity and simplicity. Walks, first and foremost, must be logical.

Staying on the right path. Given the chance, people will generally take the shortest, most direct walk from where they are to where they want to go. We've all seen these lines etched into lawn areas where people cut corners, so to speak, to take a more direct route to their destination. In fact, some professional site planners deliberately leave the sidewalks out of the initial construction phase and, a year or so later, when the walks have been worn into the turf, go back in and build the walks. This may not be a practical approach for you, but it is an argument against laying out strict 90-degree angled walks. Stay flexible and ask yourself where you really think you'll be walking to get from one place to another on your site. And try to locate your walks so that the privacy of rooms such as bedrooms and bathrooms is not compromised.

Shape and size. Simply put, the major walks should be larger and built out of more elaborate or textured materials than the minor walks.

As for the shape of your walks, the basic choices are straight, curved, and angled. Straight walks convey a formal sense to your site. They can also be a little rigid. Curved walks tend to convey an informal or organic feeling to your site. Curved walks are inherently more flexible and adapt better to sites with slopes and other unusual topography. They can also be more difficult, and therefore more expensive, to construct. Angled (or diagonal) walks lie somewhere in between straight and curved walks in terms of flexibility and cost, but are often the most efficient line between two offset points. Don't be afraid to mix different shapes if you feel that's appropriate to your site and needs.

Topography. Topography gets back to one of the main design strategies: Always work with the site and not against it. In terms of locating walks, this means avoiding both the steepest areas, which are generally unsafe for most walks, and the lowest spots on your site, where water will collect and damage your walks. On some sites, avoiding slopes and wet spots may be hard. But building through them will also increase your overall costs. The lowest spots on your site may require additional drainage structures, additional fill dirt or gravel to raise the walk above the surrounding grade, or extensive maintenance to keep those portions safe and usable throughout the year.

Safety. Above all, walks must be safe. Features that add to the safety of walks include textured surfaces such as broom finishes for concrete walks (instead of smooth finishes), lighting at critical points such as steps and landings, and sloped "washes" so that water does not collect or remain on the walkway surface itself. Broom finishes are made by using a common straw broom to add a light, medium, or heavy texture to a concrete surface after it has been troweled smooth and just before it finishes setting up. Low-level lighting (5 to 25 footcandles) at critical points (steps, landings, changes in direction, and entries) not only makes these places safer for use at night but also adds to the attractiveness of the overall site. Inexpensive

and easily installed walkway lighting fixtures are readily available at home-improvement stores and can take the form of small (1 foot or less) ground fixtures, pole-mounted fixtures, or wall-mounted fixtures (attached to the side of your house or garage). Washes are slight tilts of the walk itself to one side or the other so that water will drain off instead of forming puddles on a level walkway (and icing up in the winter in northern climates).

Accessibility. Accessiblity goes hand in hand with safety. Any walkway that rises or drops more than 6 inches per 10 feet of horizontal run or length is considered a ramp. In northern climates, ramps can be extremely dangerous when they are covered in snow or ice. If you are designing to meet current Americans with Disabilities Act (ADA) standards, for wheelchair- or walker-dependent users, the maximum rise permitted for every 12 feet of horizontal run is 1 foot. In addition, current ADA standards require that for every 30 feet of horizontal run or length, a level landing of at least 5 feet must be provided for resting. Also, handrails must be provided on both sides of the ramp.

Materials and patterns. In the following sections of this book you will find more complete and practical

information on the various materials for walks and the many patterns available. In general, professional landscape designers consider the materials used for walks to be either flexible or rigid. Flexible materials, such as pea gravel and bark chips, have the advantage of being inexpensive and relatively easy to install. They tend, however, to scatter into other areas, disappear over time, require frequent replacement, and they are not user friendly for the disabled.

Rigid materials, such as concrete or mortared masonry walkways, besides being more permanent, also come in a great range of colors, patterns, and textures. Concrete can be tinted with a variety of colors, which are added to the wet concrete as it is being mixed. Most homeowners choose the reddish tints, which tend to imitate traditional brick colors. Also available for concrete walks are numerous patterns that imitate everything from flagstone to cobblestone to basket-weave brick. These patterns come in the form of metal or rigid plastic stamps that are applied to the wet concrete. Combine the many colors and patterns that are available to suit your personal preferences.

The middle ground is dry-laid masonry systems—bricks, stones, or pavers

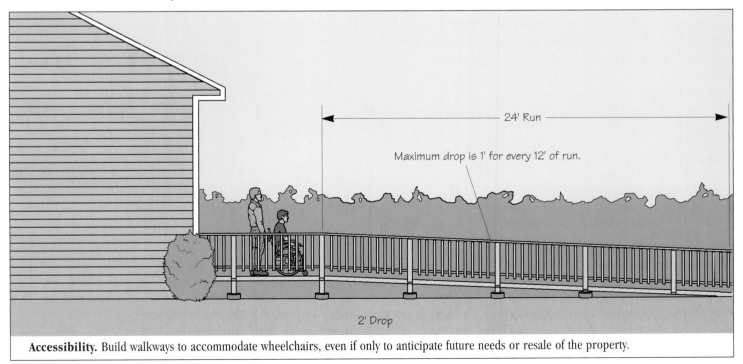

Accessibility. Build walkways to accommodate wheelchairs, even if only to anticipate future needs or resale of the property.

set without mortar in a bed of sand and gravel. Dry-laid masonry offers, to some degree, the best of both worlds—flexibility, ease of installation, durability, and accessibility.

TREES AND PLANTS

It's no secret that just about any type of plant and vegetation (with the exception of dandelions and crabgrass) can considerably enhance any site or property. Plants of all types provide comfort from the hard,

angular lines of our manmade living and working environments. When properly located, plants and vegetation can also modify the outdoor temperatures of our site. Also, plants and vegetation can add measurable value to any property. Real estate appraisers actually have tables that assign monetary values to trees and other significant plantings.

As you think about incorporating plants and planting areas into your site, consider the many functional uses of trees and plants and how your particular site might profit from them.

Benefits of Trees and Plants

Simply put, trees and plantings will make your site look good. It's difficult to imagine any property as looking complete without plants, trees, and shrubs. Plants can act as focal points, provide color accents, and intensify edges and give definition to areas. They provide visual texture to otherwise bland settings, create moods and evoke memories, provide seasonal variety, and frame special views or vistas. For all of these reasons, integrate plantings and trees with your plans from the very start, not as an afterthought or just to fill up unused spaces. Careful planning from the start is essential to reap the full benefits that plants can provide.

Among other things, plants

■ Are extremely effective modifiers.

■ Are perhaps the least expensive erosion control materials available.

■ Provide natural habitat for our furry and feathered friends.

■ Act as visual screens that provide privacy.

■ Are effective sound dampers.

■ Block or screen undesirable glare from nearby bodies of water, large areas of pavement, or the reflective siding and windows of adjacent buildings.

■ Filter and purify dust or particle-laden air as it passes through branches and/or leaves.

■ Add needed humidity to the site through the natural process of transpiration, especially in hot and dry places.

DESIGNING YOUR SITE

It's time to put pencil to paper, and design the wall, walk, or patio that's right for your yard. The key to it all is a simple scale drawing of your yard that takes into account the terrain, the house, and the neighborhood.

Take a look at your yard. What size is it? Where is the house? The building department is going to ask you the same questions, and the easiest and most precise answer is a simple map. If you know where the property corners are, you can draw your own. If not, look at the plat map, found at the local title company or county tax assessor's office. (A quick search through your house purchase records might also produce a small copy of the plat map.) Depending on the age of your house, you might also be able to obtain a site plan with these dimensions from the builder or from the building department, which typically requires a dimensioned site plan before issuing a building permit. Once you've verified the size and shape of the house and lot, take an inventory of a few other important things.

Utility easements and street rights of way. You may own it, but you don't want to build on part of the land that's been given to a utility company as an easement. A quick call to your local utility companies can tell you if there are any utility easements running through or alongside your property. Sometimes this information can be found on your title insurance report as well. Depending on your situation, you might also want to check with the local transportation department about the street and alley right-of-way. Often, there are restrictions on what can be constructed within a right of way. Street widening or improvement projects could have an adverse affect on your plans.

Utility lines. While you're talking to the utility companies, find out where the sewer, gas, water, power, cable TV, and telephone lines are. All utility companies have maps that show the approximate location of their under-

---

Tree and Plant Guidelines

Landscapers and landscape architects have a few simple tricks that help them design plantings for a yard. These same tricks can help you.

• Try to group trees and shrubs into twos and threes. Single plantings appear unnatural and sparse.

• Limit the overall variety of plants around your site so that there is a sense of unity and order versus randomness and chaos.

• Use groundcovers and grasses as the floors of the site. Bushes, hedges, and shrubs are the outdoor walls. Tree trunks are the columns when defining outdoor spaces, and tree canopies are the outdoor equivalent of ceilings. With these visual images in mind, your task of designing outdoor spaces becomes much easier.

• Trees and plantings, although obviously natural and organic, can be used in geometric or formal arrangements as well. A well-balanced variety of formal and informal planting arrangements can provide a pleasing contrast and enhance the mood you are looking for.

• Be careful not to plant deep-rooted trees next to your house or directly over underground utility lines.

• Use trees to define and frame your best views and screen or block the undesirable ones.

ground utilities. This is accurate enough for your site plan. Before you begin actual construction, though, call and have these companies locate their lines and the depths exactly. This service is normally free to all utility customers, and many utility districts have a single toll-free number to call for this service. Check the front of your phone book. Once notified and given the address, utility companies will come to your house and mark the site (usually with different colors of spray paint) to show exactly where and how deep their respective lines are located. Take advantage of this free service. Water and sewer utilities are normally buried quite deep to avoid frost and freezing. Other utilities, however, are often in rather shallow trenches and can easily be cut when digging trenches.

Zoning. City and county zoning ordinances usually have no affect on site-related improvements. Walks, walls, and patios are normally excluded from front-, side-, and rear-yard setbacks. Only enclosed buildings such as houses, garages, and sheds are required to stay behind these setback lines. On the other hand, it pays to visit the local planning department and verify just how your property is zoned and what effect that could have on your plans.

Legal restrictions. Most newer subdivisions will have a set of Covenants, Codes, and Restrictions (CCRs) that can affect the type of materials used and perhaps some other aspects of your project. Your property deed or your title insurance report should have this information. Become familiar with these requirements before designing: this will help you avoid any unpleasant surprises down the road. If you live in an older neighborhood, check with the local planning department to see if any historic district restrictions apply to your site.

Natural physical features. The majority of this information can be collected simply by walking around your site, taking notes and measurements, and perhaps taking some photos from different angles. Note and record existing trees and vegetation

you'll want to save. Be on the lookout for rock outcrops, shallow layers of bedrock, or extremely rocky soils you'll want to avoid. Note drainage swales, ditches, ponds, or streams and the soil type(s) on your site. Perhaps the most important natural feature to observe and record is the topography of your site. This means accurately measuring and locating all the sloping areas, flat areas, high points, ridges, mounds, low points, and valleys. This is important for two reasons: First, it tells you what the drainage patterns are. Second, it provides a basis for working with your site contours instead of against them.

Manmade features. Along with the natural features of your site, record any manmade improvements, such as existing fences, walks, retaining walls, curb cuts, utility poles, fire hydrants, and any other elements or details that will impact your plans. Measure and record these items in relation to a fixed reference point, such as the corner of your house or garage.

Walks. Note walks and access points. Consider changing these routes to improve their efficiency.

Climate conditions. Unless you live in a one-season climate, check with your local weather bureau, airport, or university to find information on your particular climate. Things to look for include average monthly amounts of rainfall and snowfall, average monthly temperatures, typical wind directions for both summer and winter months, and the seasonal sun angles for your location. This type of information is easy to obtain and can be extremely helpful when you get ready to locate features such as patios or planting beds.

Views and vistas. No site inventory would be complete without noting the best, and worst, views from the site. Good views are a special site amenity that should be preserved and, if possible, enhanced through careful planning and design. Technically, a view is an open sweep of landscape such as distant mountains or the seaside, while a vista is a portion of that view, usual-

ly with a single element as its focus. As you design your new site plan, make the most of your best views by opening them up from important locations on your site. Conversely, use this chance to screen or block unwanted, undesirable views.

Noise, nosy neighbors, and other nuisances. Finish off your site inventory by noting problems, such as unwanted noise or upper-story windows that overlook your anticipated patio. Look for unwanted glare from the windows of adjacent buildings, obnoxious streetlights at night, and areas that get too much sun, particularly early in the morning or late in the afternoon. Then include defensive measures in your plans.

MAKING A SITE PLAN

Now that you've spent some time inventorying your yard and thinking about what you want to include on your site, it's time to organize your thoughts by drawing up a site plan. There's a logical sequence to preparing site plans and drawings. In general terms, the drawings proceed from the large elements of the plan and progress toward the smallest elements and details. The first step is to make a rough sketch of your site, including the house and the shape of the yard.

Begin with the existing deed map, site plan, or plot map you gathered earlier. Reproduce it exactly on a large piece of tracing paper with graph lines on it (available at stationery shops or art supply stores). For large landscape projects, draw the entire property: Show its overall dimensions, its orientation (relative to north), the location of the house, and setback distances and easements from property lines, buildings, and street(s). For smaller projects, just draw the affected portion of the property.

The base map should also show your house's floor plan. If you have architect's blueprints of your house, use them to show the location of egress doors; as well as windows for views.

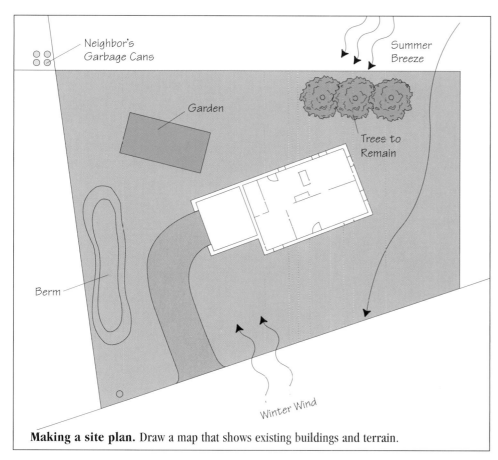

Making a site plan. Draw a map that shows existing buildings and terrain.

walls, and patio(s) on your site. The quicker and looser these early sketches are, the better. This allows you to try out many different ideas, locations, and configurations rapidly and without having to commit to the very first plan layout or idea that pops into your head.

You might consider doing a series of bubble diagrams where spaces or use areas are represented literally by bubbles in the form of circles or rounded squares. Link these bubbles together and the links start to represent your new walks. When you've worked out the large strokes, add another overlay, and refine them.

Final layout. Don't like what you've done? Tear off the overlay and start over. Want to improve on a pretty good design? Add another overlay, and edit your design as you trace it. Keep drawing and improving until you're happy with what you see. Then take a little time to reflect on the design itself. Ask someone familiar with your site to review your design. Oftentimes, designers get so close to and wrapped up in their designs that it is literally hard to see the forest for the trees.

Show the location of other buildings and permanent structures on the property, such as existing walks, walls, fences, detached garages, storage sheds, decks, patios, and the like. Show the location of underground utility lines, pipes, and cables. Draw in the size and location of existing plantings, such as trees, hedges, and shrubs as well as lawn areas, planting beds, and borders. Indicate which trees and shrubs are to be kept and which will need to be removed or relocated.

Indicate the direction of prevailing winds and existing sun/shade patterns in the yard (direction of morning and afternoon sun). Note the existing drainage patterns, along with any outside factors that affect the yard, such as noise or privacy problems, and views that you want to retain or obscure. If you find that the base map is becoming too cluttered, you can show these features on a separate overlay attached to the map.

Rough layout. Now the fun begins. Attach an overlay of tracing paper to the base map. This is where you

should begin sketching and actually placing your outdoor areas. Begin with very loose diagrams as you try out different locations for the walks,

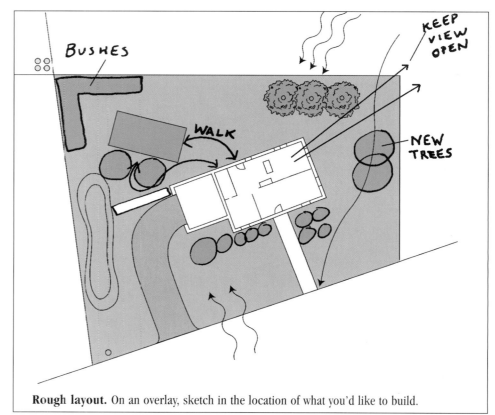

Rough layout. On an overlay, sketch in the location of what you'd like to build.

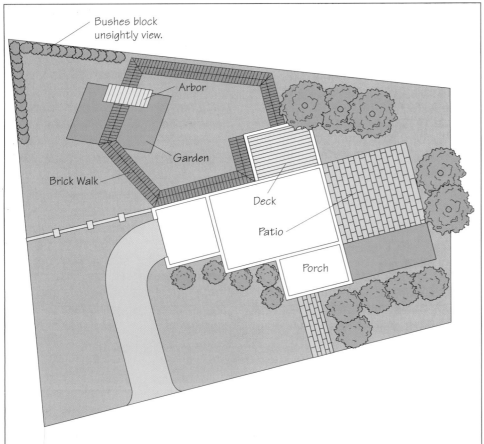

Bushes block unsightly view.

Arbor

Garden

Brick Walk

Deck

Patio

Porch

Final layout. Keep adding and refining overlays until you have the design you want.

Make sure the design fulfills your intended purpose. If you plan to do a lot of entertaining on your patio, make sure it is large enough to comfortably accommodate the number of guests that you expect will visit at one time. Ask yourself if the design fits the site, the house, and the surrounding neighborhood.

Make sure the design creates a memorable experience for friends and family. Does it have physical or sensory elements that would make the typical visitor want to return? Have you combined walks, walls, and patios in such a way as to create a pleasing atmosphere or mood that will be remembered?

Make sure you can build your design on your budget. We all want the moon, but take a hard look at the estimated costs for what you intend to build. All building projects consist of three aspects: scope (size, quantity, etc.), quality (quality and expense of the materials and finishes), and budget. If scope or quality exceed budget, one or both of them must be adjusted.

Make sure your design minimizes maintenance requirements, such as cleaning, sweeping, mowing, watering, snow removal, painting, or sealing. Some designs look fantastic on paper and then turn out to be real maintenance headaches.

If someone in your family or among your friends is physically handicapped, review your plans—especially walkways—in light of this fact. How easy will it be for him or her to get around? Will your friend be able to get to all parts of your site or only certain areas? Are the walks wide enough to accommodate someone in a wheelchair? Have you provided ramps from one level to the next? Could your design accommodate ramps in the future if necessary?

Once you've answered these questions, you may go back and make some final revisions. But when you're happy with what you see, you're ready to build. Take a copy of the final site plan with you when you go to obtain the building permit.

CONSTRUCTION

If you plan to do the work yourself, take the plans to your building supply store and ask for help developing a materials list. Most building supply stores will be happy to help develop a list of the materials, the quantity needed, and the sequence that they need to be delivered in. This can save you a lot of time on the phone or running back and forth to the store.

If you decide to subcontract portions of your project, you will need to locate the right subcontractors, give them each copies of your drawings and specifications, and ask for bids that clearly spell out what they intend to supply and install. The construction drawings you give them must include all materials to be used, all sizes and dimensions, exact locations, and construction notes pointing out both typical and unusual elements of plan. If you have a single subcontractor in mind, this will be the time to sit down and negotiate prices and schedules.

Depending on your budget and the amount of time you can devote to your project, consider scheduling your project in distinct stages so that you can order the necessary materials just in time to use them. This reduces the space needed to store materials and reduces the possibility of misfortures, such as sacks of cement getting wet in a sudden downpour. A phasing plan will also be helpful if you bid out portions of the work and want to clearly define what is to be done now and what will be completed at a later date. Prioritize or rank your individual project elements in a logical fashion. The phasing plan itself can be as simple as making a photocopy of your new site plan and then drawing borders around those projects to be completed first, second, and so on. Even if you intend to complete the entire project in one season, a phasing plan is a good tool to help you organize the sequence and schedule of work and materials.

WALLS

With a coat of stucco, a simple concrete block wall becomes an elegant backdrop to a garden.

Stone walls are durable and traditional. A dry stone wall like this one requires no foundation or pointing.

Weight and engineering, not mortar, hold a dry stone wall together. Each stone should span a gap so there are no weak spots in the wall. For stability, the wall is two rows wide. Every few feet, a stone is laid across both rows to tie the wall together.

Like dry stone walls, landscape block walls require no foundation or mortar. The blocks have the added advantage of being easy to stack.

A counterfort retaining wall consists of landscape timbers stacked on top of each other, held in place by landscape timbers stuck in the ground.

A retaining wall doesn't have to be complicated. This wall is simply landscape timbers set in trench that was then backfilled.

DRY STONE WALLS

Stonework is one of the few crafts that requires little more than a strong back and some patience. It doesn't require any specialized skills or tools; it's just plain hard work. As long as you are prepared for the physical work and the mental challenge of putting together what is, in effect, a three-dimensional jigsaw puzzle in stone, building a stone wall can be enjoyable.

A dry stone wall is the simplest of masonry jobs. No footing is required (as long as the wall is less than 3 feet high). There is no mortar to mix, and no joints to fuss over. Walls laid 100 years ago are still standing in excellent shape, so a dry wall can be a beautiful and permanent part of your landscape.

The tools you'll need for a dry-laid wall are elementary. Get a tape measure, a sharp-bladed shovel, a pickax for removing stones in the way of the wall, and a stonemason's hammer and chisel. Stakes, string, a mason's level, and a site-made batter gauge will aid in laying out and stacking the wall. A prybar comes in handy for moving stones. Wear heavy leather gloves for handling stones and safety glasses when splitting them.

Stone walls more than 3 feet high may require special construction techniques and are best left to an experienced stonemason.

A dry stone wall is held together by the weight of the stones, some of which run the width of the wall. While the walls require no foundation or pointing, building one requires patience and a strong back.

TYPES OF STONES

Stones used for wall construction can be divided into two broad categories: cut stone and rubble. Generally, the exact kinds of stone are limited to the types found in your area. Stones sold at masonry and patio supply houses and at stone yards can be expensive. You may save money by finding stones elsewhere. Stones from road-construction sites, local farmers, building-demolition sites, and landscape-remodeling projects may be free for the hauling. Also check the classified section of the newspaper.

If you decide to scrounge your own stones, you'll need a sturdy pickup truck or a trailer with good springs and tires to haul the rock away. It doesn't take many stones to add up to a ton, so you may find yourself making more trips than anticipated. Factor in your time, labor, gasoline, and wear-and-tear on the vehicle to find out if you're really saving money.

Rubble and fieldstone. Rubble consists of irregularly shaped stones. The stones are often those blasted or bulldozed from road construction sites or pieces left over from cutting trimmed stones at the quarry. Rubble is usually the least expensive stone you can buy.

Fieldstones generally have rounded edges as a result of glacial or water action. As the name implies, some of these stones are taken from plowed fields. Others are from along a creek or river.

Generally, rubble and fieldstones are set in a random, uncoursed pattern, either dry-laid or set in mortar. To strengthen the wall, stones are placed so that they straddle the two stones below them.

Cut stone. Cut stone, also referred to as quarried stone, is available semidressed or fully dressed from stone yards and landscape suppliers. Semidressed stones, such as cobblestones, are roughly square with smooth sides and uniform thickness. These stones can be laid with or without mortar, in either straight courses or

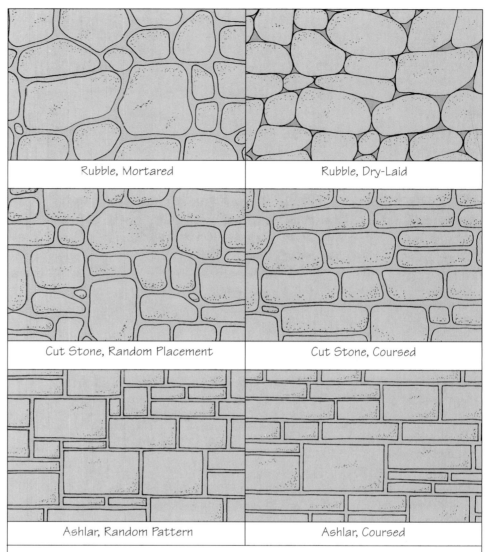

Rubble, Mortared

Rubble, Dry-Laid

Cut Stone, Random Placement

Cut Stone, Coursed

Ashlar, Random Pattern

Ashlar, Coursed

Rubble and fieldstone. Because of their irregular shapes, rubble (*top*) is usually laid in a random pattern. Cut stones (*center*) can be laid in random or coursed patterns, with or without mortar. Ashlar (*bottom*) looks best when mortared, either coursed or in a random pattern. In all cases, vertical (head) joints are staggered to provide stability.

random patterns. Fully dressed stones, called ashlar, are trimmed to more precise rectangular shapes. They are usually laid much like brick—in courses with neat mortar joints.

SELECTING STONES

Whether you buy them or scrounge them, choose stones with flat sides and edges. This is especially important if you're building a dry-laid wall, because the only thing holding the stone in place is its weight. Select stones with at least three flat sides: the top, bottom, and the side to be used for the face of the wall. Avoid large egg-shaped or round stones, but

make sure you have a good variety of sizes and shapes to provide the best design and construction.

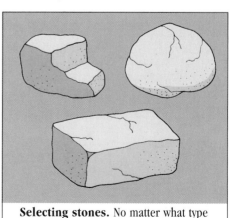

Selecting stones. No matter what type of stone you choose, those with flat sides and edges will be easier to lay.

Walls look best if they contain a good mixture of large and small stones of different colors, set randomly over the entire surface. Set small stones around large ones. Avoid grouping too many stones of one size or color in one area of the wall.

Although the project will go faster if you use large stones, make sure that they move easily and aren't too large or heavy to lift. Generally, stones that weigh from 15 to 30 pounds are easy to work with and will be in scale with most backyard garden projects.

Estimating Amounts

Stone is sold by the cubic yard or by the ton. To estimate the cubic yards of stone you'll need, multiply wall width by length by height—all measured in feet. Divide this number by 27. It's a good idea to order an extra 10 percent to compensate for breakage. If the stone is sold by the ton, have the stone dealer determine the number of tons needed to fill the volume of your wall project.

If you're scrounging your own rubble or fieldstone, simply measure the volume of each truckload, then divide this figure into the volume of the wall to determine the number of loads needed. Allow 25 percent extra to compensate for voids between the stones when they are tossed randomly in the truck.

When you get the stones home, sort them by size into different groups near the construction site. First find flat stones wide enough to span the full thickness of the wall. You'll put these stones every 4 to 6 feet in the wall to tie together the two parallel rows that make up the front and back of the wall. Place these stones, called bond stones, near where they will be laid. Then find other stones with straight edges and sides. Place them at the ends, or corners, of the wall. Place them near where they will be laid, too. It's best to spread the end and bond stones in groups one layer thick about 4 to 6 feet away from the proposed base, so that you can spot the stone you need.

DRY-LAYING A STONE WALL

Dry-laid stone walls lend a rustic appearance to the landscape, and are easy to build once you develop an eye for picking the right stones and fitting them together. A dry-laid stone wall makes a good low retaining wall: The spaces between the stones prevent water from building up behind the wall, as can sometimes happen with a mortared wall. (For more on building retaining walls, see "Dry-Laid Stone Retaining Wall," page 92.)

General Requirements

A freestanding dry-laid wall can be straight or can have corners, curves, or any combination of these. Because the wall is held together by nothing more than gravity, your main goal is to avoid building a wall that is top heavy or easily knocked over.

A rule of thumb is that a wall up to 3 feet high must be at least 2 feet wide. Freestanding walls more than 2 feet high generally have a slight inward slope, or batter, from the bottom to the top. Battered wall faces lean against each other, holding the stones in place. Walls up to 3 feet high should have 1 inch of batter for each 2 feet of rise, though a wall 2 feet or less can be built with a plumb face.

To maintain the correct batter as you build the wall, build a batter gauge, like the one shown in the drawing. Used in combination with a 2-foot level, the gauge is placed vertically against the outside faces of the wall to check the batter angle as you stack the courses.

Footings. Dry-laid walls less than 3 feet high usually require no footings. If the soil is firm, you can lay the stones directly on the ground. For best appearance and stability, however, it's a good idea to lay the first course of stones below grade.

Bond patterns. Freestanding stone walls are typically stacked two stones

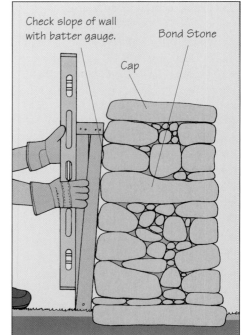

Check slope of wall with batter gauge.

Bond Stone

Cap

General requirements. Dry-laid stone walls should be set in a shallow trench. The wall is built in two halves, or wythes, with rubble between them. Bond stones at periodic intervals tie the wall together. Wall faces are sloped inward (battered) to prevent toppling.

thick; these parallel face courses are called wythes. To tie the wythes together, bond stones are placed at each end of the wall and at 4- to 6-foot intervals in each course of the wall. Usually, the more bond stones you can incorporate into the wall, the stronger it will be. As you build each successive course, stagger the joints between stones so that each stone rests on at least two stones beneath it. Gaps can be filled with small rubble stones. The top course is finished with relatively square, flat cap stones, either one or two stones wide.

CONSTRUCTING THE WALL

The work will go easier if you sort the stones you need to build the wall—bond stones, end stones, cap stones—and spread them along the wall location. Have a helper or two on hand to lend a hand when lifting heavy stones into position.

1. Excavate the site. After deciding on the location and the length of the wall, drive temporary stakes into the ground to mark the ends of the wall. Stretch mason's line between the stakes to mark the sides of the wall. Dig a trench between the lines. Remove any sod or loose topsoil with a flat-bladed shovel. Dig the actual trench with a pointed shovel. Dig the trench so that at least half of—but preferably the entire—first course will be below grade. Firmly tamp any loose soil in the bottom of the trench.

2. Stake out the wall. Double-check the position of the end stakes and drive them firmly into the ground. Attach a line level to the strings and reposition them so that they're level and about 3 inches above the anticipated height of the first course. You'll measure down from the strings as you lay the first course to make sure the course is level. Drive additional stakes every 4 feet along the line. Position the stakes so that they just touch, but do not deflect the line.

3. Lay out the first course. Select large, relatively flat stones for the base, but save the flattest stones for capping the wall, as described in Step 6, "Cap the Wall." Start by placing large bond stones at each end of the wall, with the flattest side up. Dig out the ground, if necessary, so that the stones sit firmly in the trench without rocking.

You'll find it easier to lay the front and back of the wall simultaneously: Lay two parallel wythes so that the outside of each stone is directly below the string. Place bond stones every 4 to 6 feet. Measure down from the string as you work to make sure the course is level. The base stones can lean slightly toward the center of the wall. This helps create wall sides that lean against each other for stability. Fill the void in the center of the wall with small stones.

4. Lay the second course. Move your strings so that they're about 3 inches above the top of the second course. If the wall has a batter, place the top outside edge of the stones slightly inside the string. Stagger the

1. Dig a trench deep enough to house at least half the height of the first course of stones.

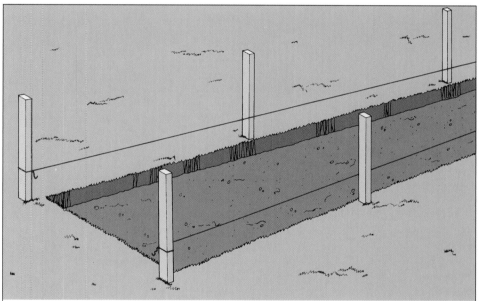

2. Drive stakes marking the ends of the wall and drive additional stakes every few feet marking the path of the wall.

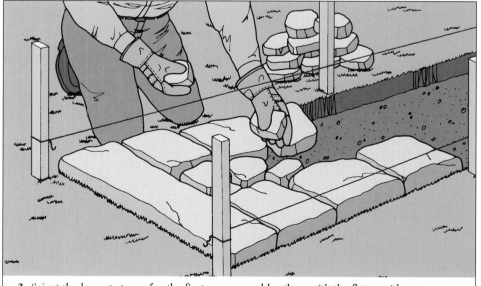

3. Select the largest stones for the first course, and lay them with the flattest side up.

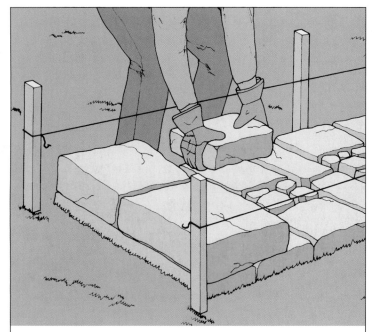

4. Adjust the strings and lay the second course, placing one stone over two stones and two stones over one.

5. Continue building the wall, checking the batter as you go. Lay bond stones every 4 to 6 feet.

joints along the faces and along the ends of the wall as well. Place one stone over two, and two stones over one. Set the front and back wythes simultaneously, filling in the gaps with small stones as you go. Check frequently with your batter gauge and level to maintain the proper batter angle on the sides and ends of the wall. Measure down from the string to make sure the course is level.

If a stone teeters on a point or sharp corner, you may be able to chisel off the projection to make the stone sit firmly. In some cases, you can place small wedge-shaped stones between larger ones to hold them in position and prevent rocking. If possible, place these small wedges toward the inside of the wall where they won't be knocked out of place.

5. Build up the remaining courses. Continue laying up courses in the same manner, maintaining the correct batter angle as you go. Ideally, bond stones should be placed in each course and staggered so that they don't fall in line with the bond stones underneath. If you don't have enough large stones, place bond stones in every other course. As you build the wall, use the squarest stones at the ends. If the wall turns a corner, use

6. The cap of the wall is the only part that is mortared. Build a slightly mounded bed so that water will run off.

overlapping bond stones to link the two meeting walls.

To fill in large gaps in the faces of the wall, gently tap in smaller stones with a hammer, being careful not to dislodge the stones already in place. When laying the top course, try to keep the top of the wall level so that the cap stones will rest firmly.

6. Cap the wall. Use the flattest, broadest, and best-looking stones for

the top course, or cap. Because cap stones are often easily knocked off low walls, you may want to mortar the cap in place. If so, spread a 2-inch-thick layer of mortar over the top course and embed the cap stones in the mortar (see "Mortar," page 75).

An alternative to cap stones is to finish off the top with a solid mortar cap. The cap should be 2 to 4 inches thick and crowned slightly to facilitate water runoff, as shown.

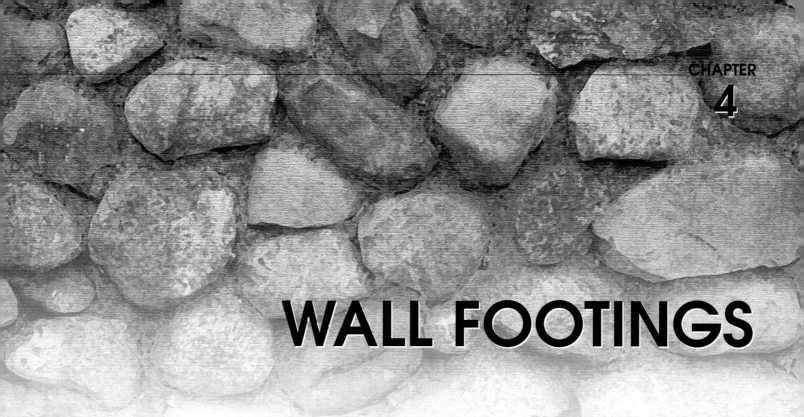

WALL FOOTINGS

Without a foundation, mortared walls will crack as the ground shifts with the seasons. A poured concrete foundation like the one shown here provides a rigid base for brick, concrete block, and mortared stone walls.

A mortared wall is rigid. Unfortunately, the ground below it isn't. As a result, mortared walls should have a strip of concrete, called a footing, beneath them. Without a footing, a wall is at the mercy of the soil, which may not offer enough support or stability to keep the wall from sinking, cracking, or collapsing. A concrete footing spreads the weight of the wall over the soil, bridges soft spots that can cause walls to crack, and provides support as the soil settles or moves.

Because they can move with the ground, dry-laid stone walls usually don't need footings. Walls taller than 3 feet require special techniques and should be designed and built by professionals. But the footing required for mortared walls 3 feet and under is well within the skill of most homeowners.

GENERAL REQUIREMENTS

The size of the footing and the way you construct it depends on the climate, soil conditions, and the height and weight of the wall it must support. Building codes are very specific on footing requirements, so be sure to check with your local building department before you start your project.

Footing Size and Depth

As a rule of thumb, footing width should be either twice that of the wall, or two-thirds the wall height, whichever is greater. If you plan to build a brick wall that incorporates pilasters into the design, make sure the footing follows the shape of the wall, or make the footing wide enough to accommodate the extra width of the pilasters. (For more on constructing brick walls with this feature, see "Pilasters," page 75.) As with all masonry walls, the top of the footing should be several inches below ground level so that it won't show once the wall is built.

Footings should be at least 6 inches thick. If frost heave is a problem, the footing should be set below the frost line. Codes vary as to the exact depth, so check with your building department for standards in your area.

In areas with extremely deep frost lines, it may not be practical to dig the wall footing below the frost line—you could end up with more wall beneath the ground than above it. In such cases, lay the footing on at least 8 inches of compacted, well-drained gravel above the frost line. If at all

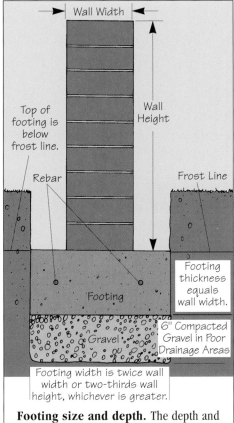

Footing size and depth. The depth and thickness of a footing depend on the depth and thickness of the wall.

possible, however, it's always best to set footings below the frost line, where freezing and thawing soil won't push the wall up and down.

In soil with poor drainage, (regardless of frost-line depth) place the footing on a tamped gravel base at least 6 inches thick. The gravel base prevents water from accumulating beneath the footing, keeping soil movement to a minimum. If you are unsure of the drainage in your area, ask local building officials about the types of wall footings they recommend.

Footing Forms

Forms, usually two-by boards, hold wet concrete to the shape required for the footing. In firm soil that retains its shape after digging, the excavation itself can be the form. In this case, place leveled 2x4s as shown at left below. You'll need the 2x4s as a guide when you level the concrete. For loose soil, use wide boards (2x6s, 2x8s, 2x10s, etc.) that extend the full depth of the footing. Once the concrete hardens, the forms are usually removed.

Poured concrete can exert considerable pressure on the forms. Anchor them by driving 1x4 stakes into the ground and nailing them to the forms every few feet. Nail 1x4 spreaders every few feet along the top of the form boards. Use duplex (double-headed) nails so that

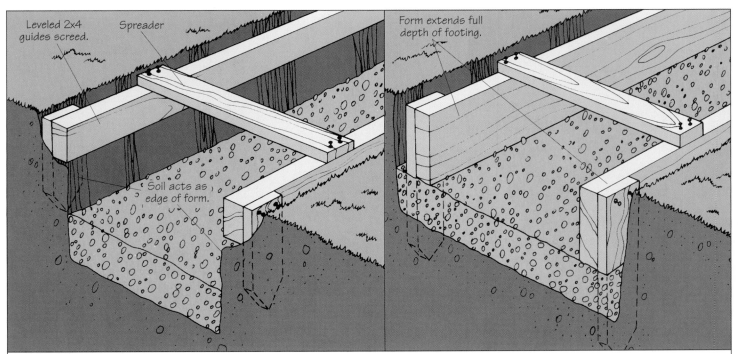

Footing forms. Footing forms help hold the concrete in place after it's poured and provide a level edge you can use as a guide when finishing the concrete. Use partial forms for firm soil (left). Use full forms for loose soil (right).

you can dismantle the forms easily after the footings have set.

Reinforcement

Poured-concrete footings should be reinforced with steel rebar, which will keep the footing structurally sound, even if it cracks. Typically, #2 or thicker rebar runs the entire length of the footing. It usually runs 1 to 2 inches from each edge of the footing about 3 to 4 inches above the bottom of the trench. Some masons prop the rebar on pieces of brick or broken concrete. Others drive short vertical rods into the ground roughly every 3 feet, and tie the horizontal rods to the vertical rods with wire. Check local codes for required rebar sizes and spacing requirements.

BUYING CONCRETE

Concrete consists of a mixture of portland cement, sand, and gravel. Depending on the size of the job and your budget, you can buy bags of pre-mixed concrete and add water; you can buy the ingredients separately and mix your own, or you can have a wet-concrete mix delivered by truck.

Dry Mixes

Purchasing dry concrete mix in 60- or 80-pound bags may prove convenient for jobs requiring less than ½ cubic yard of concrete. But since it takes about twenty 80-pound sacks to make a ½ cubic yard, larger jobs can be quite expensive and labor intensive. If you use premixed bags, it may be worth-while to have them delivered. Make sure none of the sacks has already hardened. Be sure to store the concrete somewhere dry and off the ground on something like a pallet. If the bags are stored outdoors, cover them with plastic sheeting or a waterproof tarp. If you live in a humid climate, buy the concrete no more than a day or two before you intend to use it.

You can usually save money on jobs requiring more than ½ cubic yard of concrete by buying cement and aggregates separately and mixing them yourself. Cement is sold by the 94-pound sack. (Type I cement is commonly used in residential work. Types II through IV are used in more massive structures.) Masons refer to sand as fine aggregate and gravel as coarse aggregate. Both are sold by the cubic yard. For home use, cement is commonly mixed with bank-run sand, because the round particles make for a stronger mix. For coarse aggregate, use stone or gravel ranging from ½ to 1½ inches in diameter.

All aggregates must be free of silt and debris. To test, place about 2 inches of aggregate in a glass jar. Pour in water, and shake gently. Wait for the water to clear. If there is more than ⅛ inch of silt on top of the aggregate, you'll have to wash it. Simply dump the aggregate on a clean, hard surface, and hose it down. Rake the material to make sure you are cleaning all of it.

A mix of 1 part cement, 3 parts sand, and 5 parts gravel (called a 1:3:5 mix) is typical for footings. Ask your local masonry supplier to recommend an appropriate mix for your situation.

Wet Mixes

For concrete footings and walls requiring 1 or more cubic yards of concrete, ordering a wet, or transit mix, may be your best bet. The wet concrete can be poured directly into the footings from the truck, saving hours of back-breaking labor. If the truck can't get to within about 20 feet of the forms, the concrete can be pumped from the truck through a hose. This method usually costs extra. A cheaper but more difficult method is to cart the concrete to the forms with a few wheelbarrows and some strong backs.

Specify the type of project you're doing when you order the concrete, and the supplier will provide you with the appropriate mix. If possible, schedule an early-morning delivery so that you have plenty of time to pour and work the concrete. Let the concrete supplier know in advance how you'll be unloading, in order to allow enough time before their next delivery.

Air-entrained concrete. In cold climates subject to severe freeze/thaw conditions, air-entrained concrete is common. This type of concrete contains millions of tiny air pockets that allow water to freeze and expand without damaging the concrete. The air-entraining agent can be added to Types I, II, and III concrete, but you'll need a power mixer to activate the agent in the mix. (For more information on power mixers, see "Using a Power Mixer," page 45.) Check with your concrete supplier to find out if air-entrained concrete is commonly used in your area.

Estimating Amounts

The amount of concrete required for a footing is the biggest determining factor when deciding how to order concrete. To figure out the amount needed, multiply the footing width by its depth, working in inches. Divide by 12 to get square feet. Then multiply this figure by the over-all length of the footing in feet to get cubic feet. To figure cubic yards, divide the number of cubic feet by 27.

For estimating purposes, it takes about forty 80-pound sacks of concrete mix to make 1 cubic yard of concrete. You can make 1 cubic yard of 1:3:5 concrete with five 94-pound sacks of cement, 14 cubic feet of sand, and 24 cubic feet of gravel. When you buy the concrete, order about 10 percent extra to allow for settling in the forms. However, the easiest way to determine quantities is to provide a concrete supplier with the footing dimensions and let them compute the amounts of each ingredient and an overall price.

MIXING CONCRETE

Whether you're using a premix or separate ingredients, decide if you want to mix the concrete by hand or rent a power mixer. Weigh the rental costs against the time and effort you'll save by using a power mixer. A power mixer also ensures a more even mix and is a necessity when mixing air-entrained concrete.

Mixing by Hand

Hand mixing concrete involves a square-point shovel or a mason's hoe to combine concrete ingredients. Hand mixing is hard work. While you can mix the ingredients in a wheelbarrow, it's usually easier to mix them on a clean, flat surface, such as an old sheet of plywood, or in a mortar box (also called a concrete barge).

1. Measure the ingredients.

The table "Concrete Ingredients by Proportion" shows the proportions of cement, sand, aggregate, and water needed to make concrete. Use 1½-inch aggregate for concrete used in footings. For mixing purposes, you can measure proportions by the bucket or shovel or with a measuring box like the one shown. A measuring box is built to measure exactly 1 cubic foot of dry ingredients. Make the box from lumber or plywood so the inside dimensions are 12x12x12 inches. Use the same amount of ingredients for each batch. Place the materials in layers on top of each other. Begin with the gravel; then add sand and then cement.

2. Mix the dry ingredients.
If you're working on a flat surface or mixing the ingredients in a wheelbarrow, use a mason's hoe or rake to mix the dry ingredients thoroughly before adding the water. When using a mortar box, you can either premix the dry ingredients or mix them together as you add the water. (See Step 3, "Add Water".)

3. Add water.
The water should be dirt free—clean enough to drink. The exact amount of water varies, in part because of the moisture content of the aggregate. To determine the amount of water generally required in a mix, check the chart "Concrete Ingredients." As a rule of thumb, add 6 to 7 gallons of water for every 90-pound bag of cement in the mix. If you use too little water, the concrete won't be fluid enough to fill out the form. Too much water results in weak concrete. Start with 1 or 2 gallons of water, and keep track of the amount you use so that you can add the same amount to subsequent batches.

Make sure to mix all ingredients thoroughly, scraping any unmixed cement and aggregate from the sides and bottom of the box or pile. The concrete mix should be an even color and the same consistency throughout.

Concrete Ingredients by Proportion

Maximum Size Coarse Aggregate, Inches	Air-Entrained Concrete				Concrete without Air			
	Number of Parts per Ingredient				Number of Parts per Ingredient			
	Cement	Sand*	Coarse Aggregate	Water	Cement	Sand*	Coarse Aggregate	Water
⅜	1	2¼	1½	½	1	2½	1½	½
½	1	2¼	2	½	1	2½	2	½
¾	1	2¼	2½	½	1	2½	2½	½
1	1	2¼	2¾	½	1	2½	2¾	½
1½	1	2¼	3	½	1	2½	3	½

Note: 7.48 gallons of water equals 1 cubic foot. One 94-lb. bag of portland cement equals about 1 cubic foot.
* "wet" sand sold for most construction use.
The combined finished volume is approximately two-thirds the sum of the original bulk volumes.

1. A homemade measuring box, built to hold 1 cubic foot, helps measure out the sand, cement, and gravel necessary to make concrete.

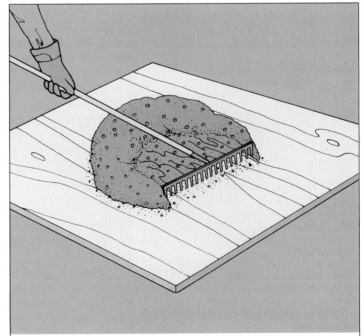

2. Mix the ingredients thoroughly with a mason's hoe or rake before adding water.

3. Make a small depression in the ingredients, pour in part of the water, and mix together. Repeat until the concrete is the right consistency.

4. Test the mixture by making ridges in it. If the ridges hold their shape, the mixture is correct.

If mixing on a flat surface, make a shallow depression in the center of the dry mix with your hoe, then pour in a little water. Mix thoroughly by pulling dry material from the edges into the depression. If using a mortar box, place the dry materials so that they fill about two-thirds of the box, leaving an empty space in the box on the side nearest the forms. Add water to the empty end, then pull the dry materials into the water, mixing them together as you go. Continue adding water in small amounts while turning over the mix until it reaches the proper consistency—not crumbly and not runny.

4. Test the mix. You can tell if the concrete has too little or too much water by using the blade of your hoe or shovel to make ridges in it. If the mix is too dry, you won't be able to make distinct ridges; if the mix is too soupy, the ridges won't hold their shape. In an overly wet mix, you'll also notice water seeping out around the edges of the pile. In a proper mix, the ridges will hold most of their shape. If the mix is too wet, it usually doesn't have enough sand and coarse aggregate for the amount of cement. Add 5 to 10 percent more aggregate, mix well, and retest. Keep careful notes of the added amounts.

Using a Power Mixer

Power mixers come in two varieties: electrically powered and gas powered. If you rent a gas-powered mixer, have the rental people start the engine to make sure it operates easily. If you use an electric mixer, make

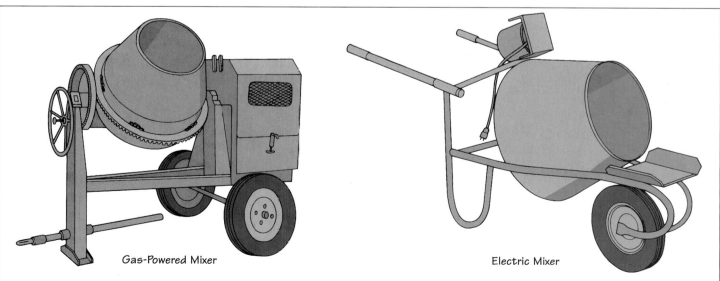

Gas-Powered Mixer

Electric Mixer

Using a power mixer. When mixing large amounts of concrete, a power mixer saves hours of back-breaking work and ensures that the ingredients will be well mixed.

sure you can provide electricity to the mixing site. If an extension cord is required, check that the wire gauge is heavy enough to handle the amperage drawn by the motor. If the cord is long, use a wire gauge that is even heavier than required: The available voltage drops as electricity travels along a wire. The rental people can advise you on the appropriate type of cord for the job. Position the mixer close to the sand and gravel piles.

With the mixer turned off, add the amounts of dry ingredients needed. Measure carefully and keep track of the amounts so that subsequent batches are consistent. Turn on the mixer and run it for a few minutes to allow the dry ingredients to mix thoroughly. With the mixer running, pour in a small amount of water, and allow it to mix in. Continue adding water a little at a time until the mixture reaches the correct consistency. If you're not familiar with this method, it's a good idea to stop the mixer periodically and check the mix, as described above. Once the concrete is mixed, tilt the mixer barrel to pour the concrete into a wheelbarrow for transport to the forms. Have a helper hold the wheelbarrow steady.

LOCATING THE FOOTING

Once you've established where to build a wall, use stakes, string, and batter boards to mark the footing location and to guide in digging trenches and positioning forms. If your wall will define property lines, be sure the footing is properly positioned so that you don't have to tear down the wall later.

1. Locate the wall ends and corners. For a straight wall, drive stakes in the ground to mark the four corners. For a wall that turns a corner, drive a stake at each end of the wall and one at the outside corner.

2. Erect the batter boards. Measure out 3 to 4 feet beyond each stake, and erect a set of batter boards, as shown. The horizontal boards

Finding a Square Corner with the 3-4-5 Method

Framing squares are much too small for laying out the corner of something as long as a wall. Instead, builders use simple geometry: A triangle with sides that measure 3 units by 4 units by 5 units, will always be a right triangle. The corner opposite the "five side" is always the right angle.

To lay out a corner of a walk, wall, or patio, you stretch strings along what will be the path of the sides. Tie the strings to batter boards. Mark one string 3 feet from the corner. Mark the other string 4 feet from the corner. Measure between the marks. Have a helper stand at the far end of either one of the strings and slide it along the batter board until the diagonal distance between the 3- and 4-foot marks equals 5 feet. At this point, the walls are square. Mark where the strings meet the batter boards, so you can reattach the strings if necessary.

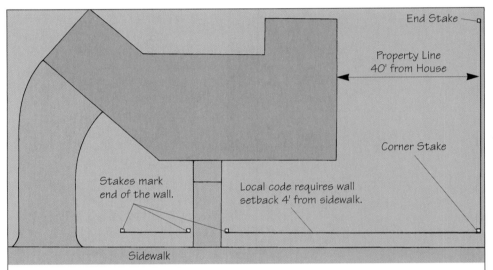

1. Begin by laying out one edge of the wall with stakes. Make sure you comply with setback and other code requirements before you pour the footing.

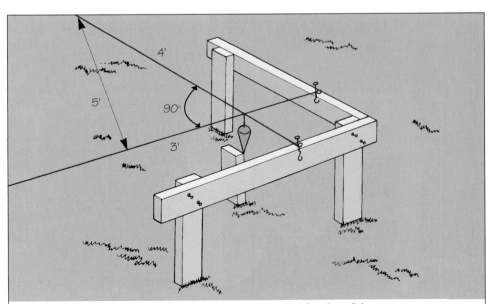

2. A wall is square when the diagonal between a 3- and 4-foot leg of the corner measures 5 feet. Slide one of the strings along the batter board until you get the proper measurement.

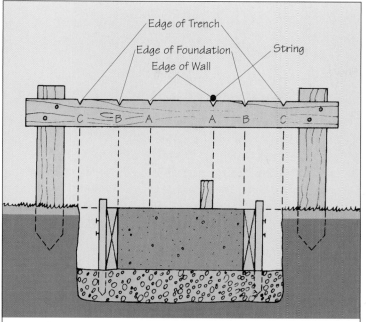

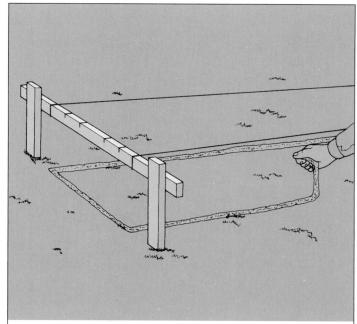

3. Make saw kerfs on the batter board to mark both outside edges of the subbase, foundation, and wall.

4. Pour a line of sand on the ground to mark the trench edge, and remove layout lines before digging.

should be at least 1 foot wider than the anticipated width of the footing trench. Align the center of the board with the rough center point of the proposed wall.

Using the stakes as guides, stretch a string from batter board to batter board to lay out the outside face of the wall.

If the wall turns a corner, check it for square as described in "Finding a Square Corner with the 3-4-5 Method," page 46.

3. Mark the batter boards. On the crosspieces, measure the wall width from the string and mark the other face of the wall (labeled A in the drawing). Measure to find the inside and outside faces of the footing (B) and the outside edges of the footing trench (C); mark them on the board, too. Remember that the footing width is either twice as wide as the wall or two-thirds the wall height, whichever is greater. The trench itself should be 1 or 2 feet wider than the footing to provide room for installing the formwork. At each mark, use a handsaw to make shallow cuts in the crosspieces to hold the strings in place.

4. Locate outside edges of excavation. Attach strings to represent the inside and outside edges of the trench.

Then, using the strings as a guide, pour a line of flour or clean sand on the ground beneath the string to aid in digging a straight trench. Remove the strings before digging.

EXCAVATION AND FORMWORK

Excavating the footing trench can be done by hand or by machine, depending on the size of the job and your budget. Before deciding on a specific approach, check out the alternatives and the relative costs of each. You probably can handle a shallow

footing with picks and shovels. However, if you need to dig a large, deep trench, hand digging may be impractical in terms of time and cost. Consider renting a small backhoe or trenching machine or hiring an excavation contractor. Small excavation firms often advertise their services in the classified section of the newspaper. Many landscaping contractors also provide excavation services.

Digging the Trench

If you're digging by hand, use a flat-blade spade or shovel to dig a trench along the sand or flour guidelines.

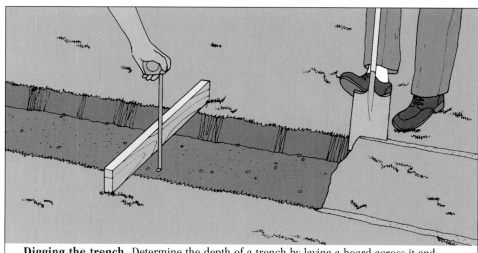

Digging the trench. Determine the depth of a trench by laying a board across it and measuring with a tape.

The trench depth should accommodate any portion of the wall that will be below grade, plus the concrete footing, plus a gravel subbase if there is one. Check the trench depth by laying a 2x4 across the excavation and measuring the distance to the bottom of the trench. Keep the sides of the trench as vertical as possible and the bottom as level as possible.

Tamp the bottom. After you dig the trench, compact the soil in the trench bottom with a hand tamper to prevent settling. Then fill the entire trench bottom with at least 6 inches of gravel. The gravel helps drain water away from the footing. Rake the gravel level, then use a tamper to compact the gravel to about 4 inches.

Tamp the bottom. Compact the soil in the bottom of the trench by pounding it with a hand tamper; then pour at least 6 inches of gravel into the trench.

Installing the Forms

Select straight pieces of lumber for the form boards. Gather some 1x4s you can use as stakes and spreader bars. Later, when the concrete dries, you'll need to disassemble the forms. You can make this easier by putting the forms together with 16d duplex nails or galvanized deck screws.

1. Locate the footing corners. Reattach the strings representing the edges of the footing to the batter boards. At the ends of the footing, or where corner strings intersect, hang a plumb bob to the bottom of the trench. Mark these points by driving short lengths of rebar into the ground, well below the top of proposed footing.

2. Install the corner stakes. Corner stakes will hold the form in place. To position them, hold a small piece of form material against the rebar at the outside corners. Drive two stakes snugly against the form material. The tops of the stakes should be level with each other and at the same height as the top of the form boards. If you're placing an L-shaped

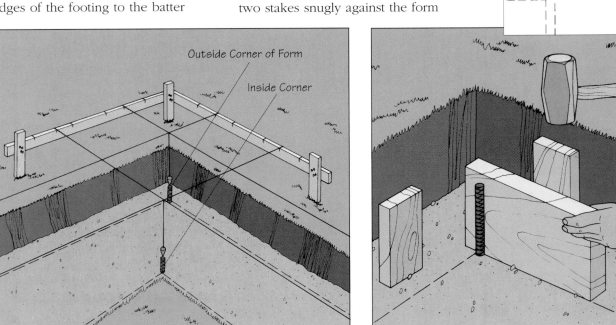

1. Mark the corners of the footings by driving rebar into the ground. To locate the corner, hang a plumb bob from intersections of the strings attached to the batter boards.

2. A spacer made from a scrap of the form helps you position the stakes that will hold the form.

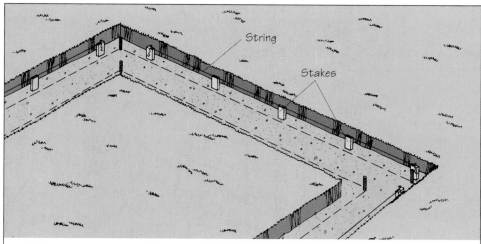

String

Stakes

3. Stretch a string to mark the edge of the form, and drive stakes along the string at intervals of 4 feet or less.

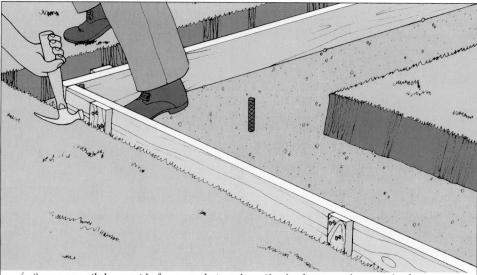

4. Screw or nail the outside forms to their stakes. Check often to make sure the forms are level.

5. Install the inside forms, making sure they are level with the outside forms.

footing, you can, for now, ignore the rebar driven at inside corners.

3. Install the intermediate stakes.

Stretch string between the corner stakes and level it with the help of a string level. Use the string as a guide to install intermediate stakes about every 2 feet. If the form boards are long enough to reach between the corner stakes, you may find it easier to attach and level the form boards first, then use them as a guide to install the intermediate stakes.

4. Install the form boards.

Attach the form boards by driving nails or screws through the stakes into the boards. While nailing, place your foot, a large stone, or a sledge-hammer head against the inside of the board to keep from knocking the stake out of position. As long as the stakes are level, you can align the top edges of the boards with the tops of the stakes. Double-check the form boards frequently with a 4-foot level to make sure they remain level.

5. Set up the inside forms.

Use the outside form boards to locate the stakes for the inside forms. Beginning a few inches from the inside-corner rebar, drive 1x2 stakes every 2 feet or so. Locate the stakes so that when you attach the form boards the space between the forms equals the footing width.

If there is an inside corner, put a form board against the rebar you drove earlier to mark the inside corner. When the board is positioned as shown, attach the stakes. Every few feet, lay a level across the inside and outside form boards, as shown, to be sure they are level with each other. Adjust as necessary.

Set the stakes for the adjacent inside form; then attach the form board. Butt the end of this board against the one you just put in place. Toenail the top edge to keep the boards flush. Make sure it is level.

6. Brace the formwork. If the
form boards are 2x6s or wider, install

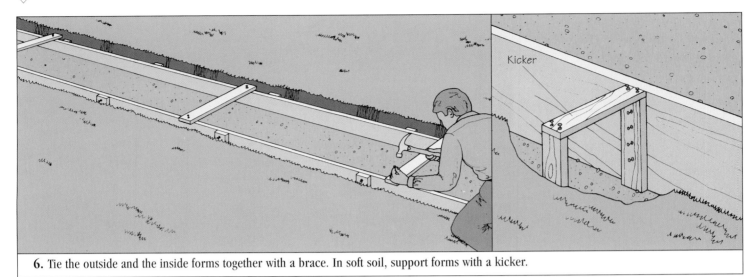

6. Tie the outside and the inside forms together with a brace. In soft soil, support forms with a kicker.

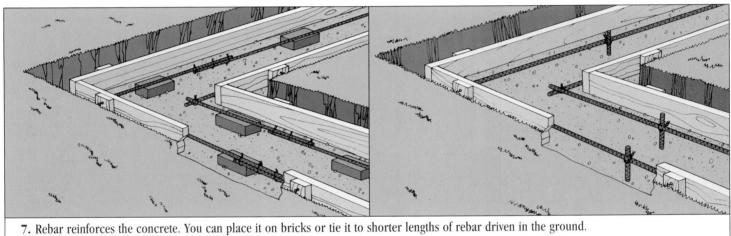

7. Rebar reinforces the concrete. You can place it on bricks or tie it to shorter lengths of rebar driven in the ground.

1x4 stretchers across the board tops at 4- to 6-foot intervals to keep the concrete from spreading the forms.

7. Add reinforcement. Place rebar between the forms, according to local building codes. Rebar should be about one-third of the way up from the bottom of the footing. For shallow footings, prop the rebar above the trench bottom on bricks. For deeper footings, you can tie the rebar to short rebar driven into the ground. Overlap rebar ends by at least 12 inches and tie them together with wire. Keep the bars at least 1 inch away from the form boards or trench sides.

POURING CONCRETE

After the formwork is complete, prepare the site for pouring concrete. Clean up anything that will be in the way. Make sure you can get the con-

crete to the forms. Brush some clean motor oil onto the inside of the form boards so that the concrete won't bond to them. Sprinkle the trench with water. The gravel should be moist so that it won't suck water from the concrete, but do not allow puddles to form.

1. Pour the concrete. Starting at one end of the form, pour the concrete. Have several helpers with shovels available to spread the concrete in the forms as it is poured. Do not allow the concrete to mound up in one area. If you are pouring wet-mix concrete, move the chute along the form, placing the concrete in an even layer. (For deeper forms, make successive pours in layers about 6 inches deep.) Stop the pour a foot or so short of the form end to provide space for concrete that you'll move around as you level the footing. Use a shovel to spread the concrete evenly in the form and to

1. Don't let the concrete mound when you pour it. Have a helper spread it along the trench with a shovel.

tamp it in place. Work the shovel with a slicing motion to eliminate any voids or air pockets in the concrete, especially along the edges of the form and in the corners.

2. Screed the forms. Pull a scrap piece of 2x4 along the tops of the forms to level off, or screed, the concrete. Work in a zigzag motion from one end of the form to the other. The purpose of screeding is to knock down any high spots and fill in any voids. The surface can be left slightly rough to provide good "tooth" for the mortar bed on which you'll set the masonry units for the wall. If you plan to build a double-thickness brick wall or hollow concrete-block retaining wall, vertical rebar may be required. Place the rebar in the footing while the concrete is still wet.

3. Let the concrete cure. Although concrete hardens in a few hours, it takes longer to cure to its full strength. So wait about a week before building the wall. During this time, keep the concrete moist by sprinkling it with water several times a day, then covering it with plastic sheeting. Do not remove the forms until the curing process is complete. To remove the forms, carefully pull out the nails or screws securing the form boards to the stakes, and gently pry the form boards away from the footing, taking care not to chip or crack the concrete.

Stepped Footings

If you're building the wall on a slope, you'll need to build a stepped footing. Think of this footing as a narrow set of stairs. The length, height, and number of steps needed depends mostly on the size of the blocks you will use to build the wall and the angle of the slope. Steeper slopes require more steps than gradual slopes.

At the top of the slope, dig a level footing trench. When the slope of the hill results in a trench that is shallower than the footing required, dig down to create a step, as shown. Make the step at least the depth of the footing. If the footing is for a concrete block wall, make the step equal to the height of the block. Once you've dug the step, dig a level trench, working down the hill until the trench is too shallow. If the footing is for a cement block wall, adjust the length of the trench so it's a multiple of the block length. When using 16-inch blocks, for example, steps could be 16, 32, or 48 inches long.

Continue digging steps and level trenches along the length of the slope.

When setting up the form boards, overlap them at each step as shown. Splice them together with closely spaced 1x4 or 2x4 stakes. Nail on a riser form, and dig a space behind the form to allow concrete to flow into the lower footing trench. Use short lengths of rebar to suspend the reinforcement above the bottom of the footing trench, as shown.

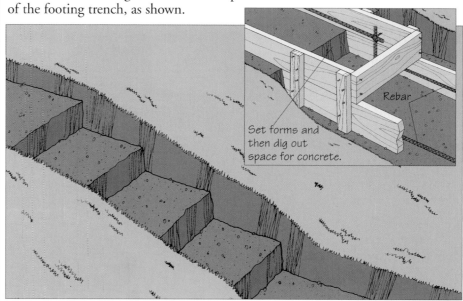

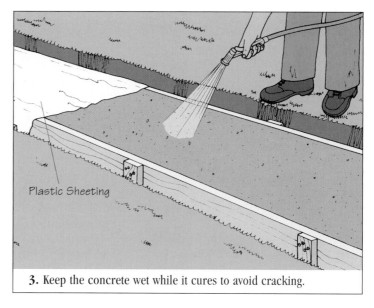

Set forms and then dig out space for concrete.

Rebar

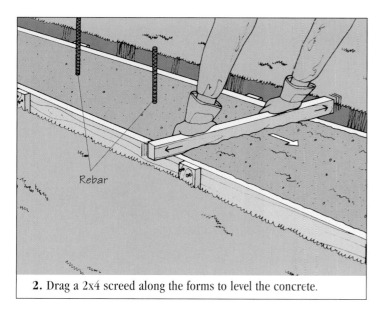

Rebar

2. Drag a 2x4 screed along the forms to level the concrete.

Plastic Sheeting

3. Keep the concrete wet while it cures to avoid cracking.

MORTARED STONE WALLS

Building a mortared stone wall
requires more time and effort than
constructing a dry-laid wall, but the
mortared wall is sturdier and has
a more formal, solid appearance.
Because the wall will have a foundation, check with your local building
department to find out if you need
a building permit.

GENERAL REQUIREMENTS

Fitting the stones in a mortared wall
is not as demanding as it is for a
dry-laid wall—the mortar fills in gaps.
For this reason, a mortared wall is a
good option when you have a limited
selection of stone shapes and sizes.
It's the only option when you're
working with river or creek stones:
Round creekbed stones won't work
in a dry-laid wall. Mortar allows you
to set irregularly shaped or rounded
stones firmly, with the best faces
exposed. Unlike dry-laid walls, which
must slope inward as they go up,
stone walls 3 feet and under are built
with plumb sides. For a strong wall,
however, it is good practice to use
bond stones and to stagger the joints.

Footings. Mortared stone walls
are inflexible, and they require con-

A mortared stone wall is more formal looking than a dry stone wall, and it is
more durable. It is built much like a dry stone wall, but you'll need to pour a
foundation and apply a bed of mortar between courses.

crete footings as a result. For walls
less than 2 feet high, the footing may
be as simple as a shallow trench dug
to the width of the wall and filled
with several inches of concrete. For
higher, wider walls, the footing should
be twice the width of the wall. The
footing should be as thick as the wall
is wide. In cold climates, the footing
should extend below the frost line.
Check with your building department
to see what local code requires. The

top of the footing should be several
inches below ground level so that it
won't show once you build the wall.
For complete instructions on installing
wall footings, see Chapter 4, "Wall
Footings," page 41. Allow the footing
to cure for at least three days before
building the wall.

Mortar. The mortar mix used for
stone walls is called a Type N mix.
It consists of 1 part portland cement,

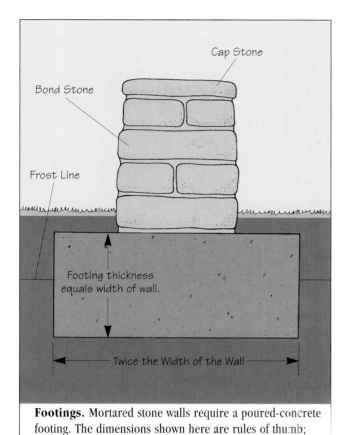

Footings. Mortared stone walls require a poured-concrete footing. The dimensions shown here are rules of thumb; check local codes for required footing size and depth.

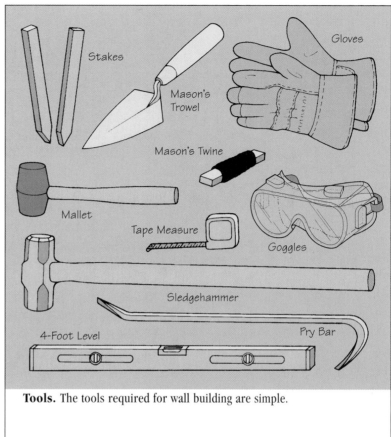

Tools. The tools required for wall building are simple.

1 part lime, and 6 parts sand, all mixed with about 5 parts water. For small projects, it's usually best to buy pre-mixed mortar in sacks; you add the water. For larger projects, you can save money by buying the dry ingredients separately and making your own mortar mix. Some masons prefer to substitute fireclay for lime in the mix to make it more workable. Mixes containing lime can stain the stones, so if you use a lime mix, test it on your stones. Add water sparingly to make a dry, stiff mix that supports the stones and won't squeeze out of the joints.

The best way to compute the amount of mortar needed is to build a short section of mortared wall (say, 3 feet tall by 5 feet long) and note the amount of mortar required. Multiply this amount by the number of 5-foot sections in the wall to figure the amount needed for the rest of the wall. Rubble and fieldstone walls will require more mortar than walls constructed of neatly fitting cut stones or ashlar.

Tools. You will need tools for mixing and applying concrete and mortar,

including a shovel, wheelbarrow, mason's trowel, and tape measure. You'll also need a sharp-bladed shovel and a pickax for removing stones in the way of the wall. Stakes, string, and a mason's level help in laying out and stacking the wall. A prybar comes in handy for moving stones. Wear heavy leather gloves for handling stones.

CONSTRUCTING THE WALL

Mortared stone walls are built much like dry-laid walls, although the work will progress considerably more slowly. Select bond stones, end stones, and cap stones and spread them along the course of the wall. Select the remaining stones one course at a time and test-fit them without mortar first.

1. Take a trial run. About one week after placing the footing, mark the wall's sides and ends on it with a chalkline. Place the end stones, and set bond stones every 4 to 6 inches along the foundation. Fit the remaining stones so that joints between them

are narrow but no less than about ½ inch wide. Fill voids between large stones with smaller ones. Arrange the stones with the flattest, broadest sides facing down to ensure a good mortar bond to the footing.

Once you're satisfied with the fit, remove the stones and lay them in order on their respective sides of the footing. Make sure the stones are clean and dry before you set them permanently.

2. Lay the first course. Starting at an end, spread a 2-inch layer of mortar about 3 feet long between the chalk lines on the footing. Carefully set the end stone, and tap it lightly with a mallet or hammer until it is approximately level. Then lay two stones next to the end stone to start the wythes that will be the front and back of the wall.

3. Mortar between the stones. Once you've laid enough stones to cover the mortar bed, use a pointed trowel to mortar all the joints between the stones. Pick up a glob of mortar on the trowel; hold the trowel several inches above the joint and parallel to

1. Make a trial run to find the right stones before you set the mortar.

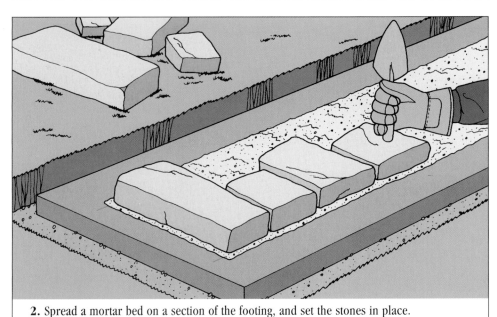

2. Spread a mortar bed on a section of the footing, and set the stones in place.

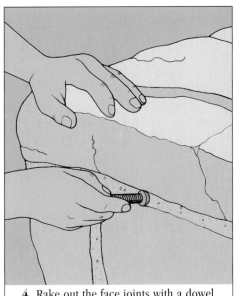

it; and with a downward flip, fling the mortar into the joint. Generally, the mortar will settle by itself to fill in any voids; you needn't tamp it in. Remove excess or squeezed-out mortar from joints with your trowel. If some mortar gets on the stone face, immediately wipe away the mortar with a damp sponge.

4. Tool the joints. After finishing each section of wall, recess, or rake, the outside joints to a depth of ½ to 1 inch. You can use a mason's jointing tool to rake the joints and make them smooth, although a ⅜ x 6-inch round-head bolt or rounded wooden stick works almost as well. Deep, 1-inch joints emphasize shadows and have a natural appearance. Shallow, ½-inch joints are better suited for semidressed and fully dressed cut stones. In any case, the joints between cap stones at the top of the wall are usually left flush.

Timing is critical in this step. The mortar should set up enough that pushing your thumb into it barely leaves a print (usually about ½ hour after the stone is set). Keep an eye on your watch as you work; it's easy to lose track of time when you're laying stones.

5. Clean the stone. After striking the joints for each section, use a whisk broom to remove loose mortar parti-

3. Once the mortar bed is covered with stone, fill spaces between the stones by flinging mortar into them.

4. Rake out the face joints with a dowel or a round-head bolt.

cles and smooth out the scraped joints. Use a stiff-bristle brush to remove any mortar that has adhered to the face of the stone. A steel brush may work on some stones but may mar others; test in an inconspicuous area before using. If you've worked carefully while setting the stones, there shouldn't be much mortar to clean off.

6. Extend the mortar bed. Trowel another 3-foot-long mortar bed onto the footing, set more stones, fill the joints, and repeat until the first course is laid. Although the stones will vary in height, try to keep the course level. Set up stakes and level strings so that they are about 3 inches above the top outside edges of the first course. Measure down from the strings, making sure both ends of the stones are the same distance from the string. If a stone is too low, raise it by placing more mortar underneath it. If it's too high, push down on it to squeeze out more mortar.

7. Build end and corner leads. Once you've laid the first course, you build up the ends and corners before filling in the rest of the other courses. This is called "building the leads" and ensures that the ends and corners will be plumb, square, and level.

To build a lead, trowel out a patch of mortar at the end or corner of the base course. Make sure that you use the best stones for the leads. Set the stones one course at a time. Allow the mortar to set up slightly, then tool the joints. This helps ensure that the mortar in the lower courses will be strong enough to hold the weight of the stones above. Stagger vertical joints and check frequently with a mason's level to make sure the lead faces are plumb and the courses are level.

8. Fill in the remaining courses. After building up the leads, move the string lines up for the second course, again placing them about 3 inches higher than the desired top edge of the stones. As with the first course, dry-fit the stones before applying mortar. Lay a 2-inch-thick bed of mortar, about 3 to 5 feet long, over the first course. Keep the mortar to within

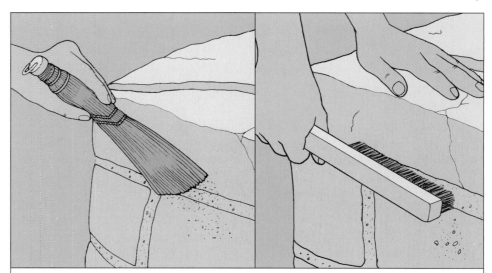

5. Brush off excess mortar with a whisk broom. Mortar that has adhered to the stone can be removed with a steel brush.

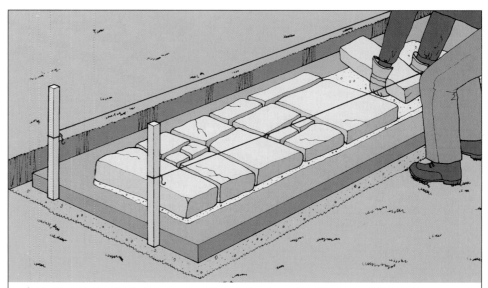

6. Continue laying the first course, working section by section. First spread 3 feet of mortar, then lay stones on it. Spread more mortar and lay more stones until the first course is complete.

7. Once the first course is laid, build up the corners. The corners, or "leads," help provide plumb, level surfaces that aid in laying out the rest of the wall.

about 2 inches from the outside edges of the wall so that the mortar won't squeeze out when you set the stones. If it squeezes out, scrape it away with the trowel. Place bond stones every 4 to 6 feet, and check the wall frequently for plumb.

9. Cap the wall. Use the flattest, broadest, and best-looking stones for the top course, or cap. Spread a 2-inch-thick layer of mortar over the top course, and embed the cap stones in the mortar. For more on mortar see "Mortar," page 75.

An alternative to cap stones is to finish off the top with a solid mortar cap. The cap should be 2 to 4 inches thick and crowned slightly to facilitate water runoff, as shown.

10. Clean the wall. Once the mortar is hard, wash down the wall with clear water to remove any mortar stains. If a mortar film still adheres to the stones, scrub the wall with a stiff brush and a mild detergent or a light solution of trisodium phosphate (TSP) and water.

Working with Large Stones

Large stones, such as those used for bond stones, may be so heavy that they squeeze the mortar out of their bed joints. If this is the case, you can support the stones with wood wedges, as shown, to maintain the proper joint spacing. When you lay the mortar bed, position the wedges on the outside face of the wall, as shown, then set the stone in place. After the mortar stiffens enough to support the stone, remove the wedges and pack mortar in the holes.

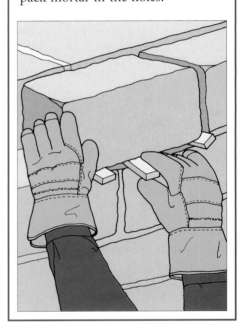

8. Position strings and use them as a guide to fill in between the leads, one course at a time. Continue to lay bond stones in the wall.

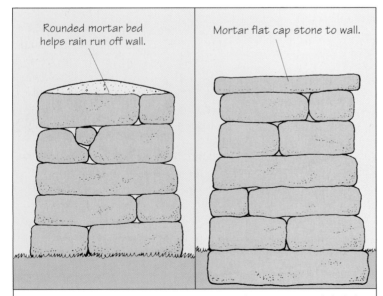

Rounded mortar bed helps rain run off wall.

Mortar flat cap stone to wall.

9. The cap on a stone wall is either a layer of mortar, mounded slightly to help water run off, or a series of flat stones, mortared in place.

10. When you've finished the wall, hose it down to remove dirt and stray mortar.

CONCRETE-BLOCK WALLS

Concrete blocks provide a relatively fast, inexpensive means of building a sturdy masonry wall. It doesn't take many tools or skills to build a concrete-block wall. The large, uniform size of the blocks makes the work go quickly. Granted, you won't be able to build the wall as quickly as an experienced mason. However, you don't have to build the wall all at once. Because you're working with individual units, you can build the wall in stages, doing as little or as much work as your time allows.

Building concrete-block walls requires a lot of heavy lifting and hard work, so it's best to pace yourself according to your physical ability. Spend a few hours each evening after work, or spread the job out over several weekends.

Unlike stone walls, which are usually built with two stacks of stones, or wythes, a freestanding concrete-block wall can be built with a single stack of blocks. Walls up to 3 feet tall usually require no steel reinforcement, unless they serve as a retaining wall. (Higher walls require special techniques and are best left to professionals.)

TYPES OF BLOCKS

Conventional concrete blocks are composed of portland cement, graded aggregate (crushed stone), and water. They weigh about 40 to 45 pounds apiece. The blocks are usually gray, although you can find them in several pastel or earth colors. Lighter-weight blocks, called cinder blocks, contain lightweight aggregate, such as expanded shale, clay, slate, or even pumice stone. Cinder blocks may be as light as 25 pounds. They are usually less expensive and easier to work with, but they don't have the structural strength and impact resistance of heavier blocks. Cinder blocks aren't recommended for building retaining walls or any wall that could be hit accidentally by a car or snow thrower. For building 3-foot garden walls, however, cinder blocks will usually suffice. Local building codes may limit their use, so check to see which types of blocks are allowed for use in your particular project.

Most blocks for walls have two or three hollow cores—called cells—to reduce their weight and to provide a place for rebar. The solid sections

Because concrete block is uniform and stacks quickly, it is often used in gardens as a backdrop for plantings.

between the cores are called webs. On some blocks, the faces and webs are tapered to provide additional surface on the top of the block for mortar. Lay these blocks with the large surface up.

Shapes and Sizes

Standard concrete blocks have a nominal measurement of 8x8x16 inches long. The actual size is 7⅝x7⅝x15⅝ inches to allow for a ⅜-inch mortar joint. You use the (larger) nominal dimensions when estimating the number of blocks required for the job. Blocks also come in nominal widths of 4, 6, 8, 10, and 12 inches. Narrower sizes often are common

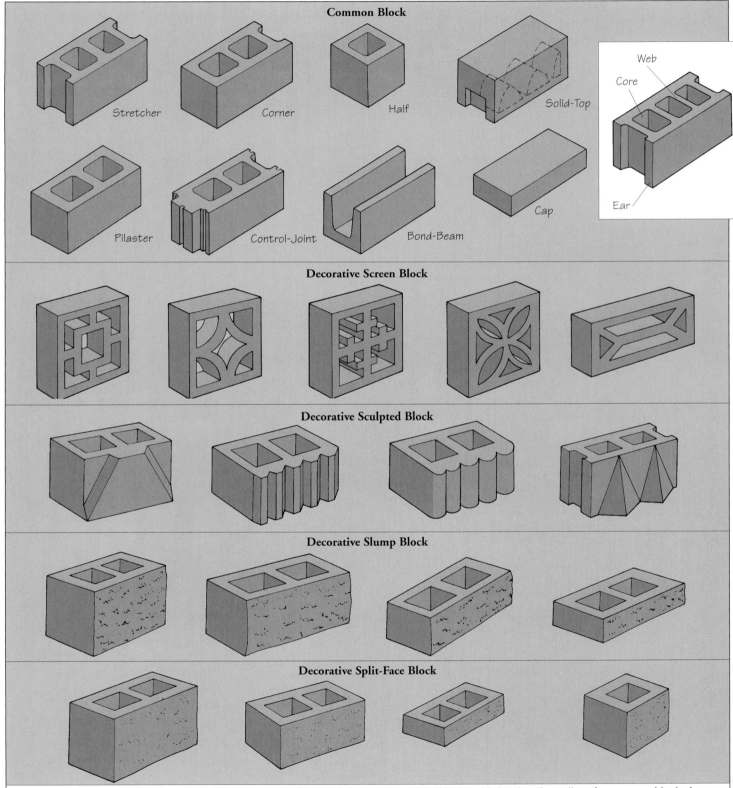

Shapes and sizes. Blocks are shaped differently, depending on their use. Decorative blocks add detail to the wall surface; screen blocks let light and air through the wall, but aren't as strong as other blocks.

in very low walls, planters, and garden borders. Wider blocks provide a more massive effect.

Most wall construction involves two types of blocks—stretcher blocks and corner blocks. Stretcher blocks have two flanges at each end. Corner blocks have one flat end to provide a finished appearance at the ends or corners of a wall. Half blocks are half the length of a standard block and are also for building wall ends. Special solid-top blocks and cap blocks have smooth tops for finishing the top of the wall.

Other specialty blocks are used for structural purposes in long or tall walls. Among these blocks are bond-beam blocks, pilaster (pier) blocks, and control-joint blocks. Bond-beam blocks have a U-shaped channel that you fill with mortar to strengthen the wall. Pilaster blocks are flat on both ends. Control-joint blocks have interlocking ends that are joined without mortar to allow for movement in the wall without cracking the blocks or mortar joints.

Decorative blocks. You can also buy various types of decorative blocks, which have sculptured or patterned surfaces to add visual interest to the wall. Decorative blocks come in the same sizes as standard blocks. One popular type, called a "split-face block," has a rough surface that resembles cut stone. A variation, called "slump block," resembles handmade adobe bricks.

Screen blocks are narrow, lightweight blocks with patterned openings. The openings allow the passage of light and air through the wall while providing some privacy. Screen blocks come in a variety of patterns and sizes; a common nominal size is 12x12x4 inches.

Because concrete blocks are usually manufactured on a local or regional basis, your choices will be limited to what's available at your local masonry supply or home center. Order decorative blocks or specialty blocks several weeks in advance to allow time for delivery.

Estimating Amounts

Base the number of blocks you'll need on the block's nominal dimensions, rather than on its actual dimensions. If possible, design the wall so that the height and length come out in multiples of the nominal dimensions of the blocks. For example, a standard block is nominally 8x8x16 inches, so a wall that's 8 inches wide, 32 inches high, and 8 feet long would require no cut blocks.

First, determine the length of the proposed wall in inches. Divide by the block length (typically 16 inches) to get the number of blocks needed for one course. Then divide the overall height of the wall by one block height (typically 8 inches) to determine the number of courses needed. To find out the total you'll need, multiply the blocks needed along the length by the number of blocks needed to create the height. Add 5 percent to allow for breakage. When figuring for walls with corners, measure the full length of each wall separately. A scale drawing of the wall will help you in your estimate. The table on this page shows the number of various-size blocks needed per 100 square feet of wall.

Storing concrete blocks. Unlike bricks, which are usually dampened before you lay them, concrete blocks are laid dry. Store them in a dry place. Stack the blocks on a pallet, waterproof tarp, or plastic sheet as close to the worksite as possible. Cover the stack with plastic sheeting to keep the blocks dry. If you are building the wall in several stages, cover the completed wall sections with plastic sheeting, as well.

BASIC REQUIREMENTS

Concrete-block walls need a poured-concrete footing for support. In some cases, reinforcement also may be needed. You can reinforce a wall by filling the cores with mortar and steel rods (called rebar) or by building a

Number of Blocks Required For 100 Square Feet of Wall	
Block Size (nominal; w x h x l)	**Number of Blocks***
4x4x16 6x4x16 8x4x16 10x4x16 12x4x16	225
4x8x16 6x8x16 8x8x16 (Standard block) 10x8x16 12x8x16	112½
8x8x8 (Half block) 10x8x8 12x8x8	225
* Add 5% for breakage	

column (called a pilaster). Even low walls can fall apart if the cores aren't filled with concrete or if no rebar is used. Check local codes to see what's required in your area.

Footings and foundations.
Before you lay the first block, the footing must be poured, screeded, floated smooth, and allowed to cure fully. (See Chapter 4, "Wall Footings," beginning on page 41.) Pour the footing to the thickness required by local codes—typically 6 inches for 3-foot garden walls. To determine the required length of the footing, measure the length of the proposed wall, and add 4 to 6 inches at each end. Typically, a footing is twice as wide as the block you'll be using.

If the top of the footing will be below the frost line, you can build a foundation up to ground level with stretchers and corner blocks. In some cases, the blocks below grade may need to be reinforced, usually by filling the block cavities with concrete or grout and inserting reinforcing rods. Check local codes for specific requirements.

Mortar. Mortar for outdoor use is generally what is called Type N—1 part portland cement, 1 part hydrated lime, and 6 parts sand. For most residential wall projects, you're better off buying premixed mortar in sacks rather than mixing mortar from separate ingredients. Mortar mix should be somewhat drier than concrete. Test for proper amount by creating a series of ridges in the mixture with a hoe or shovel. If the ridges remain sharp and distinct, you have added the right amount of water.

If you're constructing a below-grade concrete-block foundation, Type M mortar may be required. (Type N weathers better; Type M produces a stronger bond.) Type M consists of 1 part portland cement, ¼ part hydrated lime, and 3 parts sand. Check local codes to see which mortar you should be using.

Control joints. Control joints allow cracks to occur only at specific joints in the wall. On a small project, such as a short, low garden wall, you probably won't need control joints. However, long walls and those subject to unusual stresses will probably need control joints of some sort.

Because many variables determine how or where cracks may appear in a wall, there are no specific rules or guidelines on where control joints will be needed. Generally, cracks often occur at changes in wall height or at changes in footing level (such as above a stepped footing on hillside

walls). Cracks may also occur at changes in wall thickness, such as at a pilaster. Long lengths of wall usually develop cracks due to uneven settling or movement of earth beneath the footing. As a rule of thumb, long walls should have control joints placed every 20 feet.

There are several ways you can incorporate control joints into a wall, but the easiest is to use special control-joint blocks. These are cast to form an interlocking tongue-and-groove joint. (The end of one block has a tongue, the other has a groove.) Lay half-size control-joint blocks every second

Reinforcement

Although most freestanding walls under 3 feet high require no reinforcement, you may need to add it if your wall may be subject to unusual stress (such as high winds, earthquakes, or possible impact from automobiles or tractors) or frost heave. Codes are very specific concerning the type and amount of reinforcement used. Typically, a wall can be reinforced both vertically and horizontally with concrete and steel. Vertical reinforcement involves placing rebar into the footing while the concrete is still wet. The bars are spaced so that they will extend up through the block cells or cores, which are then filled with concrete or grout.

A pilaster, another type of vertical reinforcement, is a built-in column placed at the corners or ends of the wall and at 20-foot intervals along it. Even though pilasters aren't a necessity for walls under 6 feet, you may want to incorporate them into the design to add interest to the flat wall. Check with your local building department to see if pilasters are needed for your project and how they should be constructed to meet code requirements.

In some cases, horizontal reinforcement may also be required. Reinforce the wall by laying a course of special bond-beam blocks, which have no webs. Place rebar inside the blocks, and fill the cavities with concrete or grout.

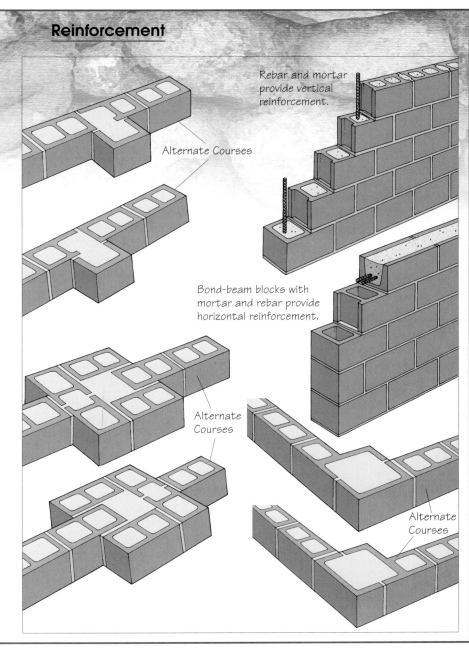

Rebar and mortar provide vertical reinforcement.

Alternate Courses

Bond-beam blocks with mortar and rebar provide horizontal reinforcement.

Alternate Courses

Alternate Courses

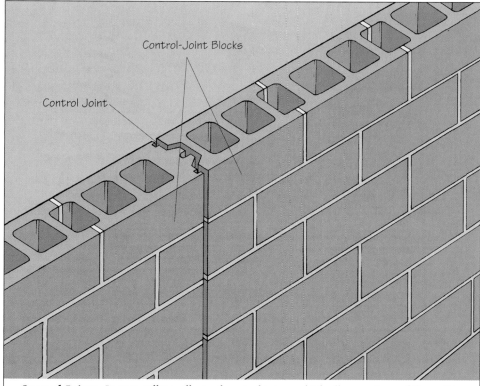

Control Joints. Longer, taller walls need control joints, which allow sections of the wall to shift independently and help keep the wall from cracking.

medium pointing trowel for applying the mortar. Tap the blocks with the trowel's wooden handle to seat the blocks in the mortar bed. To aid in aligning blocks, you'll need a mason's line and wooden or plastic line blocks. You'll also need a level (at least 3 feet long) to level and plumb the blocks as you lay them. To finish the mortar joints, the most popular tool is a convex jointer, which makes an indented joint that sheds water.

Measuring. Although not essential, a story pole comes in handy for checking the height of each course as you lay the blocks. Used like a ruler, the pole consists of a straight 1x2 or 2x4 on which you mark the height of the blocks and widths of the mortar joints.

Cutting concrete blocks. If the length of the wall isn't an exact multiple of the block length plus mortar joints, you will have to cut the blocks. The most accurate way to cut concrete blocks is with a masonry saw (available at tool rentals) or a portable circular saw fitted with a masonry blade or abrasive disc. If you have only a few blocks to cut, use a brick hammer and mason's chisel or brick set. Mark both sides of the block, then tap the chisel along the line.

course to create a straight control joint that runs from top to bottom of the wall. To allow for movement between the blocks, the joint is not mortared. Run a bead of flexible caulk into the control joint to hide the crack.

Tools. You need very few tools to lay a concrete-block wall. Tools and equipment used to mix and apply mortar include a mixer or mortar box, and a mortar board or hawk for carrying the mortar to the site. Use a

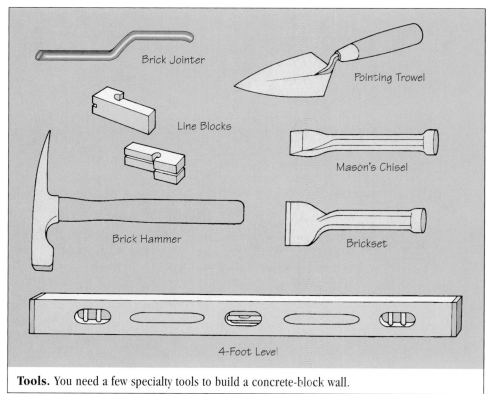

Tools. You need a few specialty tools to build a concrete-block wall.

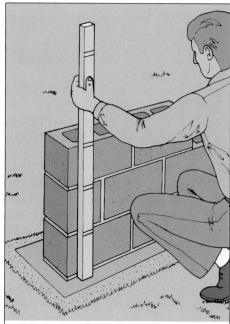

Measuring. Mark the proper height of the bricks and mortar joints on a piece of wood and use it to check the spacing of the blocks.

A few sharp blows should break the block. Most standard blocks have built-in score marks on the top and bottom edges of the block to aid in cutting half blocks.

Bond patterns. Most standard blocks are laid in a simple running bond pattern, in which the joints of each successive course are staggered, by exactly half a block. This pattern provides the greatest strength, and it makes the best use of standard block sizes with a minimum amount of cut blocks. You can add interest to a bond pattern by combining blocks of varying sizes. Other patterns

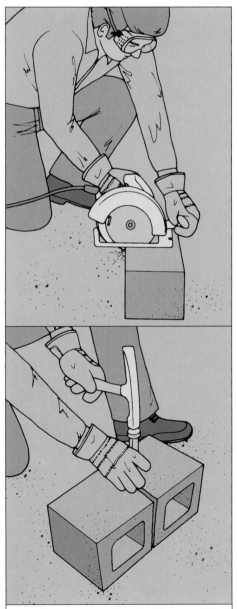

Cutting concrete blocks. If you need to cut blocks, a chisel or a saw fitted with a masonry blade will cut cleanly.

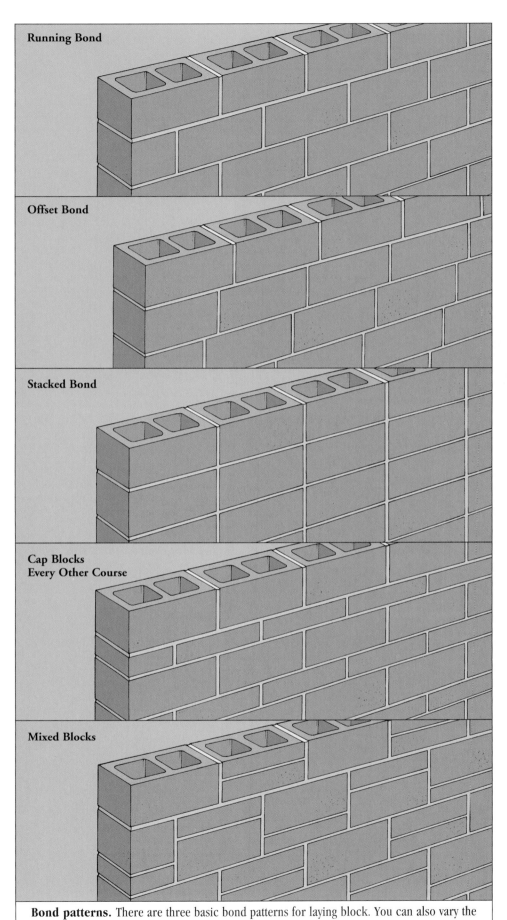

Running Bond

Offset Bond

Stacked Bond

Cap Blocks Every Other Course

Mixed Blocks

Bond patterns. There are three basic bond patterns for laying block. You can also vary the size of the blocks to create visual interest.

include an offset bond and a stacked bond. A stacked bond, with one joint directly above the next, is common on screen-block walls. It isn't as structurally sound as the others, so it usually requires vertical reinforcement. (See "Reinforcement," page 74.)

BUILDING A BLOCK WALL

The following steps show how to lay the first course of a concrete-block wall. The instructions assume that you have already placed a suit-able poured-concrete footing. You also should have the ingredients and tools for mixing mortar. As mentioned, concrete blocks do not need to be wetted before being laid.

1. Mark the wall ends or corners. First, locate the outside corners or ends of the wall by stretching lines between the batter boards that you set up for the footing. (For more information, see "Locating the Footing," page 46.) On straight walls, hang a plumb bob at the wall's ends. If your wall has corners, hang it from the intersecting lines as well. Mark these spots on the footing with a pencil.

2. Mark the footing. Sweep the footing clean. With a helper, snap chalk lines on the footing to represent the outside edges of each wall. Starting at one end or corner, make a trail run, laying the entire first course along the chalk lines. Place ⅜-inch wood spacers between the blocks to represent mortar joints. If possible, adjust the mortar joint spacing slightly so that you don't have to cut blocks. If you have to cut blocks, they must be at least a half block long. Fill smaller spaces by cutting two blocks: For a space that is a ¼-block long, for example, cut two blocks to five-eighths their full length. Remove a block next to the gap. Fill the resulting gap with the cut blocks.

Once all the blocks are laid out, check the corners to make sure that they meet at 90 degrees.

3. Spread the mortar. Remove the blocks and stand them on end as close as possible to where they will be laid. Mix a stiff batch of mortar, then starting at one corner, lay a continuous mortar bed about 1-inch thick along one of the chalk lines. Keep the edge of the mortar bed about ½ inch inside the chalk lines so that you don't cover them. Put down enough mortar to set three or four blocks. Hold the trowel at an angle so that the edge smoothes and flattens the mortar. Then use the

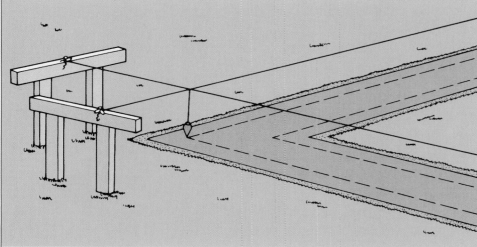

1. Mark the edges of the wall with strings and batter boards. Attach a plumb bob where the corners meet.

2. Connect the corner and endpoints by snapping a chalk line between them.

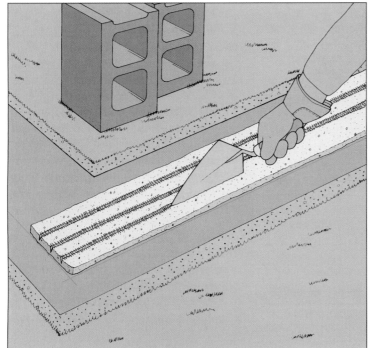

3. Make furrows in the mortar with the edge of the trowel. The weight of the block flattens the furrows, creating an even mortar bed.

4. Put the first block in the mortar and tap it with the trowel to level it.

point of the tool to create a series of shallow ridges or furrows in the mortar, as shown. The weight of the block will squeeze out the furrows and spread the mortar thoroughly over the blocks.

4. Set the first block. Set the end or corner block on the mortar bed, aligned with the chalk lines on the footing. Embed the block in the mortar by tapping on the top lightly with the trowel handle. Place a level, both crosswise and lengthwise, on top of the block to make sure it is level in all directions, and make adjustments by tapping on the block with the trowel handle. Then use a tape measure, folding rule, or a story pole to check the block height. The top of a standard block should be exactly 8 inches above the footing. If the block is too high, tap it down with the trowel handle; if the block is too low, remove it and add more mortar.

5. Add stretcher blocks. With your trowel swipe a ¾-inch-thick layer of mortar on the two flanges, or ears, at one end of a stretcher block. Grasp the top web opening and lift the block just over its location on the

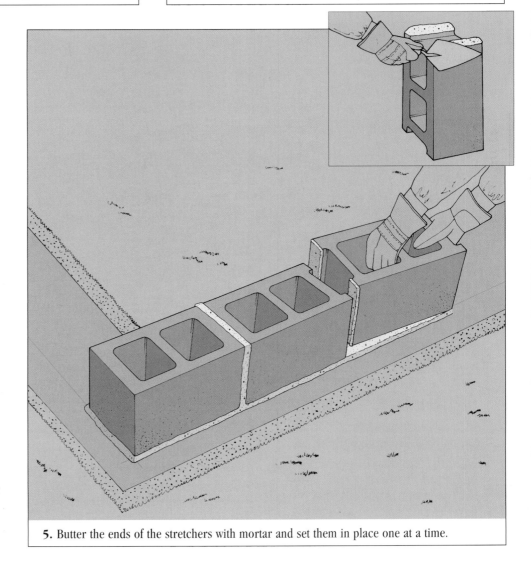

5. Butter the ends of the stretchers with mortar and set them in place one at a time.

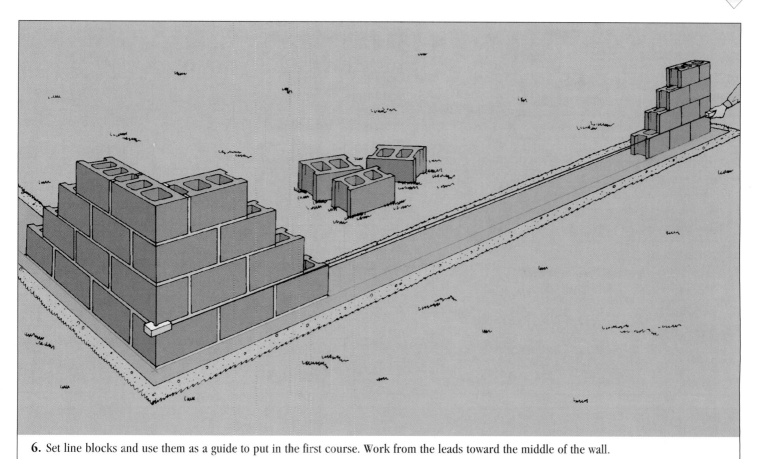

6. Set line blocks and use them as a guide to put in the first course. Work from the leads toward the middle of the wall.

mortar bed. Gently but quickly set the block in the mortar bed, nudge it against the corner block, and seat it by tapping it with the trowel handle. If the mortar falls off, remove the block and try again. Measure the mortar joint, and tap the block closer to its neighbor if necessary. Use a level to make sure the block is level in both directions and that the tops and faces of the blocks are in alignment. Repeat this procedure with the third block. If you're building a corner, lay blocks at right angles to the corner block and check for square, as shown. After laying each block, clean excess mortar off the footing with a trowel.

After you set three blocks, go to the opposite end of the wall and set three blocks there.

6. Fill in the remaining blocks.

Attach line blocks—often given away when you buy block—to the two end blocks. Stretch string between them and tighten to hold the blocks in place. Position the string even with the top of the concrete blocks and level the string with a line level. The

blocks should be level with each other. If there is only a slight difference, make succeeding mortar joints thicker or thinner on one end of the wall until both sides are level. If there is a great deal of difference, lift the blocks at the low end, and place enough mortar under them to bring them up to the level of the blocks at the opposite end of the wall.

Once these blocks are level, use the string as a guide to fill in the remaining blocks in the first course. Work from each end toward the middle of the wall.

7. Set the closure block. This is

the last block to be set in the course and is often the most difficult to lay because it must fit neatly between the blocks on either side. First, measure the opening to determine if a full-size block will fit. If not, you'll need to cut the block. (For the procedure, see "Cutting Concrete Blocks," page 61.) Swipe mortar onto the ends of the last block and onto the blocks on either side of the opening in the wall. Slowly slide the block into place.

7. Butter both ends with mortar, and slide the last block into place.

Make sure enough mortar remains in the joints to make a tight seal. If you knock too much off, remove the block, add more mortar, and try again. If a small amount of mortar falls out, leave the block in place and tuck more mortar into the joint with your trowel.

With the first course finished, check the entire course to make sure it's level and that all blocks are properly aligned with each other.

8. Finish the mortar joints. As you work, allow the mortar to set "thumbprint hard": After about 20 or 30 minutes, press a mortar joint with your thumb. If a print remains but the mortar does not stick to your thumb, the joint is ready to be smoothed and shaped, or tooled. Usually, joints are tooled with a convex jointer, which makes concave joints that provide good strength, shed water well, and look more attractive. Flush joints are used when the wall will be covered with stucco. These and other joints are shown in "Tooling Mortar Joints," page 81.

Tool the vertical joints first, then the horizontal joint. After tooling, remove any bits of excess mortar, called tags, with the top of your trowel. Finish by brushing the joints lightly with a whisk broom or soft brush.

9. Build corner leads. Once they've laid the first course, most masons prefer to "build the leads"—the corners or ends—before laying the next course. They set as many blocks as it takes to end up with a single block at the top course. The remaining blocks, or stretcher courses, are then placed between the leads.

Start by applying a 1-inch layer of mortar on the top edges of the first few blocks of the first course. For most low garden walls, you need only mortar the outer edges of the block (called face-shell mortaring). For a stronger installation, you can mortar the webbing between the cores (called full mortaring). If you're building a wall that stops instead of turning a corner, start the second course with a half block, as shown. If the wall has a corner, place a full end block at a right angle to the first.

Press the block for the second course into the mortar bed, aligned with the blocks beneath it. Tap the block level with your trowel handle, and check the height with a story pole. Continue laying up blocks to build a lead with a single block at the top course, as

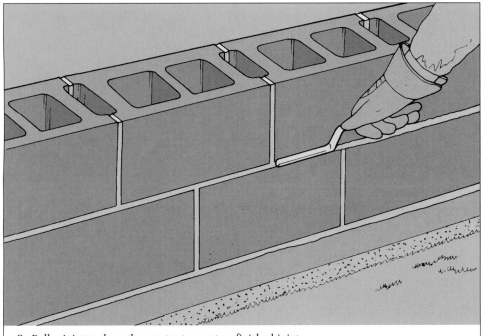

8. Pull a jointer along the mortar to create a finished joint.

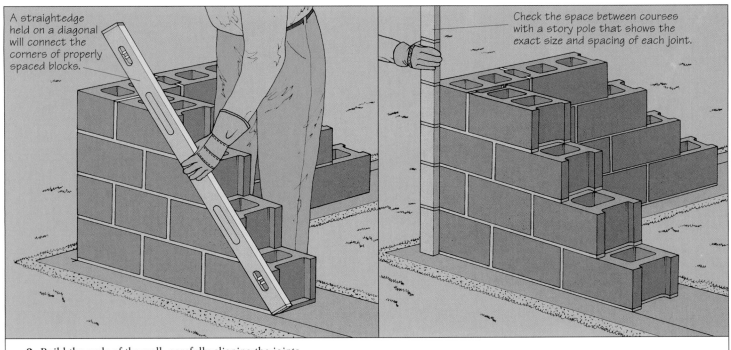

A straightedge held on a diagonal will connect the corners of properly spaced blocks.

Check the space between courses with a story pole that shows the exact size and spacing of each joint.

9. Build the ends of the wall, carefully aligning the joints.

shown. Check frequently to see that the blocks are level, plumb, and aligned. Use the story pole to ensure that each course is at the correct height. As you build up the lead, check the alignment of the bond pattern. A straightedge held diagonally should cross the top corners of all the blocks.

Tool the joints as you build the remaining sections of the wall.

10. Fill in stretcher courses. After building each end or corner lead, fill in the stretcher courses between them. For each course, attach the line block to the corner blocks. Align the string with the top edge of the blocks. Work from each end toward the middle. Check joint spacing frequently by holding a mason's level diagonally across the block corners and make any adjustments by varying the thickness of the mortar joints. Fit the final block for each course as you did for the first course.

11. Cap the wall. You can cap the wall in one of several ways, as shown in the drawings. The simplest method involves mortaring solid cap blocks on top of the wall. Another option is to fill the top block cores with mortar and create a mortared top. If you do this, cover the cores in the next-to-last course with metal screen. The screen, available from masonry suppliers, keeps the mortar from falling down into the blocks below. Fill the cores in the top course with concrete or mortar, and

10. Fill in the stretchers between the leads, guiding your work with a line stretched between line blocks.

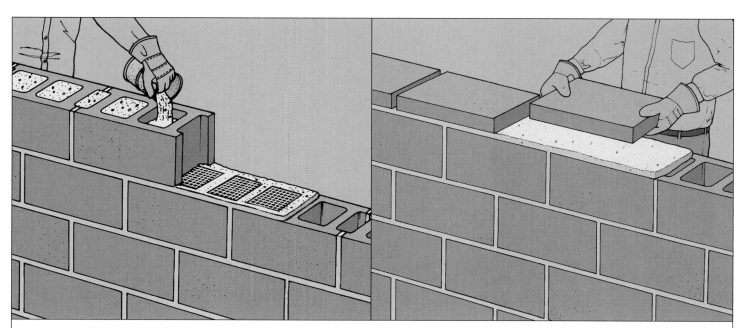

11. You can finish a wall with solid concrete cap blocks. Or you can pour mortar into the top cells, then spread a layer of mortar on top of the wall. A metal screen between the last two courses keeps the mortar from falling down into the rest of the wall.

strike it flush. For a brick cap, fill the cores as shown. Allow the mortar to set up, then trowel out a few feet of mortar and set the brick cap. (For more on brick caps, see "Cap the Wall," page 84.)

Decorative Screen Blocks

Decorative concrete screen blocks have several applications, from tall masonry screens to low, open garden walls. While other block sizes are available, the standard screen block has a nominal measurement of 4x12x12 inches. Generally, the blocks are laid directly on top of each other (stacked bond), rather than staggered. The blocks are laid much like solid concrete blocks.

Screen blocks are relatively fragile compared with solid concrete blocks, so walls or screens more than about 4 feet high usually require both horizontal and vertical reinforcement. Because reinforcement requirements vary, depending on the size of the wall, wind loads, and other design factors, it's best to have the wall designed by a landscape architect or designer. If you want to build a low garden wall with screen blocks, check with the local building department for specific structural requirements. As with other masonry-unit walls, screen-block walls require a sturdy poured-concrete foundation.

Lay out the wall location on the footing, as you would for a solid concrete-block wall. Set the blocks with full, ⅜-inch mortar joints. For a sturdier installation, install reinforcing ties in the horizontal mortar joint, as shown in the drawing.

FINISHES AND SURFACE TREATMENTS

Bare concrete-block walls aren't very attractive, no matter how you've designed and built them. At the very least, you'll probably want to give them a coat of paint. Other treatments for masonry walls include stucco and brick or stone veneers.

Metal ties reinforce the wall.

Decorative screen blocks. A screen-block wall is built like a stacked bond concrete-block wall. To strengthen the wall, put metal ties across the vertical joints.

Paint. If you want to paint the wall, choose paint recommended for exterior masonry surfaces. Because masonry walls are relatively rough, use a long-nap roller and apply at least two coats of paint. Wait until the mortar joints have dried and cured completely (five to seven days) before applying the paint. Do not paint the wall if it is damp. Scrub all surfaces with a solution of 1 cup trisodium phosphate (TSP) to 1 gallon of water to remove grease, oil, mortar smears, and minor efflorescence. Rinse thoroughly and allow to dry.

Stucco

Stucco is a popular and attractive surfacing material. Many different textures and effects are possible: Rough textures tend to hide minor imperfections on wall surfaces. Usually, stucco is applied in its natural gray color and painted later, but color powder may be mixed into the stucco before application.

If applied properly, stucco makes a durable surface coating that can be used in many climates. However, stucco work takes considerable skill, and once you start applying a coat of stucco, you must finish the entire surface. If you wish to tackle the job, here are a few guidelines for applying stucco to a new concrete-block wall.

Mixing stucco. A combination of sand, portland cement, lime, and water, stucco is mixed similarly to mortar. For small jobs, you can buy premixed stucco in sacks; for large jobs, it may be more economical to buy the ingredients separately and mix them yourself. Consult your building supplier for suitable mixes for your project. Mix the ingredients thoroughly with water until the stucco is about the consistency of mousse. For large jobs, use a power mixer. Do not mix more than you can use in about 2½ hours, and discard any stucco that has dried out on the mixing platform.

Applying Stucco

If you are planning to stucco a concrete-block wall, strike the mortar joints flush as you build. Then you can apply stucco directly to the wall in either two or three coats. Either way, the first coat is the scratch coat; it literally gets scratched to receive the second coat. The second coat is called the brown coat. It is mixed and applied the same way as the scratch coat. The optional third coat is the finish coat. It's a thinner coat made of white cement and white stucco sand for a white appearance. Or, you can add color pigment to the mix. The pigment is available in a variety of earth tones. The procedure here is for three coats. If you'll be using two coats, stop at Step 3.

The wall should be clean and damp (but not wet) before applying stucco.

1. Apply the scratch coat. Make up a mix of 1 part mortar cement and 4 parts sand, and add just enough water to make the mix workable. Start at the bottom of the wall and with a flat, square trowel, apply a ¼-inch-thick coat of stucco over the entire wall surface.

2. Prepare the scratch coat. This coat is scratched to provide a good bond for the next coat. As soon as you have finished an area, roughen it with a plasterer's rake, or make your own scratching tool by driving small nails through a short board, as shown. The scratches should run horizontally about ½ to ¾ inches apart, and should be about ⅛ inch deep.

3. Apply the brown coat. The brown coat is made of the same mixture of sand and mortar as the scratch coat, unless you're using it as the top coat. (See Step 4.) Keeping the

1. Stucco is applied in three layers. Apply a ½-inch scratch coat first.

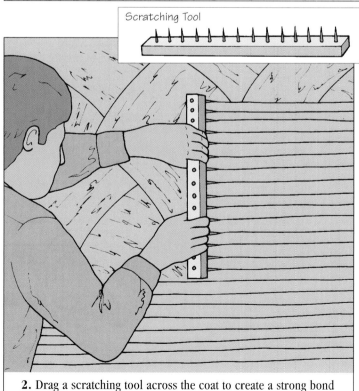

Scratching Tool

2. Drag a scratching tool across the coat to create a strong bond for the next coat.

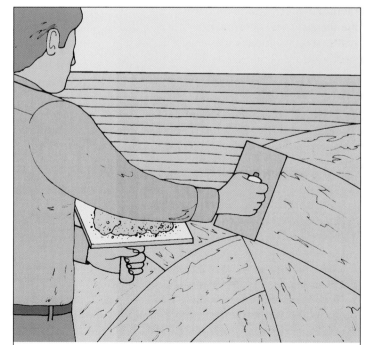

3. Shortly after you've applied the scratch coat, apply the second coat, called the brown coat.

delay between the two coats to a minimum makes for the strongest bond: Apply the brown coat as soon as the scratch coat will accept it without cracking. If you must wait longer, spray the scratch coat with a fine mist of water. Once you've applied the brown coat, allow the wall to cure for a few days, keeping it moist.

4. Apply the finish coat. Make the white coat from 1 part white cement and 3 parts white stucco sand. You can add a powder color agent to the mix if you like. Moisten the wall and, with a flat steel trowel, apply a ⅛- to ¼-inch coat.

To achieve a smooth finish, continue to trowel the surface as the stucco sets up. Make wavy or swirled surfaces by drawing a whisk broom or bristle brush lightly over the troweled surface. Pitted, or stippled, surfaces can be achieved by holding a stiff-bristle paintbrush at a slight angle and dabbing the surface. To make a skip-texture finish, trowel the surface smooth, let it harden slightly, then wipe on more stucco with a heavy brush. Let the new stucco set up, then knock down the high spots with a flat trowel held at a slight angle to the surface. Before attempting any of these techniques over the entire wall, it's best to practice on a small, inconspicuous area.

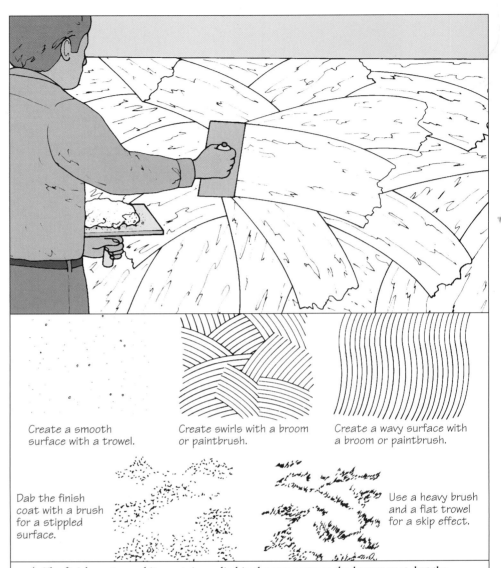

Create a smooth surface with a trowel.

Create swirls with a broom or paintbrush.

Create a wavy surface with a broom or paintbrush.

Dab the finish coat with a brush for a stippled surface.

Use a heavy brush and a flat trowel for a skip effect.

4. The finish coat, or white coat, is applied in the same way as the brown coat, but the mixture has less sand at that point. You can create a variety of textures by brushing or troweling the surface with different tools.

Veneers

When applied over a concrete-block wall, thin facings of real or simulated stone or brick have the same appearance as a solid brick or stone wall, at a fraction of the cost. To extend the lifetime of a stone-veneer wall, install metal flashing along the top course of block before laying the veneer cap.

Veneers made of real stone or full-thickness brick are applied to the wall with mortar. This type of application requires careful planning; it is not considered to be a do-it-yourself project. As the concrete block wall is built, metal masonry ties are inserted into the mortar joints every 16 inches, or as required by code to help bond the veneer to the wall. The ties should not extend beyond the thickness of the veneer.

Lightweight simulated brick or stone veneers, on the other hand, are designed to be applied by the do-it-yourselfer. These veneers are either mortared in place or attached to the wall with adhesive. Masonry ties aren't usually required. Most manufacturers of simulated brick and stone veneers provide complete installation instructions and specify appropriate bonding products. Make sure the veneer you choose is specified for exterior use.

Veeners. You can apply a brick or stone veneer over the block to give it a more finished appearance.

BRICK WALLS

Brick is one of the most attractive materials you can use to build a wall, and it comes in a variety of sizes, colors, and surface textures. You can set it in many different bond patterns and finish the joints in a number of different profiles.

A typical wall is either one brick thick, known as single wythe, or two bricks thick, known as double wythe. Usually, brick walls under 2 feet high require no steel reinforcement. Taller walls may incorporate steel ties or even metal reinforcement into the design to withstand stresses and loads placed on the wall. Consult your local building department for structural requirements.

TYPES OF BRICKS

Many different types of bricks are available, but those used for walls fall into three broad categories: building brick, face brick, and concrete brick. Within each of these categories, you'll find a wide variety of sizes, shapes, colors, and surface textures.

Building brick. Also called common brick, these economical bricks are suitable for building low, informal garden walls. They may be a bit too rustic where a neat, formal look is desired. Building bricks are usually the "seconds" or "rejects" from the brickyard. Some bricks may be chipped, warped, or broken. Color, dimensions, and density may vary from brick to brick.

Face brick. If a neat appearance is important, use face bricks. Compared with building brick, face brick is uniform in size, color, and surface texture. Face bricks come in a great variety of colors and textures, and are the standard brick used in most outdoor construction. They're more expensive than building bricks, but because they're more uniform in size and shape, they're easier to work with. They also have a better finished appearance and are suitable for formal projects.

Concrete brick. As the name implies, these bricks are formed from concrete. They cost considerably less than either type of clay brick. Concrete bricks are similar in appearance to concrete blocks, with a slightly rougher, more porous surface than

Brick is a traditional choice for building walls. The great variety of bond patterns makes it possible to tailor the look of a wall.

clay bricks. Colors usually are limited to light or medium brick red or adobe beige. Concrete bricks don't have the strength of clay bricks, so they are prone to cracking, especially under severe freeze-thaw conditions. Check with your local building department to see whether these bricks are recommended for your particular project. If you use concrete bricks, plan to seal them with a waterproof masonry sealer. Ask the dealer for the appropriate product.

Brick Sizes

Most bricks come in modular sizes. The length of the most common modular unit, a standard brick, is roughly twice its width and three times its thickness. The nominal dimensions are 2⅔x4x8 inches. The actual brick is smaller than this by the thickness of a mortar joint—either ⅜ inch or ½ inch. Size varies for another reason, too: manufacturing tolerances. In any given production run, brick sizes can vary as much as ½ inch. If you're concerned about size, ask the dealer for the dimensions of the brick you intend to use. Other types of bricks used in wall construction include jumbo, Roman, Norman, SCR, and utility.

Some bricks used for walls have hollow cores to reduce their weight, provide a better mortar bond, and allow space to insert vertical reinforcing rods into the wall, when required. While hollow-core bricks are sometimes less expensive than solid ones, you generally have fewer choices in size, color, and surface texture.

TYPES OF WALLS

Besides the look of the bricks themselves, two factors determine a brick wall's appearance. One is the number of wythes used to build up the wall thickness; the other is the bond pattern in which you lay the bricks.

Wythes. A wall that is only one brick wide (4 inches wide if using standard bricks) is called a single-wythe wall. When a second, parallel course of

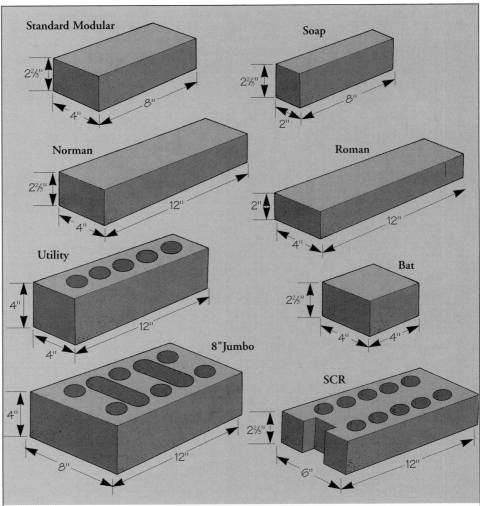

Brick sizes. Modular bricks for wall construction come in several different sizes, as shown. Modular bricks come in lengths, widths, and thicknesses that are multiples or fractions of each other, so mortar joints line up no matter which bond pattern you choose.

bricks is added next to the first, you have a double-wythe wall. A double-wythe wall is stronger than a single wythe, and the thicker wall may look more appropriate with other landscape features. Depending on the desired overall width of the wall, the wythes may be butted together (with a mortar joint between wythes) to produce a wall 8 inches wide or spaced apart to provide additional width. In the latter case, the cavity between the two wythes may be filled with grout (thinned mortar) or concrete (and sometimes reinforcing rods) to provide additional strength for tall walls. In all cases, the two wythes are tied together, either by bricks (called headers), metal masonry ties, or a combination of these, depending on the bond pattern. (For more on tying wythes together, see "Reinforcement," page 74.)

Bond patterns. The drawings show popular bond patterns for brick walls. Some patterns—such as the common bond, Flemish bond, English bond, and rowlock bond—are structural bonds. They incorporate header bricks to tie the wythes together. Running bond and stack bond usually require metal masonry ties to reinforce the wall. Single-wythe walls typically use a running bond, offset running bond, or stack bond pattern. In the first two, the vertical joints are offset to provide additional strength. In a stack bond (also called jack-on-jack), the bricks are simply stacked one atop the other so that all vertical joints are aligned. A stack bond has virtually no lateral strength, depending almost entirely on the strength of the mortar joints to hold it together. Such walls are typically reinforced with masonry ties in horizontal joints. If vertical reinforcement is needed, use hollow-core bricks and insert rebar into the cores, as required by code. Check with your local building department for specific requirements.

Anatomy of a Brick Wall

As in other trades, brick masons have terms to describe the components of a brick wall. Learning these terms will help you understand the instructions in this chapter.

One horizontal row of bricks is called a course. The courses are identified as odd courses (first, third, fifth course, etc.) and even courses (second, fourth, sixth course, etc.), starting from the base of the wall up. When building the wall, you'll get the best results by building the ends of the wall (the leads) first, rather than laying complete courses from one end of the wall to the other. Leads help

establish proper alignment of vertical mortar joints and let you attach a mason's line at each end to keep the wall straight and level. The last brick you lay in each course is called the closure brick. Even if you take considerable care in laying out the wall, the closure bricks often must be cut to fit.

Stretchers and headers. Stretchers are bricks laid flat with the long dimension parallel to the length of the wall. If the brick is laid on edge, it's called a rowlock stretcher. Headers are bricks laid flat at right angles to the stretchers, tying the two wythes together. A header laid on edge becomes a rowlock header. Header courses are often used to cap the wall as well.

Bats and soaps. Bats are bricks cut in half across their width. Bricks cut along their length are called soaps. Both are sometimes available precut, but more likely, you'll need

to cut them yourself. Commonly, bats are used in single-wythe walls to finish the ends and to produce various patterns.

Head joints and bed joints. Vertical mortar joints between bricks are called head joints; horizontal joints between courses are called bed joints.

Estimating Amounts

Bricks are more expensive than most other masonry products. You buy bricks by the piece. You may get a discount if you buy a whole pallet. As with lumber, you can sometimes go into the yard and hand-pick bricks out of the pile, if you want. Generally, if you're building a wall that requires hundreds or thousands of bricks, you order more than you need (to compensate for breakage and other waste) and have the bricks delivered.

The number of bricks you'll need to build a wall depends on the number of wythes, the size of individual bricks, mortar-joint spacing, and the bond pattern. Bond patterns that include header bricks will require more bricks than those that use only stretchers.

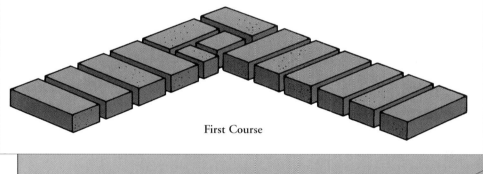

First Course

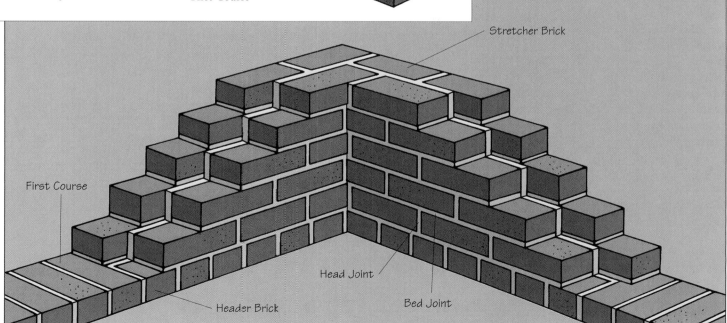

Stretcher Brick

First Course

Head Joint

Header Brick

Bed Joint

Anatomy of a brick wall. A brick wall is built in stages. Once you lay the first course, you build up the corners, called leads. The horizontal joints are called beds, the vertical joints are called heads.

Numbers of Bricks Needed for Single-Wythe Wall
(Running-bond pattern)

Brick Size		Amount per 100 sq. ft.*
2⅔"x4"x8"	(standard)	675
3⅛"x4"x8"	(engineer)	563
4"x4"x8"	(economy)	450
5⅓"x4"x8"	(double)	338
2"x4"x12"	(Roman)	600
2⅔"x4"x12"	(Norman)	450
4x4x12"	(utility)	300
5⅛"x4"x12"	(triple)	225
2⅔"x6"x12"	(SCR)	450
3⅛"x6"x12"	(Norwegian)	375
4"x6"x12"	(6" jumbo)	300

* Double amounts for double-wythe walls

Note: Data from Brick Institute of America, McLean, VA

A simple way to calculate the number of bricks you'll need is to make a scale elevation drawing for a 2- to 4-foot section of the wall you're building. In your drawing, include the bond pattern and the overall height of the wall. Draw in the bricks at their nominal, rather than actual size, and you'll be able to leave the mortar joints out of your drawing. Count the bricks in the section, and multiply the number of bricks required for each section by the number of sections required to complete the wall. Add 5 to 10 percent extra to allow for miscuts, breakage, and future repairs.

The chart shows the number of bricks (of various sizes) required for 100 square feet of wall in a running-bond pattern. Using this pattern, seven standard modular bricks (4x2⅔x8 inches) cover 1 square foot. If you're building a double-wythe wall, double the amount.

BASIC REQUIREMENTS

Building a sturdy brick wall depends on three factors: a strong footing, adequate reinforcement, and proper mortar mix to bond the bricks together. Lacking any one of these elements, the wall will soon crack and eventually fall apart. But if you pay special attention to each factor, your wall will last a lifetime.

Footings

As a rule, a poured-concrete footing should be two times wider than the wall it supports and as thick as the wall is wide, as shown on the drawing. The footing should also extend 4 to 6 inches beyond the ends of the wall. In severe winter climates, the footing must be below the frost line. You can build the foundation up to ground level with concrete blocks. Usually, the top of the footing or foundation will be a few inches below grade, where it won't be seen. Fill the foundation-block cavities with mortar and insert reinforcing rods. Be sure to check local codes for specific footing and foundation requirements. (Complete instructions for constructing footings appear in Chapter 4, beginning on page 41.)

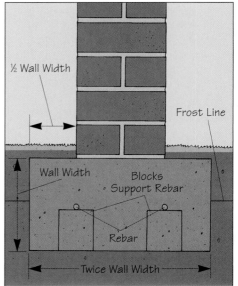

Footings. Most brick walls require a poured-concrete footing to provide a strong, stable, and level base. The surface of the footing is rough, which allows the brick wall's mortar bed to adhere to the footing. Steel reinforcement (rebar) is placed on blocks before you pour the concrete. The dimensions shown are minimum sizes; footings in cold climates must extend below the frost line.

Reinforcement

Requirements for wall reinforcement will vary depending on wall height, bond pattern, soil stability, wind load, and other factors. Check with your building department for accepted

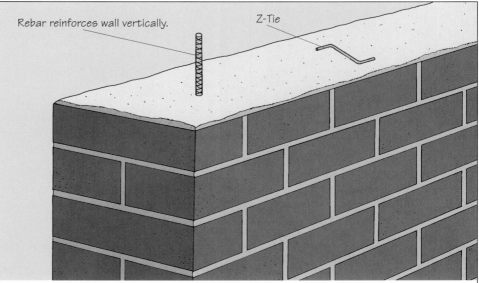

Reinforcement. Shown here are two ways to reinforce a brick wall. Check local code for reinforcement and spacing requirements. As shown, double-wythe cavity walls use large Z-ties to hold the two wythes together.

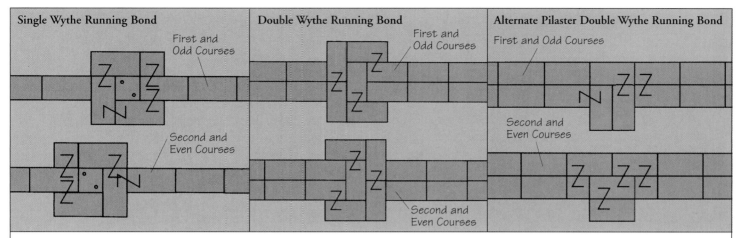

| Single Wythe Running Bond | Double Wythe Running Bond | Alternate Pilaster Double Wythe Running Bond |

First and Odd Courses

Second and Even Courses

Pilasters. Long, tall walls usually require pilasters to provide additional strength. In most cases, the pilasters are located at ends or corners and are spaced 12 feet apart along the length of the wall. Walls less than 12 feet long and 3 feet high usually don't need pilasters, but you may want to add pilasters for aesthetic reasons.

practices and code requirements for your particular project. For most walls up to 3 feet high, a structural bond pattern, such as common bond, provides sufficient strength, so no additional reinforcement will be needed. Walls set in a stacked-bond or running-bond pattern are usually tied together with metal Z-ties embedded in the mortar, as shown in the drawing. Tall walls may also require reinforcement with metal rebar, as shown.

Z-ties. These steel ties are used to tie wythes together in a double-wythe wall. Typically, the ties are placed in a bed joint, spaced 36 inches apart (or as required by code) along every third or fourth course. Stagger the ties so that they do not align vertically.

Reinforcement bar. Steel bars, known as "rebar," come in many different diameters and are designated by a number, such as #3, #4, etc. These numbers correspond to ⅛-inch increments: #3 rebar is ⅜ inch in diameter, #4 is ½ inch in diameter, and so on. Rebar is inserted into the concrete footing; it extends up between wythes in a double-wythe wall or through brick cores in a sin-gle-wythe wall. You can cut rebar with a hacksaw. Cut about halfway through the bar and bend it a few times until it breaks.

Pilasters. Pilasters, or built-in columns, are sometimes incorporated into brick walls to provide additional

strength. Typically, the pilasters are located at both ends or corners and at 10- to 12-foot intervals along the length of the wall. The use of pilasters is especially recommended for single-wythe walls.

Pilasters are tied into the wall with header bricks and Z-ties. In double-wythe walls, the cavity in the pilaster is filled with grout (mortar that has been thinned so it can be poured) or concrete and reinforced with rebar. In all cases, the poured concrete footing should follow the shape of the pilasters. Consult your building department to see if pilasters are required for your wall design and which type is recommended for your particular project. Even if they aren't required, pilasters can lend visual

interest to a wall. Several basic designs are shown in the drawing.

Mortar

Mortar is a mixture of cement, hydrated lime, sand, and water. Type N mortar is most often used for freestanding brick garden walls. However, you should consult a local masonry dealer for the best type to use in your area. As a rule, increasing the proportions of lime and sand in relationship to cement makes mortar less expensive and more workable, but weaker. Colored pigments can be added to the dry mix, if desired. The chart shows the various types of mortar mixtures used for different applications.

Mortar Types		
Type	Proportions of Ingredients	Recommended for
M	1 Cement ¼ Hydrated lime 3 Sand	Below-grade foundations, walks, retaining walls, and wherever masonry will have long-term contact with water or damp earth.
S	1 Cement ¼-½ Hydrated lime 4½ Sand	Reinforced masonry and wherever high-bond strength is needed, such as in walls in windy areas.
N	1 Cement ½-1½ Hydrated lime 6 Sand	Weather-exposed structures, such as above-grade garden walls.

For most residential walls, it's more convenient to buy premixed mortar in bags than to mix the components yourself. A 70-pound bag of premixed mortar is enough to set about 40 standard bricks.

Mortar consistency. As with bagged dry-mix concrete, you'll need to add the correct amount of water to achieve the desired consistency. This may take some experimentation. Generally, stiffer mixes are used for concrete block, while wetter mixes are used for bricks. You can mix mortar with a shovel or hoe in a wheelbarrow, in a concrete barge, or on a large sheet of plywood. A power mixer is recommended for large jobs to speed the mixing and to save your back. Start with small batches, then work your way up to larger ones as you learn to gauge your working time. If the mortar starts to dry out, you can add a bit more water to bring it back to the proper consistency. This process, called "retempering the mortar," can be done only one time for each batch. Additional retempering severely weakens the mix.

Grout. Grout is mortar that's thin enough to pour. It's made by adding enough water to the mortar mix to make it soupy. You can use grout, and sometimes vertical rebar, to fill the cavity between a double-wythe wall. Pour the grout as you work: After laying several courses of a wall, pour grout into the cavity with a coffee can. Then lay a few more courses. Repeat the process to the full height of the wall. Whether or not you need to add grout or other reinforcement depends on soil conditions and the wall's function and design. Check with your building department.

Tools

Bricklaying requires most of the same tools as laying concrete blocks: tape measure, trowel, story pole, line blocks, string, level, brick hammer, and brickset or mason's chisel. Brick walls can have a wide variety of joints, so you'll need to use the appropriate striking tool for the joint you've chosen.

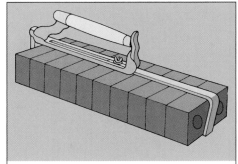

Tools. Brick tongs come in handy for transporting bricks from the pile to the section of wall you're working on.

(See "Tooling Mortar Joints," page 81.) Brick tongs are another handy tool. They consist of a sliding clamp and a handle for carrying a stack of bricks.

BUILDING A SINGLE-WYTHE WALL

The following steps show how to lay a single-wythe brick wall in a running-bond pattern. The instructions assume that you have already poured a suitable footing and will be providing any reinforcement required by local building codes.

Unlike concrete blocks, bricks need to be dampened before you lay them. Dry bricks absorb moisture from the

mortar joint, resulting in a poor bond. Thoroughly spray all the bricks in the pile with a garden hose an hour or two before laying them. By the time you get the mortar mixed, the surface water should have evaporated from the bricks, leaving them slightly damp. Do not lay the bricks if they are dripping wet.

1. Mark the footing. For straight walls with no corners, you can simply mark the center of the footing and center the wall on the mark. On walls that turn a corner, lay out the wall with the help of the batter boards you set up for the footing. Stretch string across the batter boards to mark the outside of the wall. Where strings intersect at corners, drop a plumb bob from the intersecting lines and mark this point on the footing. Snap chalk lines on the footing to represent the outside wall edges.

2. Do a trial run. Starting at one end or corner, dry lay the first course along the chalk line. Place ½-inch wood spacers between the bricks to represent mortar joints. You may want to adjust the joint widths slightly to avoid cutting a brick. Do not, however, make joints narrower than ⅜ inch or wider than ⅝ inch. If you must cut a brick, try to make it a bat (half

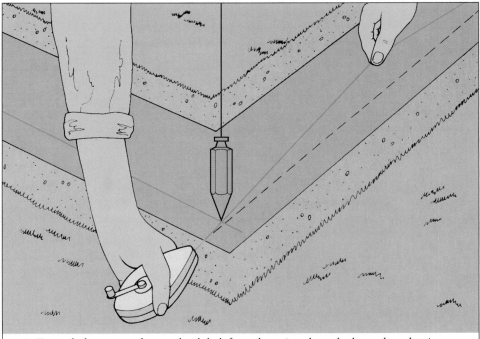

1. To mark the corner, drop a plumb bob from the point where the batter board strings meet. Connect the corners by snapping a line between them.

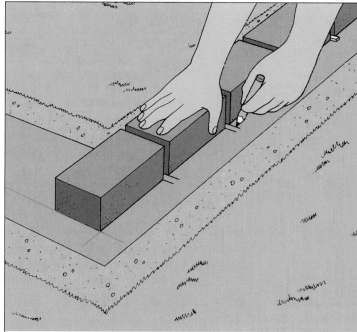

2. Position the bricks on the footing without mortar. If necessary, adjust the spacing to avoid cutting a brick. Mark the spacing on the foundation.

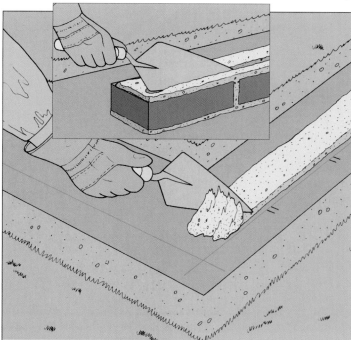

3. Lay mortar on the foundation to a depth of 1 inch. Use the trowel to cut a furrow in second and subsequent courses.

brick), and place it at the end of the wall. After the course is laid, remove the wood spacers. Mark every joint with a pencil, as shown, then set the bricks aside where they'll be within easy reach as you lay up the wall.

3. Spread the mortar. Mix a batch of mortar; then, starting at one corner, lay a 1-inch-thick mortar bed long enough to place four or five bricks, but slightly narrower than the width of a brick. Be careful not to cover the chalk lines. On second and subsequent courses, use your trowel to make a furrow down the center of the mortar bed so that the edges are thicker than the center.

4. Set the first bricks. Set the end or corner brick in the mortar even with the chalk lines. Embed the brick by tapping on the top lightly with the trowel handle until the mortar joint compresses to ½ inch. Check to see that the brick is level. Swipe a ¾-inch layer of mortar on one end of the next brick, place it on the mortar bed about 1 to 2 inches away from the corner brick, and slide it in place with a slight downward motion. A small amount of mortar should squeeze out of the joints. With the edge of the trowel, scrape off any

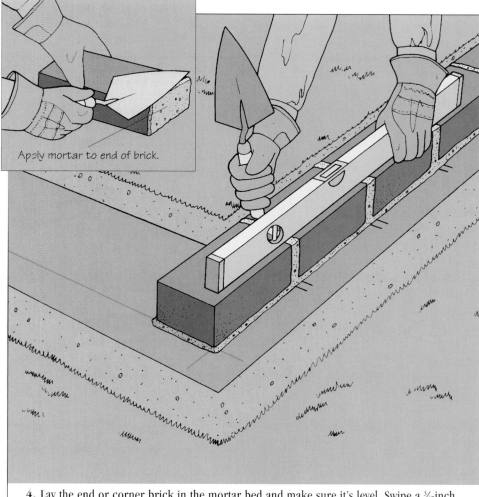

Apply mortar to end of brick.

4. Lay the end or corner brick in the mortar bed and make sure it's level. Swipe a ¾-inch layer of mortar on one end of the next brick, and slide it in place.

squeezed-out mortar and reuse it. Set two or three more bricks in this fashion, then move to the opposite end of the wall, and repeat the process.

Check with a level to make sure all the bricks are aligned. If a brick is too high, tap it down with the trowel handle. If a brick is too low, remove it and add more mortar. Once you've trued up the two ends of the wall, attach a string to line blocks at the ends of the wall. Position the string even with the tops of the bricks, and check the string with a line level. The bricks at each end should be level with each other. If they are slightly out of level (less than about ¾ inch), trowel mortar under the low end and reset the bricks. If the bricks are more than ¾ inch out of level, compensate by laying thicker bed joints at the low end over several courses.

5. Build the end leads. For a straight wall with no corners, build the leads. Working from the end, lay three bricks, lay two bricks on top of them, and then a single brick at the very top. (When you've got the experience, you can build a lead as many as five courses high.) If Z-ties are required, insert these in the horizontal joints where needed. (See "Reinforcement," page 74.)

Be sure to include the bond pattern in your lead. In a typical running bond, the end bricks for the second course are half bricks, or bats. The third course is a full brick, and so on. If you haven't bought half bricks for this purpose, cut them. (See "Cutting Bricks," page 82.)

Build up the leads three to five courses high before you fill in the center sections of the courses. Check course heights with a tape measure or a board called a story pole, which has the top of each course marked on it. Check the leads for plumb and level. Hold the level diagonally across the corners of the bricks as shown. The level should touch each brick to make sure the corners align. If it doesn't, adjust the width of your head joints.

6. Build any corner leads. For a wall with corners, build corner leads

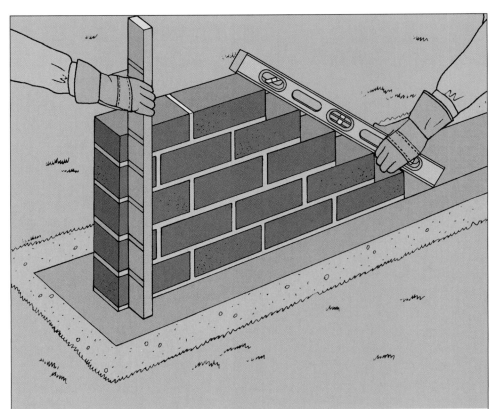

5. Build the leads of the wall before completing the courses. Check to make sure the leads are level and plumb. The corners of the bricks should connect on a diagonal. Check them with a level or a straightedge.

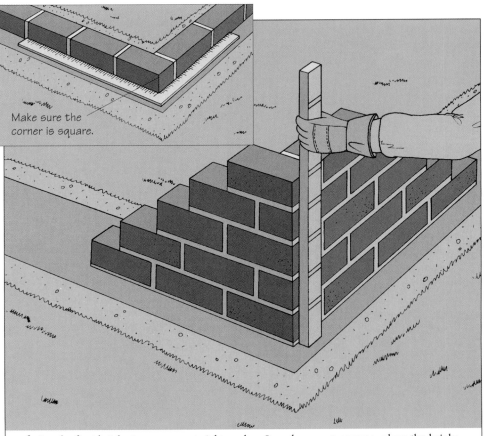

Make sure the corner is square.

6. Lay the first bricks in a corner at right angles. On subsequent courses, place the bricks so that each spans a joint below it.

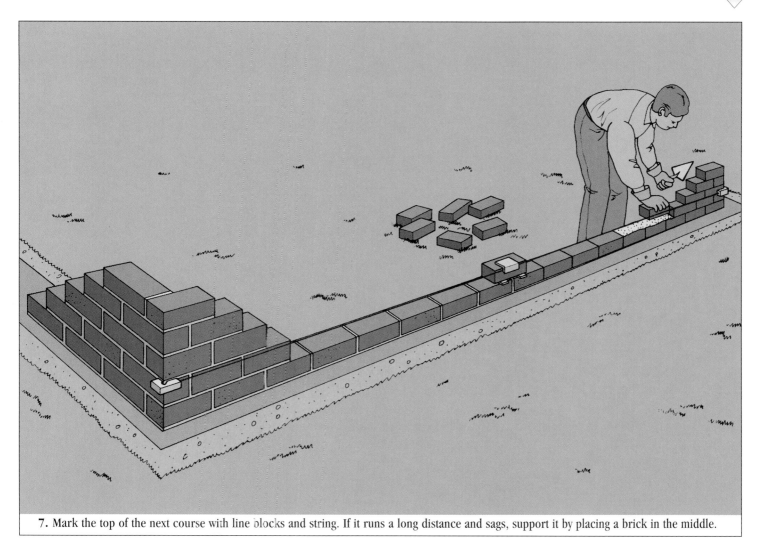

7. Mark the top of the next course with line blocks and string. If it runs a long distance and sags, support it by placing a brick in the middle.

by laying four or five bricks in each direction for the first course, as shown in the drawing. For the second course, place the corner brick at right angles to the one underneath to create a running bond. Mortar the ends of a few bricks, and lay them in a furrowed mortar bed. Continue alternating courses in this fashion until you have built up three to five stepped courses, making frequent checks of the leads for plumb, level, and head-joint alignment. Repeat at each corner.

7. Fill in between leads. Attach
line blocks to the second course of bricks in each lead, aligning the string with the top edge of the bricks. If the line has to reach a long distance, it may sag, so temporarily support it in the middle with a brick. Use wood spacers to raise the brick ½ inch to simulate a mortar bed, and place a fold of flashing over the brick to hold the string in place, as shown. Then fill

in the bricks in the second course, working from both leads toward the middle. Align the tops of the bricks with the string as you work.

8. Set the closure brick. The
last brick in each course is called a closure brick and must fit neatly between the two bricks on either side. If possible, plan the job so that you can use a full-size brick for the closure. If you must cut a brick, make sure it fits before applying mortar. Then swipe generous amounts of mortar on each end of the brick, and on the ends of the bricks on either side. Carefully slip the closure brick into place, dislodging as little mortar as possible. Clean up any excess mortar with your trowel.

9. Lay the rest of the bricks.
Set the rest of the brick courses to fill in between the leads. For the best appearance, stagger the closure bricks so that they do not align vertically.

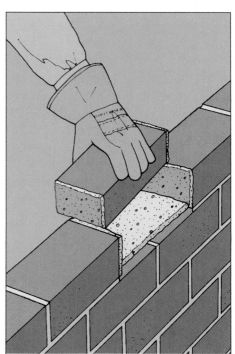

8. Work from each corner toward the middle. The last brick slides into place between its neighbors.

9. Continue laying bricks between the leads, adjusting the line blocks and string to mark the height of each course.

Build new leads once you've filled in between existing ones and repeat the process until the wall is complete.

10. Finish the mortar joints.

As you work, use your trowel to smooth any squeezed-out mortar flush along the joints. Keep your eye on the joints as you work and test them by pressing your thumb gently into the mortar. If your thumbprint remains and the mortar doesn't stick to your hand, then it's time to tool the mortar joints. Select the appropriate tool for the type of joint you want to make. (For more information, see "Tooling Mortar Joints," page 81.) Tool the vertical joints first, then the horizontal joints. Remove any bits of excess mortar, called "tags," with your trowel. Finish by brushing the joints lightly with a whisk broom or soft-bristle brush.

10. Shape the joints between bricks with a jointing tool, remove excess mortar with a trowel, and brush the joints clean with a whisk broom.

Tooling Mortar Joints

Mortar joints can be tooled in several ways, depending on the desired finished appearance of the wall. Each type of joint creates its own visual effect. The drawing shows common mortar joints. Some of these can be made with a pointed mason's trowel; others require special striking tools, called jointers, available at masonry suppliers.

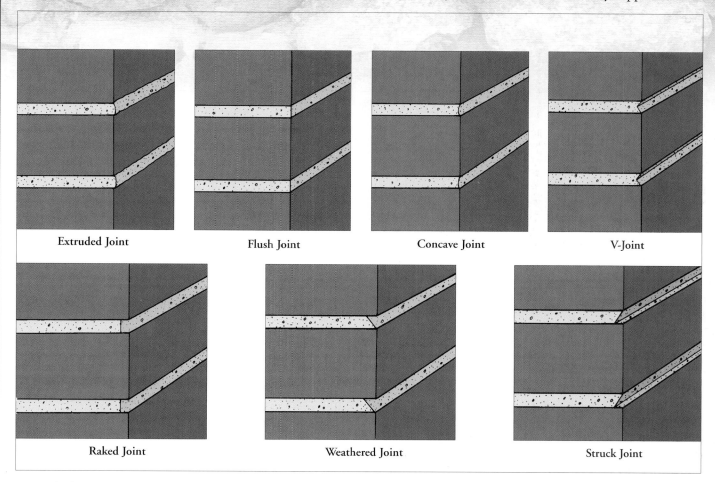

Extruded Joint   Flush Joint   Concave Joint   V-Joint

Raked Joint   Weathered Joint   Struck Joint

Extruded joints. Extruded joints require no tooling; they are formed as mortar squeezes out between the bricks when you tap them in place. Such joints are used where a rustic appearance or texture is desired, but they tend to trap water, making them relatively weak. Also, pieces of mortar tend to break away, leaving an unattractive finish. Using a masonry sealer will help extend the life of these joints. (Ask your masonry dealer for the appropriate product.)

Flush joints. To create a flush joint, simply cut away the excess mortar with the edge of your trowel as you lay the bricks. Flush joints produce a smooth surface and are often used for brick walls that will be painted or stuccoed. Left unpainted, the joints are not particularly watertight, and surface layers may eventually flake off or crack.

Concave joints. These joints are the most popular because they shed water well. To make these joints, press a convex jointer into the mortar and slide it along the joint. The tool compresses the mortar, making a strong, watertight joint. Walls with concave joints have a flat look, with little or no shadow.

V-joints. These joints are made by removing mortar with a pointed tool called a V-jointer. V-joints emphasize shadows and allow good water runoff, making them relatively watertight.

Raked joints. These joints are recessed about ½ inch back from the face of the wall, using a tool called a rake-out jointer. Raked joints create dark shadows for a dramatic effect. However, they collect water and may encourage the growth of moss in the mortar joints, which will eventually crack or erode them.

Weathered joints and struck joints. Make these by removing mortar with the point of a mason's trowel. Orient the trowel tip upward for weathered joints, downward for struck joints. Both joints produce attractive shadow line. Weathered joints shed water better than struck joints.

Cutting Bricks

Most types of bricks cut easily with a wide chisel, called a brickset, and a small sledgehammer or mallet. (Do not use a carpenter's hammer. Striking the chisel will damage the hammer face.) Place the brick on a flat, solid surface, such as a bed of compacted damp sand, earth, or a piece of scrap lumber. Wear safety goggles and gloves. Mark the cut with chalk or a pencil on all sides of the brick, and score a line along the mark with the chisel. Center the chisel on the score line and make several sharp, light taps with the hammer. In most cases, the brick will break along the cut line after the second or third tap. If it doesn't, turn the brick over and give the chisel a light, sharp blow on the backside to break the brick.

If you want very precise cuts or want to make angle cuts (such as for a mitered brick cap), rent a water-cooled masonry saw (also called a wet saw). These are available at tool rental shops.

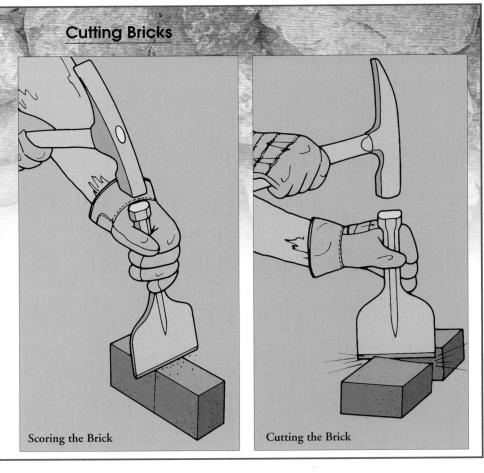

Scoring the Brick

Cutting the Brick

BUILDING A DOUBLE-WYTHE WALL

The procedures for laying a double-wythe wall are similar to those for a single-wythe wall, except that you'll be laying each course two bricks wide and tying the wythes together, either with header bricks, masonry ties, or a combination of these. The following instructions show how to lay a double-wythe wall in a running bond pattern. Sequences for other bond patterns are shown on page 85.

1. Start the first course. Mark the footing to locate the outside and inside edges of the wall. For straight walls with no corners, lay a dry course of spaced bricks, following Steps 1 and 2 under "Building a Single-Wythe Wall," page 76. In most cases, space the wythes so that the cap bricks will overhang each side of the wall by about ¼ inch. Mark the brick locations, remove them from the foundation, and lay a mortar bed. The bed should be long enough for three

bricks, and should be narrower than the wall by ½ inch on each side.

Place and level an end brick for each wythe. Swipe mortar on the ends of two bricks and set them next to the

end bricks. Continue laying bricks until you have a base two bricks wide by three bricks long. Check to make sure the bricks are level and aligned, as shown on the drawing. Repeat this

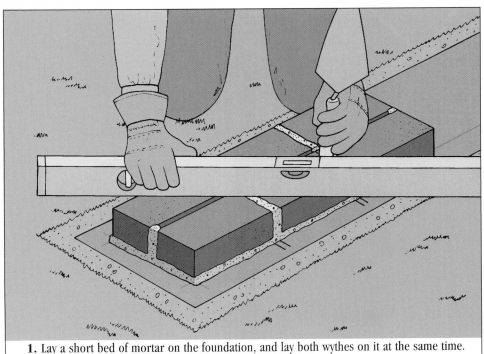

1. Lay a short bed of mortar on the foundation, and lay both wythes on it at the same time.

procedure at the other end of the wall. Run a string from the end bricks to check if the ends are level with each other. Build up the mortar bed under one end if necessary, then fill in the rest of the course.

2. Start a corner. For walls with corners, lay the wythes as shown and mark their locations. Then lay down two mortar beds about 2 feet long just inside the chalk lines. Lay the first brick on the outer corner, then swipe a ¾-inch layer of mortar on the end of another brick and lay it at right angles to the first brick. Use a framing square to make sure the bricks are square to each other. Adjust as necessary. Then lay two more bricks in each direction. Check frequently with a level and square to make sure the bricks are level and aligned to form a 90-degree angle. Form the backup wythe in the same manner, laying out bricks in the order shown.

3. Build the Leads. At ends or corners, build leads up to a height of five courses. As you build the leads, lay metal reinforcing ties in the mortar bed at regular intervals (as required by code) to tie the wythes together. The ties should be about 1 inch shorter than the wall width so that the tie ends don't protrude. Check constantly for plumb, level, and square. Use a story pole to ensure consistent course heights. Corner leads will affect construction of end leads, as shown.

4. Fill in between the leads. Attach line blocks and string at the top of the lowest course. Fill in the course, working from both leads toward the middle. Rather than filling in all the bricks for one wythe, then moving to the other, lay both wythes as you move down the course. Check frequently with a level to make sure the wythes are level with each other. After filling in two or three courses, fill the cavity between the wythes with mortar or grout, if required. If the wall will be taller than the initial lead, continue to build up the lead, keeping it three courses higher than the stretcher courses. Complete each course with a closure brick. (See Step 8 under "Building a Single-Wythe Wall," page 76.)

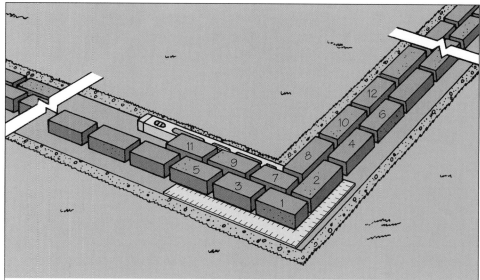

2. At corners, lay the corner brick first and then alternate between sides, in the order shown, to create the rest of the wall.

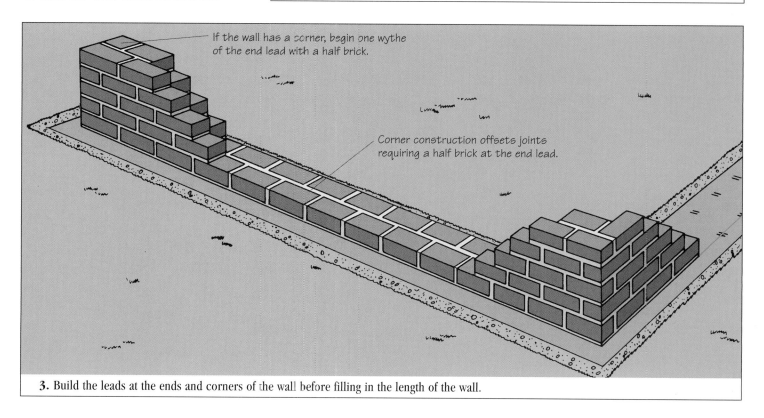

If the wall has a corner, begin one wythe of the end lead with a half brick.

Corner construction offsets joints requiring a half brick at the end lead.

3. Build the leads at the ends and corners of the wall before filling in the length of the wall.

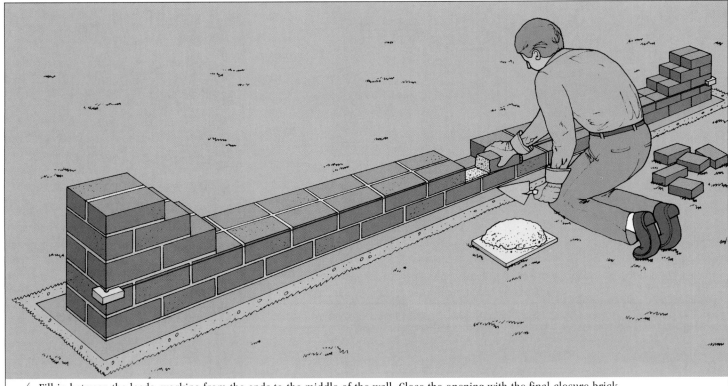

4. Fill in between the leads, working from the ends to the middle of the wall. Close the opening with the final closure brick.

When the mortar will hold a thumb-print, clean up and strike the joints with a jointing tool as described in Step 10 under "Building a Single-Wythe Wall," page 76.

5. Cap the wall. If the wythes are separated only by a ½-inch mortar joint, a cap is optional. A cavity wall, however, requires a cap to keep water out of the wall. The wall may be capped with header bricks placed flat across the width of the wall. For a stronger cap, use rowlock headers laid on edge, as shown. Precast concrete copings are also available.

It's usually best to begin with a trial run. Lay all of the bricks dry, with the proper space for mortar joints between them. If the last brick over-hangs the end of the wall by more than ¼ inch, adjust the joint spacing or else mark the brick, score it, and cut it.

Place metal flashing in the bed joint between the top course, and cap bricks for additional moisture protection. Trowel out a mortar bed that covers the wythes and wall cavity. Apply mortar to each brick as shown. Hide the cut brick four or five bricks in from the end of the wall.

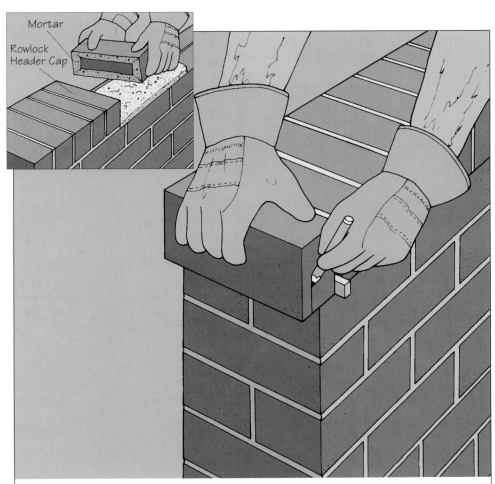

5. First lay out the wall cap without mortar. If you need to cut a brick, mark it and place it in the middle. Then lay a short bed of mortar and set the bricks.

Other Bond Patterns

The drawings on this page show the basic sequence for laying up corner leads for several popular bond patterns. The numbers indicate the order in which the bricks should be laid. After building leads five courses high, fill in between them by repeating the pattern used for each course of the leads.

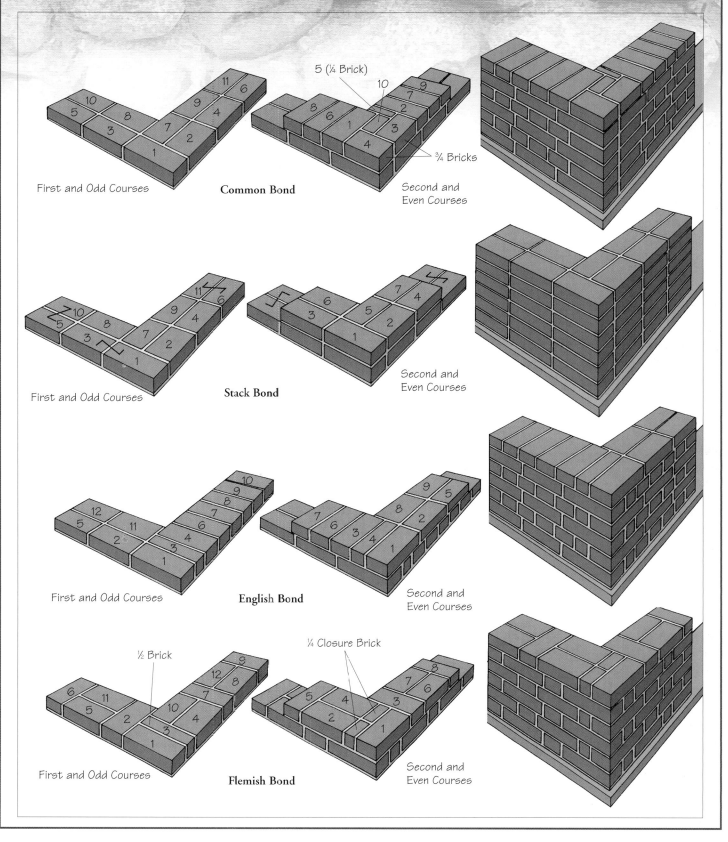

Common Bond

First and Odd Courses

Second and Even Courses

5 (¼ Brick)

¾ Bricks

Stack Bond

First and Odd Courses

Second and Even Courses

English Bond

First and Odd Courses

Second and Even Courses

Flemish Bond

First and Odd Courses

Second and Even Courses

½ Brick

¼ Closure Brick

RETAINING WALLS

Retaining walls prevent soil at a higher grade from tumbling down or eroding to a lower grade. Retaining walls can transform a slope into a series of terraces for lawns, planting beds, or patio areas. On flat sites, low retaining walls can create raised planting beds or borders, adding a sense of visual depth to the landscape.

BASIC REQUIREMENTS

You can make retaining walls from a variety of materials: timber, stone, brick, and concrete block among them. Perhaps the easiest materials for the do-it-yourselfer to work with are mortarless interlocking concrete blocks designed especially for retaining walls. These blocks are discussed in "Interlocking Concrete-Block Walls," page 94. Low timber retaining walls are also easy to build and require little or no experience.

No matter which material you choose, retaining walls must be strong enough to hold the weight of the soil placed against them. And you must make provisions for drainage. With tall retaining walls, structural and drainage issues become critical, so it's best to leave the design and construction of tall walls to professionals. Retaining walls

Retaining walls help turn sloped land into usable space. Stone walls like this one require a lot of work but are unmatched for natural beauty. Newer landscape block walls are foundation free and stack quickly and easily.

smaller than 3 feet high may be designed and built by the do-it-yourselfer, but take your plans to the local building department to make sure they meet code requirements.

Excavation

The type and amount of excavation required to install the wall depend on wall height, the angle of the slope, and the amount of flat space you wish to create on the downhill side of the wall. On sloped ground, you'll

generally cut and fill to create a flat area bounded by a low retaining wall. In the cut-and-fill process, you remove the soil downhill from the proposed wall. If you're building a single retaining wall, it's easiest to cart the soil just downhill and fill in the slope with it. Fill the excavated area behind the wall with tamped sand or gravel to facilitate drainage, and top it off with a layer of topsoil. If you're building a series of terraces and walls, it's easiest to dump the soil into a pile uphill. Fill the area immediately behind the wall as before. Level off the slope with soil from the pile.

You can excavate low, short walls with a shovel, pick, and wheelbarrow. Heavy equipment, such as bulldozers, backhoes, and front-end loaders, may be required for larger projects. Unless you know how to operate such equipment, leave the job to an excavation contractor. Even for low walls, you'll need to move a lot of soil, so consider hiring a few strong backs to help with the shovel work.

Drainage

Because wet soil can exert considerable force on a retaining wall, you should build a drainage system into the wall. Typically, you backfill the wall with gravel, lay perforated pipe in it, and build weepholes into the wall. The gravel drains water away from the wall, and the drainpipe carries water away from the wall footing to an opening in the ground. Line the excavation with permeable landscape fabric to keep the gravel from clogging with silt. When planning a drainage system, make sure that you're not directing the water runoff into a neighbor's yard.

Weepholes allow subsurface water to drain through the wall. For brick and block walls, you can make weepholes by omitting the mortar from some of the vertical (head) joints near the wall base. Or you can insert 1- or 2-inch diameter PVC pipes in the head joints every 4 to 6 feet along the base of the wall as you build it. If you are building a timber wall, the pipes can be inserted in holes drilled in the wood. In all cases, cover the back of the hole with landscape fabric or fine galvanized wire mesh to help prevent clogging.

Dry-laid retaining walls of stone or interlocking blocks usually require no weepholes because there's no mortar between joints to block drainage. Placing a layer of landscape fabric directly behind the wall will help hold the soil in place while allowing water to seep through the cracks.

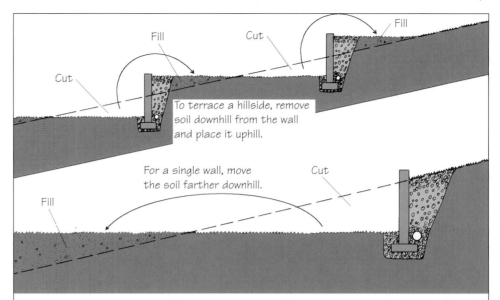

To terrace a hillside, remove soil downhill from the wall and place it uphill.

For a single wall, move the soil farther downhill.

Fill   Cut   Fill   Cut   Fill

Cut   Fill

Excavation. You can cut and fill to create a series of terraces with low walls (top) or a large, flat area in front of a taller retaining wall (bottom). In either case, the space behind the wall is backfilled with gravel to facilitate drainage.

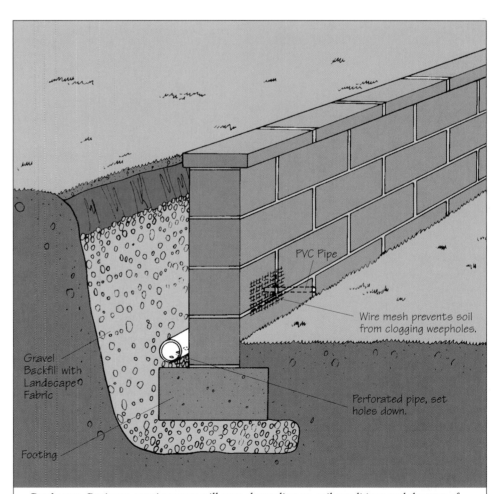

PVC Pipe

Wire mesh prevents soil from clogging weepholes.

Gravel Backfill with Landscape Fabric

Perforated pipe, set holes down.

Footing

Drainage. Drainage requirements will vary, depending on soil conditions and the type of wall you're building. In most cases, a perforated drainpipe is placed near the bottom of the excavation, and the space behind the wall is backfilled with gravel. Permeable landscape fabric keeps soil from migrating into the gravel while allowing the passage of water. Weepholes near the wall's base prevent water buildup behind it.

Footings and Reinforcement

Most retaining walls require large, sturdy footings for support. Specific requirements for footings depend on soil conditions, the size and type of wall you're building, and local building codes. Generally, the width of the footing should be at least two-thirds the total wall height. The top of the footing should be at least 12 inches below grade on the downhill side of the wall. The footing should be as thick as the wall width or a minimum of 8 inches. All dimensions may vary, depending on local building codes.

Mortared masonry retaining walls generally have poured-concrete footings with steel reinforcement (rebar) running the length of the footing. Separate rebar extends vertically up into the wall to tie it to the footing. (For information on building concrete footings, see "Locating the Footing," page 46.) Generally, more of the footing extends behind the wall (uphill side) than in front of it, allowing the weight of the soil to keep the wall and footing from tilting forward. The

exact orientation of the wall on the footing depends on code and specific site requirements.

Dry-laid stone retaining walls generally don't require poured-concrete footings or reinforcement. Large stones at the base of the wall serve as footings, and planting the crevices between the stones with groundcovers or vines helps stabilize the wall and prevents soil erosion.

LANDSCAPE-TIE RETAINING WALLS

Many retaining walls are made from pressure-treated landscape ties. These walls are easy to build and require no footings. Instead, timbers called deadmen are connected at right angles to the wall and extend into the bank behind it to provide additional stability.

The main drawback to using wood for retaining walls is that even pressure-treated timbers won't last as long as stone and masonry. In ideal soil conditions, the timbers may last

40 years; in wet soils, expect a shorter life span. Use pressure-treated wood rated for ground contact or foundation-grade timbers and provide a good drainage system behind the wall to ensure a maximum life span.

Used railroad ties are not recommended for most residential garden situations. Real railroad ties are warped, splintery, cut to odd lengths, and saturated with creosote, which is toxic to plants and animals. Used ties may also have gravel embedded in them, which will ruin saw blades. Although more expensive than real railroad ties, pressure-treated landscape timbers are a better bet for most home landscaping projects. Landscape ties come in standard lengths and sizes, so they're easy to work with and provide a neat, uniform appearance. Most walls are built with 4x6 timbers laid horizontally. For a more massive wall, use 6x6s.

Tools and Materials

In addition to tools required for layout and excavation, you'll need a saw capable of cutting the timbers. A small chain saw works best, although you

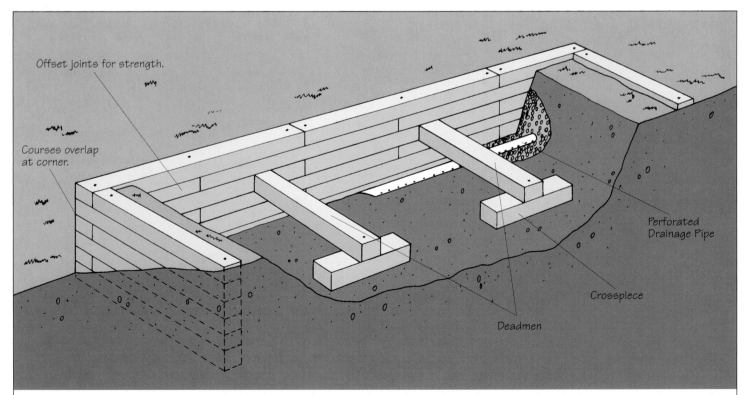

Offset joints for strength.

Courses overlap at corner.

Perforated Drainage Pipe

Crosspiece

Deadmen

Landscape-Tie Retaining Walls. Stacked landscape timbers make for quick assembly of this wall. T-shaped "deadmen" reach back into the hill to provide support. Lengths of rebar tie the timbers together.

can also use a large, coarse-toothed handsaw (such as a woodcutter's bucksaw, bow saw, or two-man cross-cut saw). Fasteners include large galvanized spikes, long bolts, and lag screws. The following text and drawings show three ways you can build a low timber retaining wall. Horizontal timber walls can be built up to 3 feet high; vertical timber walls should not exceed 2 feet. If you want to build a higher wall, consult a landscape architect or engineer.

Building a Landscape-Tie Wall

This wall is made of landscape timbers stacked on top of each other and tied together with lengths of ¾-inch rebar. To help resist the tremendous pressure of the soil against the wall, you install timbers (called deadmen) that reach back into the hillside. The deadmen should be a minimum of 3 feet long, and are cut from the same size timber as the rest of the wall.

This design works for walls up to 3 feet tall. Walls between 3 and 4 feet need additional reinforcement, and may require a concrete footing. Most codes require any wall over 4 feet tall to be designed by an engineer. If local terrain requires a wall over 3 feet tall, consider building two smaller walls several feet apart to create a terraced hillside.

After measuring the overall wall length, it's best to make a scale drawing to help determine the amount and lengths of lumber needed. Use 6x6 pressure-treated landscape ties rated for ground contact (.40) for this wall. Any length will do, but lumber over about 10 feet long will be difficult to lift and place without several helpers. Also use the drawing to show the locations of joints and deadmen. In all cases, stagger the joints so that they don't align vertically.

Consider renting a drill and bit to help you with the holes required for the rebar. You'll need a heavy-duty ¾-inch drill and a ¾-inch auger bit with extensions long enough to drill through the height of your wall.

1. Excavate the site. Lay out the wall with stakes and string, then exca-

vate a flat area behind it, allowing you room to work. Next, dig a trench approximately 12 inches deep by 16 inches wide along the length of the wall, and backfill it with 6 inches of firmly tamped gravel. In cold climates, extend the bottom of the trench below the frost line. If the wall will go around a corner, lay out, dig, and fill trenches for the side walls, too.

2. Lay the first course. The top edge of the first timber should be at ground level. Lay the first timbers end to end in the trench. Level each timber front to back and side to side using a level as a guide.

3. Lay drainage pipe and start the side wall. Water buildup behind the wall can exert considerable pressure and eventually push timbers forward. A 4-inch perforated drainpipe behind the wall helps drain it once the wall is constructed. Lay landscape fabric behind the wall, and run it up the hill for about 6 feet. You will use it later as a barrier between the gravel and the topsoil.

Lay the pipe (holes down) tight against the wall. If necessary, shovel

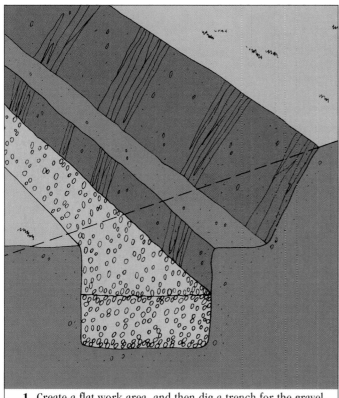

1. Create a flat work area, and then dig a trench for the gravel and landscape timbers that act as a foundation for this wall.

2. Lay the timbers end to end in the trench and fill in around them with gravel.

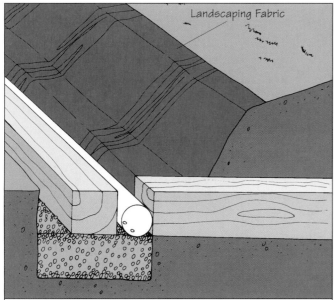

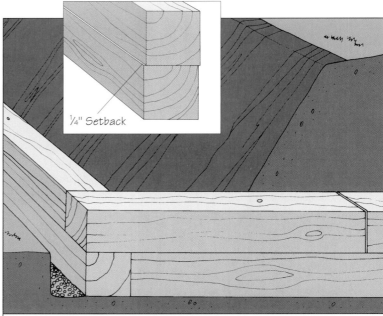

3. Perforated pipe behind the wall helps drain water away from the wall, and keeps the pressure of the water from pushing against the wall. Gaps between the ends of the timber help further drain the wall.

4. Set each course ¼ inch back from the one below it, and overlap the timbers at the corner to create a strong joint.

gravel underneath to slope it about ¼ inch per foot toward one end of the wall. Slope towards the downhill end of the wall, if there is one. Run the pipe a few inches past the end of the wall to a point where it can exit the ground.

Once the pipe is in place, set the timbers for any side walls. Snug a timber against the pipe on the side of the wall with a drain running past and against the front timbers on the other side wall. Fill in the rest of the trench with gravel.

4. Lay the second course. Each course must be set back ¼ inch from the one below it, as shown. This helps counteract the weight of the hill against the wall. Lay the second course over the first beginning at the end with a timber cut to half its original length. This strengthens the wall by staggering the joints so that no joint is directly above another. If necessary, shim the timbers to level them. Leave a small space between the ends of adjoining timbers, which will help drain the wall. Spike the courses together with 12-inch galvanized spikes placed about 2 feet from each joint in the upper course, as shown. Before nailing, drill pilot holes for the nails that are slightly smaller than the diameter of the nail.

Overlap the timbers where the side walls meet the front wall, as shown.

5. Lay the third course and install the deadmen. Set the third course back ¼ inch from the one below

it. Align the joints in this course with the joints in the first course. Spike the courses together, as before.

Now lay out the deadmen atop the third course so they will fall 4 feet

5. Build T-shaped deadmen that reach back into the hill to help support the wall.

6. Cut timbers to fit between the deadmen, and continue building, spiking each course to the one below it.

from the wall ends and roughly every 8 feet between. If necessary, move the deadmen a few inches to the side so that they won't be directly over a joint in the wall.

Cut the deadmen so that when they're installed, they will be flush with the front face of the wall and at least 3 feet long. Spike a 3-foot crosspiece to the end, as shown. Excavate into the hillside, as necessary. Tuck the landscape fabric between the hill and the crosspiece, and set the deadmen on top of the course you just laid.

6. Add remaining courses.
Cut timbers to fit between the deadmen. Spike this course to the one below it with 12-inch galvanized spikes, predrilling pilot holes before you nail. Continue laying courses, setting each course back ¼ inch from the one below, and spiking the courses together.

7. Drive the rebar. Once all the timbers are in place, drill ¾-inch diameter holes for the rebar pins

7. Drill holes for rebar, and drive the rebar down through the entire length of the wall to give the wall strength.

that tie the wall together. Drill holes about 8 to 10 inches on either side of the joints in the top of the wall and continue until they go through the wall and exit the bottom timber. Also drill a hole that goes down through each deadman and into the ground. At the other end of the deadmen, drill holes a few inches from the end of each crosspiece.

To keep the bit from jamming in the hole, drill a few inches, and then back out the bit to clear the waste. Add extensions to the bit when the bit will reach no further.

Drive 24-inch lengths of #6 (¾-inch) rebar pins through the deadman crosspiece and into the ground. Cut the rest of the pins from #6 rebar so that they're 2 feet longer than the wall is high. With a sledgehammer, drive the pins through the timbers into the ground.

8. Backfill behind the wall.

Cover the perforated drainpipe with a 6-inch layer of gravel, tamped firmly in place. Continue adding and tamping layers of gravel to within 6 inches of the top of the wall, then cover it with the landscape fabric you laid earlier. Complete the fill with topsoil.

Dry-Laid Stone Retaining Wall

Dry-laid stones create a natural-looking retaining wall. Construction is similar to building a dry-laid freestanding wall, although the retaining wall usually requires a wider base and a greater batter angle. (See "Dry-Laying a Stone Wall," page 38.) Generally, the width of the wall at the base should equal at least half the wall height. In most situations, large base stones serve as the wall footing, so no poured-concrete footing is needed. As with freestanding walls, you must pay careful attention to selecting and fitting the stones so that the wall will remain stable.

Depending on the size and shape of your stones, and the wall height, you can build the wall one, two, or even three wythes thick. Lay two stones

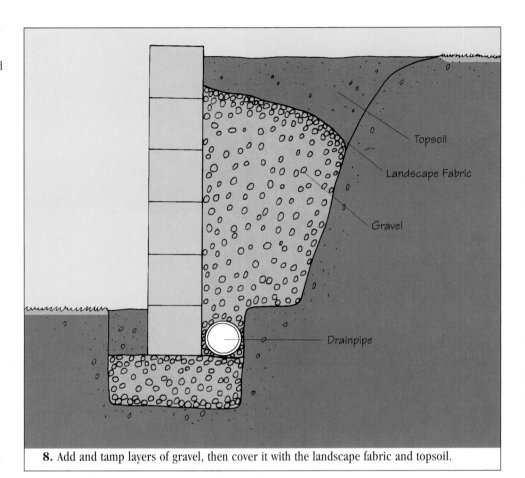

8. Add and tamp layers of gravel, then cover it with the landscape fabric and topsoil.

Topsoil
Landscape Fabric
Gravel
Drainpipe

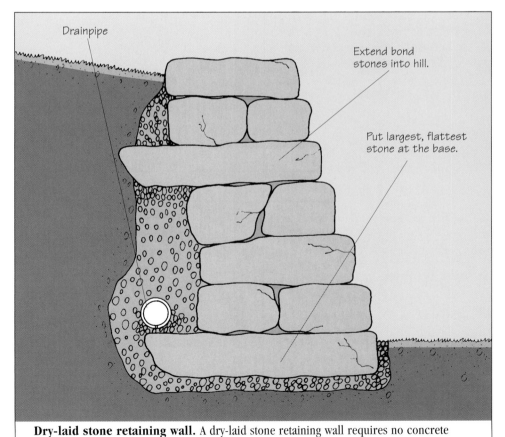

Drainpipe
Extend bond stones into hill.
Put largest, flattest stone at the base.

Dry-laid stone retaining wall. A dry-laid stone retaining wall requires no concrete footing. Large base stones provide stability, as does the sloping, or battered, face. Gravel, a perforated drainpipe, and gaps between stones help drain water.

over one and one stone over two. Use bond stones to tie the wythes together every 4 to 6 feet and at each end of the wall. Ideally, some of these stones should extend behind the wall so that the weight of the earth will hold them in place. The largest, flattest stones are used for the base.

The following instructions explain how to build a low dry-laid stone retaining wall. It's best to leave the construction of stone retaining walls more than 3 feet tall to experienced stonemasons.

1. Excavate the site. Cut and fill to create a space for the wall. Lay out the wall with stakes and strings, and excavate a level trench about twice as wide as the proposed bottom course of stones. Dig the trench deep enough to house the base stones. In wet or unstable soils, dig a deeper trench and add 2 to 3 inches of compacted sand or gravel to promote drainage. Line the cutout area with landscape fabric to keep the gravel you'll put there from clogging with silt.

2. Lay the base course. Select the largest and flattest stones for the base course. Lay them in the trench so that they tilt slightly toward the bank. Use large, flat bond stones at each end of the wall and at 4- to 6-foot intervals along it. Between the bond stones, lay stones one in front of the other to create a double-wythe wall. Long bond stones can extend behind the back of the wall and be cut into the bank to help support the wall. After laying the first course, replace any soil on the front side of the wall and tamp firmly. Install a perforated drainpipe behind the wall.

3. Add the backfill. Place the next course of stones, set back slightly from the first course to start the batter angle. Continue to add bond stones, which extend back toward the hillside. To prevent the stones from toppling, begin filling the uphill side of the wall with gravel. Add enough fill to bring the gravel to the same level as the top of the highest stones, then tamp it.

4. Add remaining courses and backfill. Build up the remaining

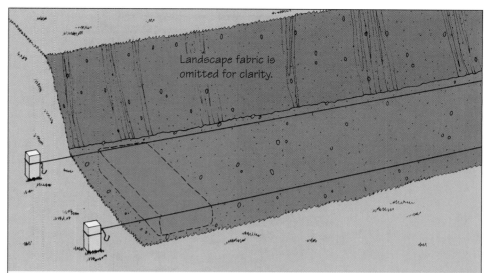

1. Cut and fill to create a site for the wall; then dig a trench about twice as wide as the bottom course of the wall. Line the cutout area with landscape fabric.

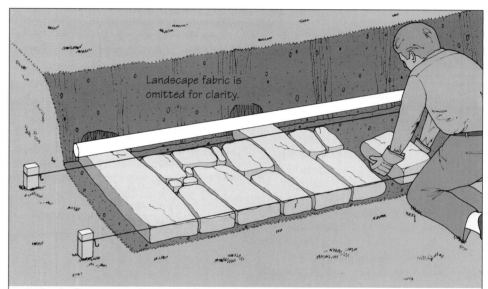

2. Set the first course of stones in the trench. Long bond stones, extending beyond the wall and toward the hill, provide extra support when covered with backfill.

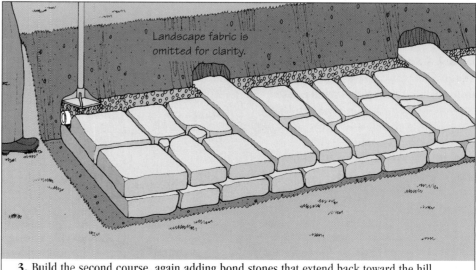

3. Build the second course, again adding bond stones that extend back toward the hill.

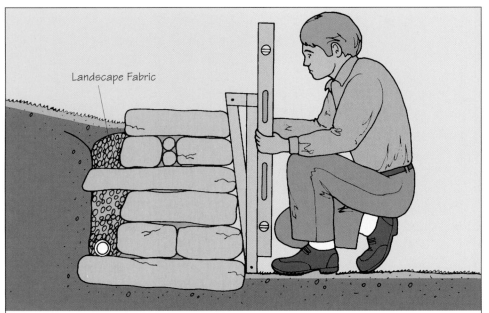

Landscape Fabric

4. Lay the rest of the courses, checking the angle of the wall constantly with a batter gauge.

means of pins, clips, or joints cast into the block itself. No mortar or reinforcing bar is required. Once you provide the required footing (for most manufacturers, a compacted sand or gravel base), you simply lay up the blocks, using the appropriate pins or other fasteners to lock them together. As each course is laid, the hollow cores are filled with well-draining soil, sand, or pea gravel to add mass to the wall.

On most types, the blocks interlock so that each horizontal course is stepped back slightly from the one beneath to create a batter angle. A few brands offer alternate pin positions to create either a plumb or a battered wall. These systems also include corner blocks and cap

courses, stepping the stones slightly back against the slope, staggering joints, and installing bond stones periodically. Fill the gaps between large stones with small rubble stones. Use a batter gauge so that you can be sure that the wall angles back 1 to 2 inches per 1 foot of height. (For more on batter gauges, see "General Requirements," page 38.)

Continue backfilling with gravel: Every time you complete one or two courses, add gravel up to the top of the wall and tamp it. Add another one or two courses, then backfill, and so on. Backfill to within 4 inches of the top of the wall and cover with topsoil.

INTERLOCKING CONCRETE-BLOCK WALLS

There are many interlocking-block retaining-wall systems on the market. These are available from most patio suppliers, masonry suppliers, major home centers, and other retail sources. The individual blocks are cast to look like natural stone and come in a variety of shapes, colors, and surface textures.

Although installation techniques vary for each brand, most interlock by

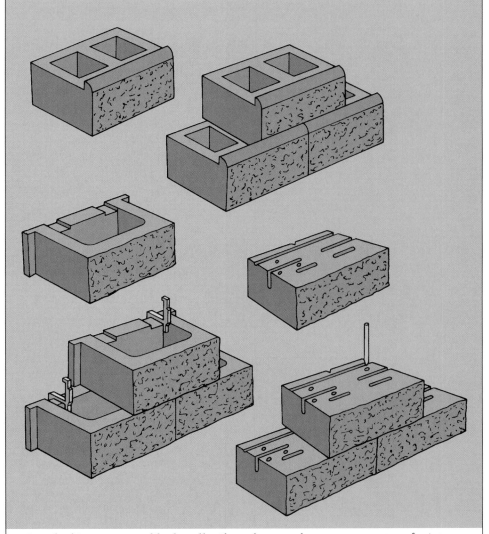

Interlocking concrete-block walls. Shown here are three common systems for interlocking concrete blocks. Set in a level sand or gravel base, these blocks create attractive retaining walls that are easy to build.

blocks to complete the installation. Some manufacturers offer specially shaped blocks for constructing serpentine walls. The steps below outline the basic procedure for laying one common type of block.

1. Prepare the foundation. Cut and fill for the wall and lay out the wall with stakes and strings. Excavate a trench along the planned wall location, and compact the soil in the trench bottom. Add a 3- to 6-inch layer of sand or pea gravel to level the trench and to provide drainage. The total depth of the trench will depend on how much of the wall must extend below grade on the downhill side. Typically, at least half of the base course is buried, but check the manufacturer's instructions.

2. Install the base course. For straight walls, set up stakes and a level string to represent the top front edge of the base course. On curved walls, check your work constantly with a level. Lay a row of blocks, orienting them so that the next course can interlock with the base course. The manufacturer's instructions will indicate how to place the blocks so that they'll interlock. As you lay each block, check it for level in both directions. Leveling the first course is extremely important as the rest of the courses will follow suit. Because the blocks fit tightly together, you can't compensate for any out-of-level conditions as you can with mortared block or brick walls. Backfill behind the first course with tamped sand or gravel, taking care not to shift the blocks out of position. Use the same fill material to fill the cores of the blocks.

3. Lay remaining courses. In the first-course blocks, install any pins or clips, following the manufacturer's assembly instructions. Then fit the second course over the first, staggering the joints to create a running-bond pattern. Backfill behind the second course and fill in the cores, as you did for the first course. Repeat the procedure for each additional course. Because the mortarless blocks are self-aligning, there's no need to build up corner or end leads as you would with a conven-

1. Cut and fill to create a site for the wall, then dig a trench to hold the first course of blocks and line it with gravel.

2. Set the first course of stones in the trench.

3. Lay additional courses, backfilling behind them and putting the fill material in the hollow cores of the bricks.

4. Finish the wall with cap blocks. Some walls can simply be covered with soil, which is then planted.

tional concrete-block wall. The batter angle is also pre-established.

4. Finish the wall. Although all manufacturers produce matching cap blocks for their walls, not all walls require a cap. Check with the manufacturer or supplier. If your wall doesn't require a cap, simply fill the cores of the top course with gravel or soil and allow plants to cover the top of the wall. If a cap is recommended, install the blocks with pins, clips, or a special high-strength adhesive recommended by the manufacturer.

MORTARED RETAINING WALLS

Other retaining-wall options include laying up brick, concrete block, and stone with mortared joints. Although the basic construction techniques used in building freestanding mortared walls are also applicable to building low retaining walls, building codes may require additional reinforcement and special drainage provisions. This usually means placing a wide, deep, reinforced-concrete footing, tying vertical rebar into the footing, and building the

wall around the rebar. Concrete-block cores or cavities between wythes should be filled completely with grout and gravel fill; a perforated drainpipe and weepholes must be provided. Basic construction techniques for mortared stone walls appear in "Constructing the Wall," page 53; for concrete-block walls, see "Building a Block Wall," page 63. Brick-wall construction is covered in "Building a Double-Wythe Wall, page 82. If you opt to take on the project yourself, be sure to consult a local building official, engineer, or architect to be sure that your wall will function properly.

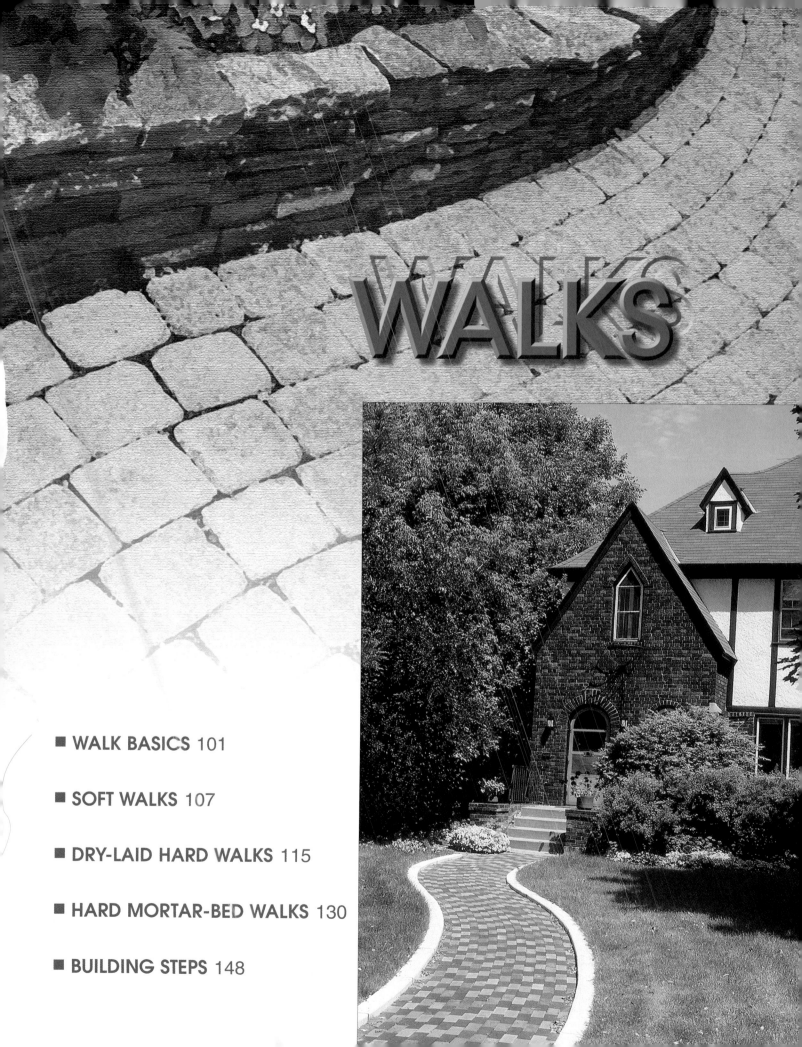

WALKS

Landscape timbers along the edge of a gravel path help keep the gravel from spreading.

Flagstone pavers can sit directly on the ground. Planting moss or a ground cover reduces mowing.

A walk may be as simple as a garden path made by spreading mulch on the ground and holding it in place with a stacked-brick border. Such loose-aggregate walks are ideal for informal locations and uses.

Brick walks often have a decorative edging, though it isn't strictly necessary. This edging, which is also brick, was laid at the same time as the walk. Other types of edging may need to be done earlier, as a separate operation.

Planting around stones controls weeds and grass while giving the walk a natural look.

Interlocking pavers sit on a simple sand bed, creating an intricate-looking walk that requires little preparation.

Redwood rounds can be set directly on the soil. Cast concrete stones that imitate wood provide a similar look.

You can change the look of a brick sidewalk by changing the edging or the pattern you choose. At the left, a half-basket weave pattern is lined by stone that also serves as garden edging. The diagonal herringbone pattern above (left) has a flush brick border. The change in levels in the walk above (right) is marked by a strong border and different brick patterns. The lower level is running bond; the upper level is a diagonal herringbone bond.

WALK BASICS

When you plan a walk, think of it as one part of the overall *land-scape scheme*, complementing fences, gates, walls, patios, decks, planting areas, and other features. These features, along with the characteristics of the site, help you determine the walk's location, design, and materials. This chapter focuses on specific design options and requirements for all kinds of walks.

But you must also think of the walk as something people will use. Even a narrow walk should be a minimum of 2 feet wide, which enables one person to walk comfortably along it. Garden walks that will bear the traffic of wheelbarrows, seed spreaders, and other wheeled equipment should be at least 3 feet wide. Walks 4 feet or wider enable two people to walk comfortably side-by-side, or to pass in opposite directions. Ideally, walks

This brick walk is laid on a concrete bed. Walks can also be laid directly on a sand base, or simply consist of mulch raked onto the ground and contained by edging.

leading to a house's front entry should be 4 feet wide. If you have a wheelchair user in the family, access walks should be at least 5 feet wide.

One of the first decisions you must make when designing a walk is which material to use. Walks can be divided into two basic categories, based on

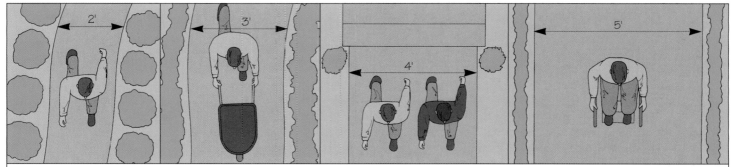

Walk basics. Consider how your walk will be used when deciding on its width. Generally, garden walks are narrow and entry walks and wheelchair-access walks are wide.

the walk's surface material: hard walks, made of brick or stone, and soft walks, which include walks made of wood or loose aggregate.

HARD WALKS

Hard walks may be poured concrete or unit masonry materials, such as brick, stone, concrete pavers, and quarry tile. While initial installation can be expensive, hard walks require little maintenance to keep them looking good for many years. Hard walks are preferable in high-traffic areas, such as front entry walks. Choose your materials carefully. A cobblestone or rough flagstone entry walk may look good, but high heels can get caught in the joints. Avoid surfaces that become slippery in the rain, such as glazed ceramic tile. Unglazed quarry tiles are a safer choice.

Most hard walks must be laid on a firm, well-drained subbase or they will tend to buckle, crack, or sink. A subbase consisting of 4 inches of compacted gravel topped by 2 inches of builder's sand (also called torpedo sand) should suffice. The subbase not only provides a solid, well-drained base but also makes it easier to level the paving units. Poorly drained soils or those subject to frost heave, settling, and erosion may require a subbase of 6 to 8 inches of gravel or crushed stone.

In mild climates, large, relatively flat stones more than 1½ inches thick can also be set directly on level, well-tamped soil or recessed into it. Such walks look quite attractive when the joints between the stones are planted with low-growing groundcovers, such as Irish moss, dichondra, or woolly thyme.

The most durable hard walk, however, is a paving material like paving brick, concrete patio blocks, flagstones, or quarry tile laid over a concrete subbase. The concrete—which can be either an existing sidewalk or a new slab—supports the paving material and keeps it from cracking or shifting with freeze-thaw cycles.

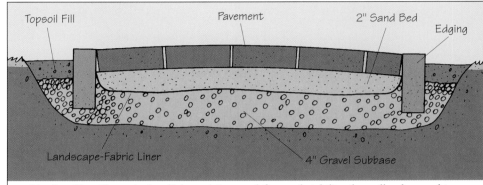

Hard walks. The typical walk has edgings to define and stabilize the walk edges and is constructed over gravel, which helps drain water. Unit masonry materials, such as bricks, may be placed in a sand bed or in a mortar bed over a concrete base.

SOFT WALKS

The term soft walks refers to walks that consist of wood or any loose aggregate, such as gravel, decorative rock, crushed shells, wood chips, and bark. Often, these materials are used for walks or paths in rustic or informal garden settings or in areas where only occasional foot traffic is expected. The main advantage of soft walks is that they're relatively easy and inexpensive to install and repair. Unlike masonry walks, soft walks aren't affected by unstable soil or frost heave, so you don't need to be as particular about the base you install beneath them. In fact, the base is often nothing more than tamped dirt.

Loose materials usually have to be replenished annually, however, because the material is kicked into surrounding areas or worked into the soil beneath. To help alleviate these problems, install a sturdy, raised edging to keep the loose paving material from spreading into surrounding areas. It also helps to place landscape fabric on the soil to prevent the

paving material from mixing with the earth and to stop weed growth.

Soft walks usually work best on flat ground—the aggregate can erode if the walk is built on a slope. Also, keep in mind that most loose aggregates make rougher going for wheeled equipment, such as lawn mowers, wheelbarrows, and wheelchairs. Some materials, such as crushed stone and gravel, are tough on bare feet and hard to navigate in dress shoes. In heavy-traffic areas, you'll need to rake the path frequently to keep up its appearance.

Wood Walks

Although naturally decay-resistant woods, such as redwood and cedar, are undeniably beautiful, they are also expensive. Fortunately, the wide availability of pressure-treated lumber has made wood practical and economical for walks and edging. Pressure-treated wood rated for ground contact may be installed below ground or on grade.

Wood is also a good material for temporary walks: Simply attach top boards

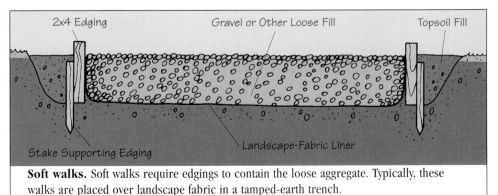

Soft walks. Soft walks require edgings to contain the loose aggregate. Typically, these walks are placed over landscape fabric in a tamped-earth trench.

to flat 2x4 stringers to create modules of any manageable size. You can relocate or rearrange the modules as your landscape requirements change.

EDGING

Edging is both decorative and functional. Edging is placed along the sides of a walk to define its borders and to contain the walk material. All soft walks (gravel, bark, and so on) require raised edging to keep the material in place. Brick and other masonry walks also need edging if they are to be dry-laid on a sand bed. In such cases, the edging not only holds the pavement in place but also serves to contain the bed on which the paving is set. If the walk materials will be mortared in place, edging is more decorative than structural, and its use is optional. If a concentrated load will be placed at the edge, however, you will need to reinforce the edges. If the walk is located where an automobile will drive over it, for example, you should either pour a thickened concrete edge along each side of the walk or install heavy timbers or railroad ties flush with the concrete surface.

Edging Materials

Edging materials may be wood, brick, concrete block, stone, or poured concrete, which either can match or contrast with the paving material. Plastic

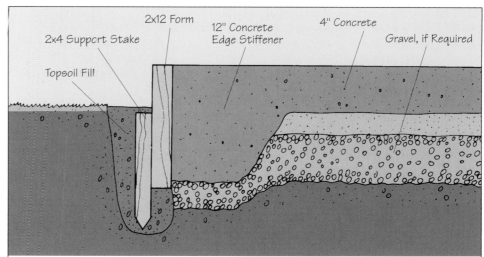

Edging. Concrete walks that must support a heavy load—such as those that cross a driveway—require reinforcement at the edges. Thickened strips of concrete along the walk edges, called edge stiffeners, keep the walk from breaking apart under a load. If the walk won't have to support heavy loads, no stiffener is required.

edging, which is completely buried after it's installed, is also available. Wood and plastic edging requires no forms and is simply anchored to the ground with stakes or spikes. When installing most masonry edging, however, you must set up temporary forms to hold the edging units in a straight line and to act as leveling guides. Once the edging is installed, the paving material is placed on its bed in the desired pattern.

In choosing edging materials, decide how you want to install them. Most walk surfaces are slightly higher than the surrounding ground. Edging is usually flush with the pavement or slightly recessed to allow for water runoff. If the walk is on or below

grade, however, a raised edging keeps surrounding soil from washing onto the walk and serves to contain plantings. A continuous edging of wood or poured concrete can prevent grass and weeds from spreading from the lawn to the walk. Raised edging also can serve as low retainers for raised planting beds adjacent to the walk or act as a curb for wheeled equipment on sloped walks or ramps.

Wood edging. Pressure-treated landscape ties (usually 4x6s or 6x6s) make massive and sturdy edging that is easy to cut and install. They work with all types of paving materials and can serve as forms for poured-concrete walks—simply leave the timbers in place after the concrete is poured.

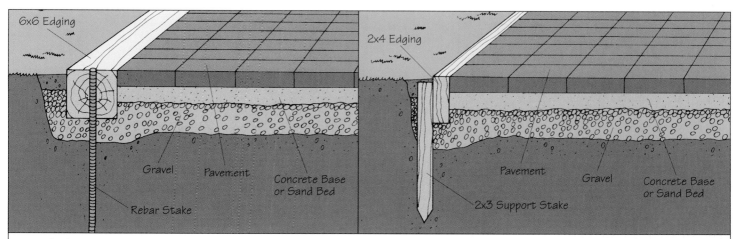

Wood edging. Wood edging helps anchor the paving material and adds a decorative detail. Landscape ties provide a massive, sturdy look and are held in place by lengths of rebar. Slimmer two-by lumber has a thinner profile and is supported by a wooden stake.

Plan the excavation so that the edging timbers rest on a 4-inch base of gravel or sand and anchor them in place with rebar spikes.

If landscape ties are too massive for your walk design, you can use pressure-treated 2x6s or 2x8s. Set these boards in the ground at the desired height and hold them in place with pressure-treated 2x3 stakes. When the walk is complete, backfill over the stakes with topsoil.

Brick edging. Bricks make attractive edging that is simple to install in a variety of patterns. It's a good choice for edging curved walks as well. Depending on soil conditions, bricks can be set directly in the ground, or they can be set over a gravel-and-sand subbase. For more stability, you can set the bricks into a poured-concrete footing.

Block edging. Concrete edging blocks, manufactured to match patio blocks, may be set in a ribbon of concrete along the walk perimeter. Edging blocks come in straight or curved shapes, with various top designs. The blocks typically measure 24 inches long, 5 inches wide, and 2 inches thick. The edging also may be used by itself as planting borders or in combination with other walk materials.

Stone edging. Cut stone, cobblestones, and small boulders make good edging for wide walkways. Cut stones, thick flagstones, and cobblestones should be set in a ribbon of

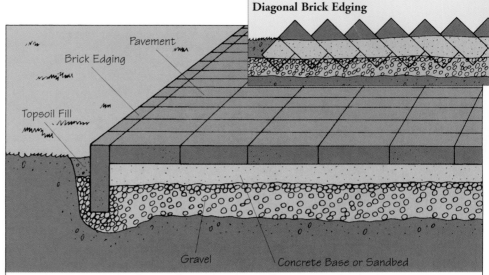

Brick edging. Set bricks on either end or diagonally to create a brick edging. For a stronger installation, edge bricks can be set in concrete.

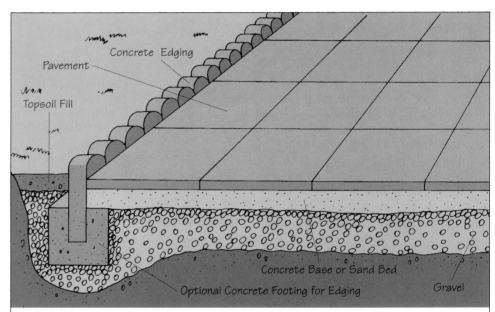

Block edging. Block edging comes in a variety of decorative shapes. Place the edging in a concrete ribbon to form a sturdy border for a walk.

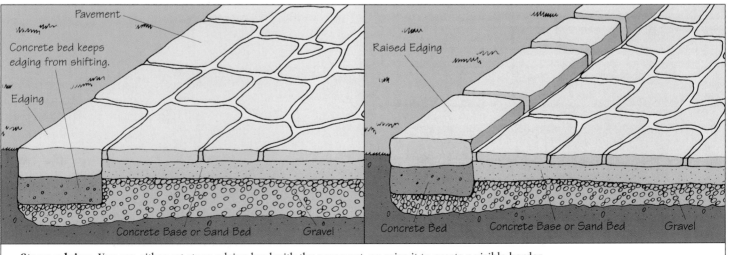

Stone edging. You can either set stone edging level with the pavement, or raise it to create a visible border.

concrete to keep them from shifting. Large, irregular boulders can be set in concrete or directly in the ground. Such edging looks best lining informal garden paths. When edging narrow walks, however, you should avoid irregularly shaped stones because they are easily tripped over or kicked out of place. If you're installing a flagstone walk, ask your dealer about the availability of thicker border stones of the same type of rock.

Concrete edging. Another alternative to edging brick and other masonry-unit walks is to pour a concrete curb. The curb will require formwork, which can be either straight or curved. A curb 6 to 8 inches wide set 6 to 8 inches in the ground should be adequate for most applications and localities. Check local building codes. Place the concrete on a 4-inch bed of gravel or gravel and sand. Before removing the forms, round over the top edges of the concrete with an edging tool.

Plastic edge restraints. If you're installing a brick or paver walk and you do not want a visible edging, you can use special molded-plastic edge restraints. Several types are available that will conform to straight or curved walks. To install them, you place the plastic strips along layout lines on the gravel subbase. The edging is held in place with 12-inch spikes driven into the ground. The tops of the plastic edging are used to guide a notched screed board that smoothes the bedding sand. After setting the paving units, you backfill on either side of the walk with topsoil, completely covering the edging, then lay sod or sow seed.

GRADING AND DRAINAGE

The characteristics of the site—terrain, soil conditions, and drainage requirements—as well as the paving materials used determine how you must prepare the ground for the walk. Virtually every walk project will require some amount of excavation to create a level surface and to provide a stable base for the paving

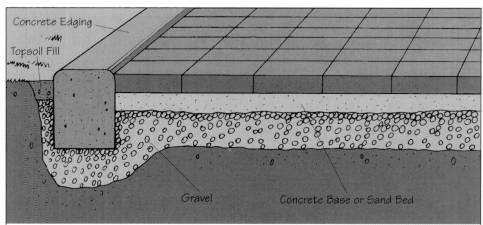

Concrete edging. A concrete curb goes well with a variety of paving materials. When set next to a lawn, the concrete edge prevents grass from spreading to the walk.

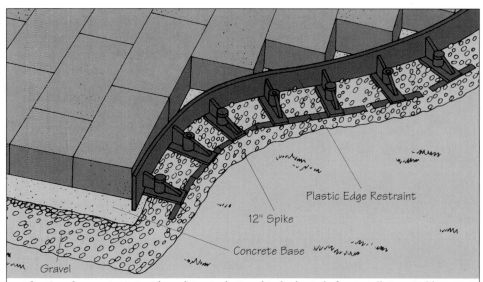

Plastic edge restraints. This edging is designed to be buried after installation. Held in place with long spikes, plastic edging conforms to both curved and straight walks.

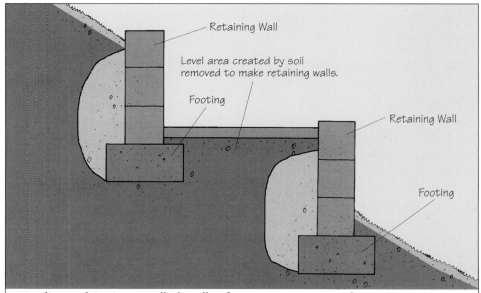

Grading and Drainage. Hillside walks often require extensive grading. Here, retaining walls create a level area for a walk that crosses a slope.

materials. Installing a walk on a sloped or uneven lot will require extensive cutting and filling to provide a level walking surface. Where the walk runs parallel to a slope, you may need to install low retaining walls on both sides of the walk, as shown, so that it will be level across its width. If your walk requires extensive grading and excavation, it's best to hire an excavation contractor to do the work.

Drainage

Drainage is usually not a major concern when building a walk. Typically, a building lot is graded so that water runs away from the house, and a walk that runs along grade level presents no problems. In some cases, however, the walk area will have to be graded to provide a slight slope for drainage. If you anticipate drainage problems, sloping the walk ¼ inch per foot along its length will provide adequate drainage in most situations.

In wet soil, you may want to install a perforated drainage pipe in a gravel subbase to assist drainage. If the walk crosses a low area subject to puddling or periodic flooding during the rainy season, loose aggregates, such as gravel or bark, will soon wash away or become mixed with dirt and debris washed in from surrounding areas. In such cases, you should install raised edging and build up the walk materials above the level of the surrounding soil. Don't install walks that cross swales or run across slopes. Such walks can act as dams that impede natural drainage patterns in the yard.

Often, walks made of bricks or concrete pavers are higher in the middle, or crowned, to prevent puddles from gathering on the walk. The crown (measured from the center of the walk to the edge) should be about ⅛ inch per foot. A 4-foot-wide walk, for example, is crowned ¼ inch in the middle. Poured-concrete and flagstone walks are often sloped across their width (about ⅛ inch per foot) to shed water. If a hard walk is next to a garden wall or the house, slope it away from the structure, as shown.

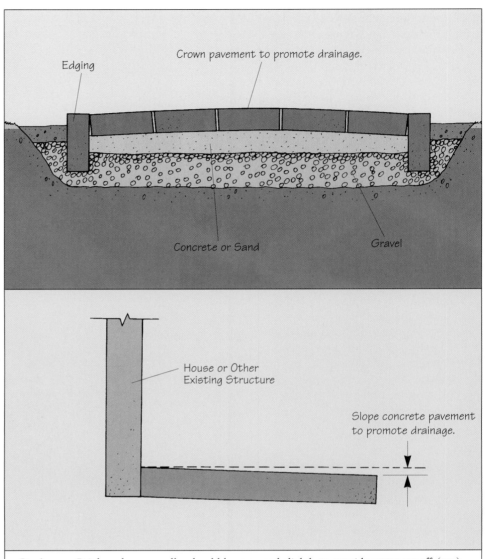

Drainage. Brick and paver walks should be crowned slightly to provide water runoff (top). Poured-concrete walks are often pitched across their width to direct runoff away from adjacent walls or buildings (bottom).

Changes in Walk Level

On lots with only minor changes in grade or terrain, a hard-surface walk may be able to follow the contour of the land, provided that the walk doesn't become submerged in low areas during the rainy season. But for soft walks the ground must be level, or the aggregate could wash away from high spots and collect in low spots, leaving bare areas. Steeper slopes or grades are usually dealt with by means of steps. If the slope is fairly gentle, you can install long sections of level walkways interspersed with single steps. For steeper slopes, flights of stairs connected by landings may be the solution. To reduce the number of steps required, you can slope the landings.

To determine how many steps are needed, first calculate the total amount of rise between the uphill side of the walk and the downhill side, then divide this measurement by the desired riser height of each step. (Risers should be no more than 8 inches high.) These procedures are described in detail in "Determining Tread and Riser Sizes," page 149.

For wheelchair access and for those who have difficulty with steps, ramps are preferable. There are strict rules concerning ramp size, angle, and materials; for more information, see "Accessibility," page 28.

SOFT WALKS

Soft walks are made of loose stones, wood, or wood products. They are less expensive and easier to install than hard walks but will require more maintenance. Because of the variety of materials, they can take on a variety of appearances. Gravel or pebbles come in an array of colors and sizes. Wood walks can be built from boards or from loose aggregate, including bark, wood chips, and mulch.

In most cases, wood walks made from boards require a gravel subbase, but stone and wood loose aggregates may be placed directly on the ground. Usually, edging will be required to contain loose aggregate. Even with edging, however, foot traffic will disperse loose aggregate into the surrounding area, and if the area is a lawn, a lawn-mower blade can turn the aggregate into dangerous projectiles. On the other hand, both stone and wood aggregates will conform to any shape walk, which makes these materials highly desirable for surfacing meandering garden paths.

Lumber walks can take many shapes and can be raised above grade level to bridge rough terrain or low areas. For high-traffic areas, a lumber walk offers the advantages of easy installation and repair and can serve to unify other wood elements, such as a deck or house siding, with the landscape.

Mulch or gravel laid directly on the ground creates a rustic path that is simple to install and maintain. Edging holds the paving material in place.

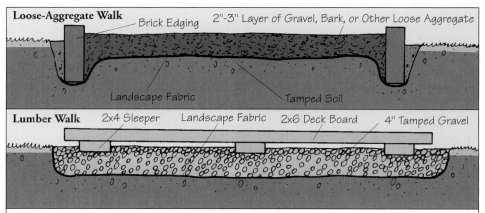

Loose-Aggregate Walk — Brick Edging — 2"-3" Layer of Gravel, Bark, or Other Loose Aggregate

Landscape Fabric — Tamped Soil

Lumber Walk — 2x4 Sleeper — Landscape Fabric — 2x6 Deck Board — 4" Tamped Gravel

Soft walks. Soft walks made from materials such as loose stones are built in a shallow, compacted excavation. Set edging materials in trenches along the walk. Lumber walks should be placed on a gravel base.

Tools

To build a loose-aggregate walk, you will need stakes and string, a level, a spade and a shovel, a pickax to remove large stones, a garden rake, and a steel tamper. If you are installing wood edging or a lumber walk, you also will need a tape measure, saw, hammer and nails or screwdriver and screws, and a framing square. Other tools that you might need are also shown in the drawing.

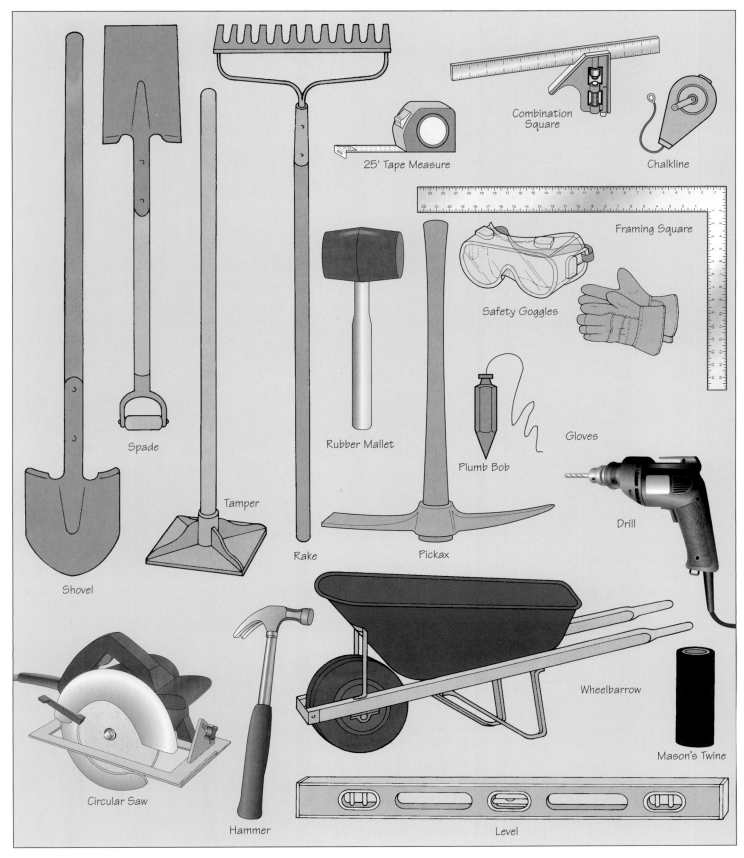

Combination Square

25' Tape Measure

Chalkline

Framing Square

Safety Goggles

Gloves

Spade

Rubber Mallet

Plumb Bob

Drill

Tamper

Rake

Pickax

Shovel

Wheelbarrow

Mason's Twine

Circular Saw

Hammer

Level

STONE

In general, stone aggregate is a good choice for walks that receive light traffic. Because it dries quickly and drains efficiently, crushed stone is a good choice for garden paths. A light spray from a garden hose is usually enough to wash away surface dirt. To cover 100 square feet of walkway with a 2-inch layer of stone, you will need about ⅔ cubic yard of material.

As for its disadvantages, stone must be replenished, raked, and tamped periodically. When compared with a hard walk surface, pushing a wheelbarrow over loose stone requires more effort, and walking in dress shoes or barefoot can be difficult, if not painful.

Types of Stone Aggregate

Stones used for soft walks may be classified by their texture, either smooth or rough. Generally, rough stones make a tighter, more compact walk than do smooth stones. Both textures are available in many colors and sizes, but choose carefully. Pick a color that won't overwhelm the landscape—blue rocks that look attractive in the bag may end up as an electric blue river in your yard. Also consider function. Light-colored stones stain easily, so they won't be appropriate for a high-traffic path, like one the rototiller takes to the garden.

Although loose aggregate ranges from ¼-inch pebbles to 3-inch stones, the best sizes are between ¾ and 1½ inches. These medium-size stones stay in place better than small pebbles, and they compact better and are more comfortable to walk on than large stones.

Gravel and crushed stone. You can buy gravel or crushed stone in uniform sizes or in random sizes, called unscreened gravel. Because gravel is jagged, it compacts well, but it's also uncomfortable to walk on barefoot. Typically blue-gray in color, gravel is also commonly available as reddish-brown redrock, white dolomite, and multicolored decomposed granite.

Smooth aggregates. River stone is smooth, which makes it more comfortable to walk on barefoot but less likely to stay compacted. River stone usually consists of white, tan, and gray rocks, which have been rounded smooth either naturally or by machine. Like gravel, river stone is sold in a variety of sizes by the bag or by the yard at stone yards and garden centers.

WOOD

Loose wood-aggregate walks are simpler and less expensive to install than lumber walks, but they won't last nearly as long. Bark, wood chips, and mulch make a soft, springy walkway that you can kneel on comfortably when gardening. Like stone, wood aggregates are recommended for light-traffic areas and are difficult to negotiate with wheeled equipment or in high heels. Most wood aggregates will last only a few years before decomposing. Bark and redwood chips will last longer but are expensive. Wood aggregates tend to hold moisture, and they will wash away in a heavy rain, leaving bare spots. Avoid them in areas subject to flooding or with poor drainage. Even under good circumstances, the wood aggregates require regular raking and replenishing. To cover 100 square feet of walkway with a 2-inch layer of wood aggregate, you will initially need about ⅔ cubic yard of the material.

Bark chips. Sold by the bag at garden centers, bark chips come in a variety of sizes, from ¼ to 3 inches. Two common types, firbark and tanbark, have a dark color and a rustic texture that complement a natural landscape. Generally, bark lasts longer but is more expensive than wood chips.

Wood chips. Typically light in color, wood chips are the by-product of milling or tree-clearing operations. Wood chips sold by the bag are purer than those sold by the yard, which often contain leaves, twigs, and bark, but the bagged form is also more expensive. Landscapers and utility companies sometimes sell wood chips at reasonable prices by the truckload.

Mulch. Mulch refers to a variety of organic materials cut to small sizes, such as ground bark, sawdust, conifer needles, and shredded roots. Among all loose aggregates, mulch offers the most comfortable walking and kneeling surface. Although mulch makes attractive, natural surfaces, it is meant to decompose and will require frequent replenishing.

INSTALLING A LOOSE-AGGREGATE WALK

In circumstances where drainage is not a problem, soft walk materials can be placed in a shallow excavation, with edging installed in trenches on each side of the walk. It's not necessary to build up a gravel subbase. Simply tamp the soil at the bottom of the excavation. It's a good idea to lay down landscape fabric to discourage weed growth.

1. Excavate the site. Begin by laying out the walk with stakes and string. First, drive two 1x2 stakes at each end of the walk, positioned to indicate the edges of the walk. Then attach string to the stakes to mark the finished height of the edging—usually about 2 inches above grade. Don't level the string; if the ground slopes, the string should slope with it. Check to make sure that the string is the same distance apart at both ends. If the walk leads straight to an entry, make sure the lines are perpendicular to the house by using the 3-4-5 triangulation method, explained in "Finding a Square Corner with the 3-4-5 Method," page 46. Lay out curved walks with a rope or garden hose, as described in "Plotting Curves," page 110. Excavate to a depth of 2 or 3 inches.

2. Dig the edging trenches. Use a flat-bladed shovel to dig narrow trenches for the edging. Dig the trenches deep enough so that the edging just touches the top of the string. Lay down landscape fabric,

Plotting Curves

Curved walks can be laid out in a freeform design or by "drawing" a series of arcs on the ground with a giant compass, made from a rope, a stake, and a sharp stick. Tie one end of the rope to the stake and drive it into the ground. Mark the desired radius on the rope, and tie the stick at the mark. Swing the rope and stick around the stake, scratching the arc on the ground. Adjust the length of the rope to lay out the other side of the walk.

Lay out an irregular curve with a rope or garden hose. Outline one side of the curve with the rope or hose. Cut a series of sticks the width of the walk, and place them at regular intervals, as shown. Outline the other side of the curve with a second rope or hose. Then sprinkle flour or sand to mark the curves. Dig a trench deep enough to accommodate a curved form (which can be made from bending thin plywood) or a permanent edging material, such as bricks.

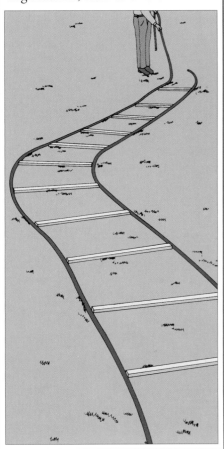

tucking it into the edging trenches. On curved walks, lay fabric across the excavation instead of running it down the length. Lap all seams by at least 6 inches.

3. **Install the edging.** Double-check to make sure the strings are at the right height, and use them as a guide in installing straight edging. Use stakes to support wood edging.

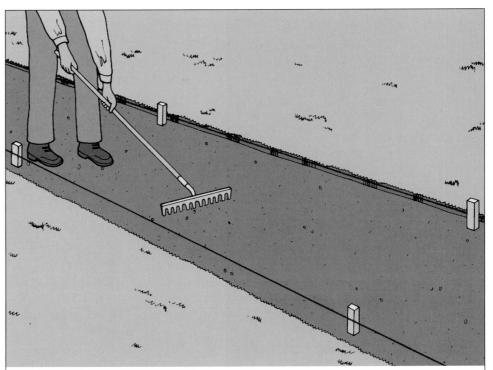

1. Set up layout strings, and remove the turf and loose soil to a depth of 2 or 3 inches. Rake the soil level and smooth, and firmly tamp it.

2. Along each side of the excavation, dig narrow trenches for the edging with a spade. Make the trenches about 6 inches deep, with the bottoms level and smooth.

For curved edging, use a rope or garden hose to guide you in creating smooth curves. As you set brick and block edging, fill behind them with compacted soil.

4. Spread the loose aggregate.
Add the soft walk material in 1-inch layers, spreading and tamping each layer until the material is within ¾ inch of the top of the edging.

The walk surface should be above the surrounding grade. Bed brick or block edging by tapping the inside face of the edging with a rubber mallet.

3. After placing landscape fabric in the excavation, set the edging into the trenches. Use layout strings or, for curved walks, a garden hose to align the edging.

4. Spread the aggregate in flat, smooth layers, and tamp each layer until the material is about ¾ inch below the edging. With a rubber mallet, tap the inside face of brick or block edging to bed it into the soil.

Subsurface Drainage

If you are building a walk in an area that is subject to flooding, such as a walk at the bottom of a slope, you'll dig the walk an extra 6 inches deep and lay a 4-inch perforated drainpipe down the middle. Dig the middle of the excavation a few inches deeper than along the sides to create a sloping bottom that aids in drainage.

Spread and tamp a 2-inch layer of gravel (crushed limestone works best) on the bottom. Set the perforated pipe in the middle of the excavation with the perforations down. Spread and tamp more crushed stone. Continue filling until you can set edging on the fill and have it protrude about 2 inches above grade. If you are setting brick edging, lean the bricks against the sides of the excavation. If the soil will not hold a vertical edge, set up forms and prop the bricks against the forms until you can add more fill. Add stone to cover the pipe, but leave enough room for a 2-inch layer of walk material. Place a layer of landscape fabric on the crushed gravel, then spread the surface material until it comes within about ¾ inch of the top of the edging.

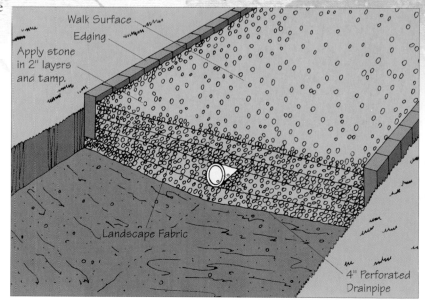

Walk Surface

Edging

Apply stone in 2" layers and tamp.

Landscape Fabric

4" Perforated Drainpipe

LUMBER WALKS

Compared with most hard walk materials, such as concrete and brick, lumber is easy to cut and install. It's less expensive than most paving materials, and depending on the type of lumber you choose, a wood walk may last as long as a hard walk. To build a lumber walk, all you need are a few basic layout and carpentry tools, a shovel, a rake, and a wheelbarrow. If you're laying the walk on or below grade, you should provide a level, well-drained base of gravel.

Some lumber species, notably redwood, cypress, and cedar, are naturally resistant to decay and can be used to construct wood walks, albeit expensive ones. A more economical approach is to use pressure-treated lumber. You can install a durable, long-lasting treated-wood walk in, on, or above the ground. Building an above-ground walk is an excellent way to avoid altering existing drainage patterns or to create a level walking surface across uneven or rocky terrain with a minimum of excavation.

Treated Lumber

Pressure-treated wood comes in a variety of dimensional sizes, from one-by boards to large landscape timbers and poles. All treated wood is rated according to usage. Lumber rated for ground contact, designated 0.40 (meaning it has a preservative retention of 0.40 pound per cubic foot), is recommended for all walk applications. Preservative doesn't completely penetrate into the center of the board, so you should apply wood preservative to the cut ends. If your design calls for large timbers, use pressure-treated landscape ties. Treated timbers are better for walking on than real railroad ties, which are splintery and have a toxic, oily creosote coating.

Untreated Lumber

Naturally decay-resistant woods, such as redwood and cedar, are often used in outdoor projects for appearance's sake. Such woods are recommended for above-ground use only, where they may last ten years or more, depending on climate and maintenance. Finishing such wood species with paint, stain, or preservative will prolong the life span. Other species, such as pine and fir, have little resistance to decay and are not recommended for walks even if finished.

Wood rounds and blocks. In some part of North America (typically in the West), redwood and cedar rounds are used as "stepping stones." Rounds are sections of log about 3 to 6 inches thick and 12 to 30 inches in diameter, with or without the bark attached. Laid directly on level, well-drained soil or on a compacted-sand base, the rounds last about five years before they begin to decay. (Simulated wood rounds, which are formed from concrete, are available at stone yards and patio suppliers and will last much longer.) Plant the spaces between rounds with a groundcover that can withstand light foot traffic. Such plants include Irish moss, lippia, sandwort, and yerba linda. You can also recess the rounds into a soft walk made from a loose aggregate, such as gravel or bark chips. The rounds should be about ½ inch higher than the surrounding loose aggregate so that it won't wash over the rounds.

If wood rounds aren't available in your area but you like exposed end-grain, you can set short timber blocks (either redwood or pressure-treated lumber) vertically in a sand bed. The procedure is similar to that for setting bricks in sand. (See "Laying Paving Units in Sand," page 125.) Cut the blocks—4x6s or larger timbers—into 3- or 4-inch lengths. Lay enough blocks to calculate the width of the walk. Excavate the walk area, add a gravel-and-sand base, and install the

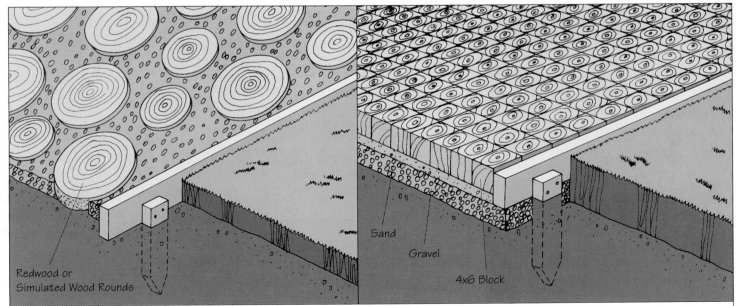

Redwood or Simulated Wood Rounds

Sand
Gravel
4x6 Block

Wood rounds and blocks. Used as pavers, redwood rounds may be placed in loose-stone aggregate or on a sand base. Simulated wood concrete rounds are also available. Short timber blocks set vertically on a sand bed with swept-sand joints make a smooth, durable walk.

edging before setting the blocks. To avoid drainage problems, set the edging so it will be flush with, or below, the walk surface. Put the blocks end-grain up, and butt them together. Sweep fine sand into the joints.

After setting rounds or timber blocks, brush on a good water sealer or a wood preservative to help prevent checking and cracking. Soaking the blocks or rounds in a wood preservative before installation will extend their life considerably, although the treatment is fairly expensive. Because many wood preservatives are toxic, follow all label precautions.

BUILDING A BOARDWALK

You can build a simple wooden boardwalk by nailing two-by cross-pieces to wood sleepers laid either in or on top of a flat, well-drained base of gravel. Make the sleepers from pressure-treated wood rated for ground contact. The deck boards can be pressure-treated wood or a decay-resistant species. Support walks more than 3 feet wide with a third sleeper running down the center of the walk. For wider walks, space sleepers no more than 3 feet apart.

The walk surface should be at least 1½ inches above grade. To keep washed soil and trash from accumulating underneath the raised walk, attach a two-by header that touches the ground at each end.

The decking can be 2x6s, 2x8s, or wider boards, or a combination of widths. The project described below uses 2x4 sleepers laid flat on top of a gravel subbase. The 3-foot-wide walk surface is 2x6 deck boards.

1. Prepare the base. At each end of the walk, drive two 1x2 stakes at least 2 feet into the ground to indicate the edges of the walk, and stretch strings between them. Double-check to make sure that the strings are the same distance apart at both ends. If the walk leads straight to an entry, make sure the lines are perpendicular

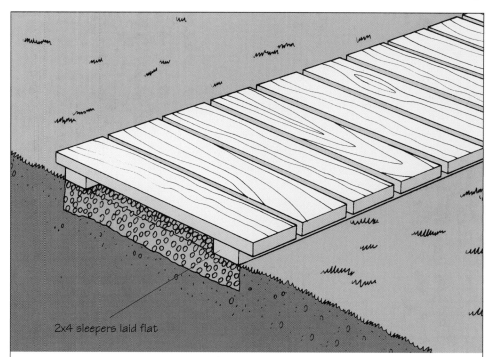

Building a boardwalk. A simple 2x6 boardwalk rests on 2x4 sleepers laid flat on a gravel base.

2x4 sleepers laid flat

to it by using the 3-4-5 triangulation method, explained in "Finding a Square Corner with the 3-4-5 Method," page 46.

If you are building on stable, well-drained soil, you can lay the walk directly on the ground. If the ground is soggy, or prone to puddles, build a gravel base for the walk. First, dig a trench at least 4 inches deep and wider than the walk by 4 to 6 inches on each side. To prevent weed growth, lay landscape fabric over the bottom of the excavation. Backfill with 4 inches of pea gravel and tamp, or with two inches of pea gravel and 2 inches of sand. Tamp each layer as you install it.

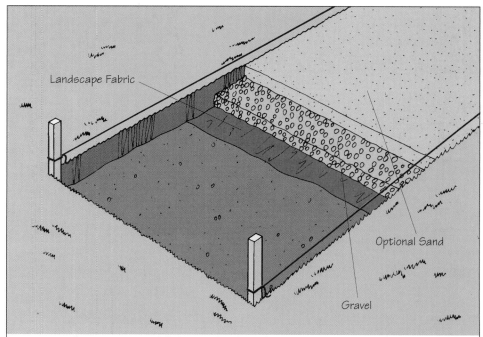

Landscape Fabric

Optional Sand

Gravel

1. Set up layout strings and dig a trench at least 4 inches deep. Put down landscape fabric to control weeds. Spread and tamp a layer of gravel, followed by sand, if desired.

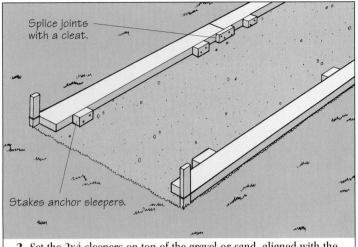

2. Set the 2x4 sleepers on top of the gravel or sand, aligned with the layout strings. Drive 2x4 stakes along the inside edges, and fasten them with 3-inch deck screws. Use 1x4 cleats to splice joints in sleepers.

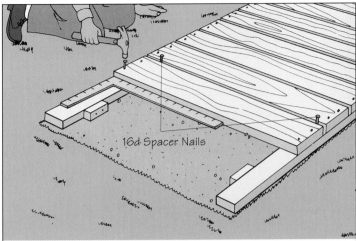

3. Cut the deck boards to length, and nail them to the sleepers. Use a framing square to keep the boards perpendicular to the sleepers. Space the boards using 16d nails.

2. Install the sleepers. Use the layout strings to position the sleepers on the gravel base. For sleepers that are flush with the ends of the boards, align the sleepers with the layout lines. For overhanging boards, align a 2x4 spacer with the lines and lay the sleeper next to the spacer. In either case, lay the sleepers flat on the ground and drive 2x4 stakes every 4 feet along the inside edges of the sleepers. Attach the sleepers to the stakes by driving 3-inch galvanized deck screws through the stakes. Where sleepers butt together, join them with 1x4 cleats on the inside of the sleepers. Drive stakes on either side of the cleat.

3. Attach the decking. Cut 2x6 decking boards to length. Align the boards with a framing square, and attach them to the sleepers with 10d galvanized nails or 3-inch deck screws. Predrill holes to avoid splitting board ends.

If you are using redwood or cedar decking, leave a ⅛- to ¼-inch space between boards to allow for wood expansion, and to facilitate water runoff—16d common nails make good spacers. Space pressure-treated wood the same way. If you are building with wet pressure-treated lumber, however, you may want to butt the boards together—they will shrink as they dry out.

Plank Walks

A variation of the boardwalk is a plank walk. In this type of wood walk, 2x8 or wider deck boards run along the length of the walk and are supported by 2x4 cleats laid across the walk excavation. Letting the deck boards overhang the cleats is not advisable, so cut the cleats to the exact walk width and set them every 3 feet directly on a gravel base. Lay the first plank over the cleats, aligned with the layout line; when the end of a cleat is flush with the edge of the plank, fasten the two together. Make sure joints between planks occur over cleats. Use a framing square to keep the cleats perpendicular to the planks. For a finished appearance (and additional stability), attach 2x4 or 2x6 edge strips around the walk perimeter.

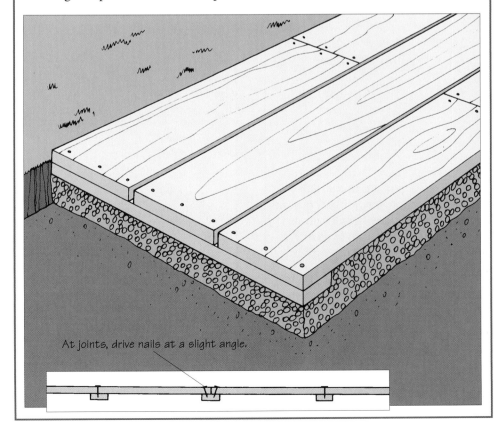

At joints, drive nails at a slight angle.

DRY-LAID HARD WALKS

This chapter and the next concern hard walks, made of unit paving materials—brick, concrete pavers, and stone—and you'll see that there are two ways to set these walks: You can dry-lay them or set them in wet mortar. This chapter discusses dry-laid walks, in which paving materials are laid on a bed of tamped sand over gravel. The next discusses laying paving material in mortar on top of a concrete bed.

In dry-laid walks, the joints between paving materials are filled with sand, topsoil, or dry mortar. The width of the joints will help you determine which material to use. Paving materials that can be laid closely together, such as bricks and interlocking pavers, are usually set with sand between the joints. In this type of construction, called flexible paving, fine mason's sand is swept into the joints, creating a stable and durable walk, even in climates subject to some frost heave. It's easy to replace damaged paving materials, fill sunken portions of the walk, or remove sections of the walk to get to buried utility lines or pipes. However, the sand must be replenished annually, and sometimes more frequently.

Joints between irregularly shaped paving materials, such as flagstones and rubble, are too wide to hold onto

Brick, stone, and pavers can be laid on a simple sand bed for a durable, attractive walk. Sand swept between the bricks in this walk keep them from shifting, as do the perpendicular border bricks.

sand, so these paving materials have topsoil or mortar joints. If you live in an area where frost heave is not a problem, you can make a simple and attractive walk by setting concrete stepping stones, flagstones (2 inches or thicker), or fieldstones directly on compacted soil. Pack the joints with topsoil. To prevent weed growth, plant the crevices with grass or a low-growing groundcover. Mortared joints make for a smoother, more formal walk than topsoil joints, but they are subject to cracking in a dry-laid walk.

TOOLS FOR DRY-LAID WALKS

The tools you will need for installing a dry-laid walk will depend on the walk material, but some tools will be used for all walks. For example, the job of compacting the soil and subbase can be done with a hand tamper; however, renting a power tamper is recommended. Power tampers compact soil, gravel, and sand better, faster, and with less effort than tamping by hand.

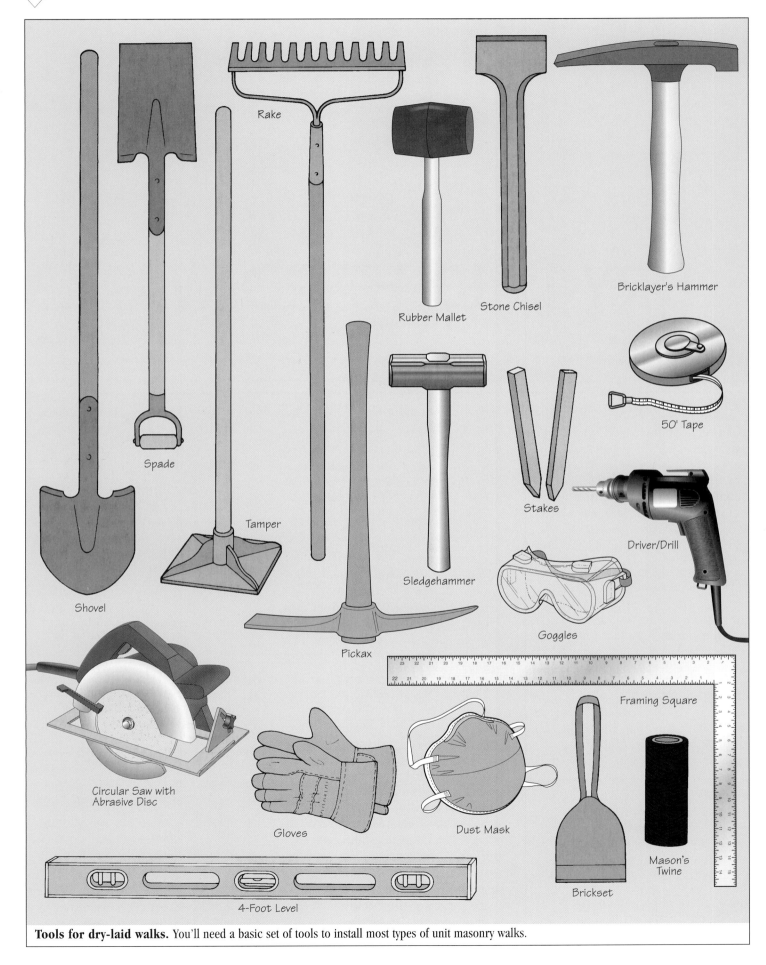

Rake

Rubber Mallet

Stone Chisel

Bricklayer's Hammer

Spade

Stakes

50' Tape

Tamper

Sledgehammer

Driver/Drill

Shovel

Goggles

Pickax

Framing Square

Circular Saw with
Abrasive Disc

Gloves

Dust Mask

Mason's
Twine

Brickset

4-Foot Level

Tools for dry-laid walks. You'll need a basic set of tools to install most types of unit masonry walks.

Screed board. A tool you can make yourself is a screed board for smoothing the sand bed. The screed board is a piece of 1x6 whose ends are notched to fit loosely inside the walk borders or edgings. Because the notched ends usually ride on top of the edgings, the notch depth equals the thickness of the paving material. If you're laying dimensional paving materials, such as brick or dressed stone, cut the screed board so that the bottom edge is arched the proper amount to create a crowned walk. When setting irregular paving materials, such as flagstones and rubble, the walk is pitched sideways to shed water, and the bottom of the screed board is straight.

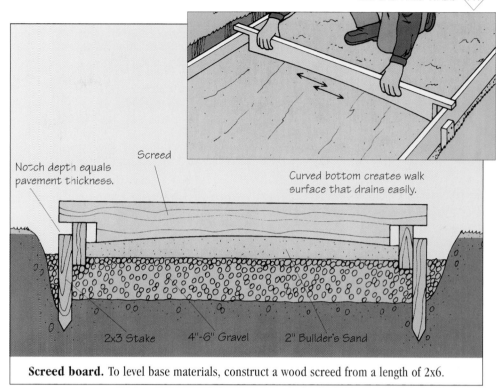

Notch depth equals pavement thickness.

Screed

Curved bottom creates walk surface that drains easily.

2x3 Stake   4"-6" Gravel   2" Builder's Sand

Screed board. To level base materials, construct a wood screed from a length of 2x6.

PAVING UNITS FOR DRY-LAID WALKS

Paving materials that can be laid in a sand bed over a gravel subbase include brick, stone, adobe, concrete patio blocks, and interlocking pavers. Among these choices, some materials are cut to more precise sizes and shapes than others; some materials are better suited to particular climates. Otherwise, walk construction techniques and required substrates are similar. Exceptions are noted under each heading below. As with any masonry project, check local building codes for specific requirements and accepted practices in your area.

Types of Brick

Bricks provide a beautiful walk surface that will last for many years, provided that you choose the right kind of brick. That's a formidable task, considering that bricks come in a bewildering array of sizes, colors, and textures, not all of which are suitable for walks. Some bricks are designed for interior applications and won't hold up under wet or freezing conditions; some have smooth or glazed surfaces that can make for a dangerously slippery walk when wet. The ideal brick is hard and dense and has a slightly rough surface to provide good traction in wet weather. Paving

brick is designed especially for walks and patios and meets these criteria. The next best choice is face brick, followed by concrete brick.

Paving brick. Designed especially for ground contact, paving brick is sealed, so it has a high resistance to abrasion and moisture penetration. Most paving bricks are cut to uniform dimensions in modular sizes, so they can be set with perfectly aligned, mortarless joints. You can also get pavers that are sized to work with mortar joints. Some paving bricks, called repress pavers, have chamfered or rounded edges on one or both faces. Repress pavers are preferred in some climates because the chamfered edges facilitate water runoff and are less likely to chip if struck by a snow shovel.

Concrete brick. If you live in a mild climate and your walk will receive only light traffic, you can save money by using concrete brick. Concrete bricks are not quite as durable as pavers, and their colors, sizes, and textures are often limited. A typical concrete brick measures $2\frac{1}{4} \times 3\frac{5}{8} \times 7\frac{5}{8}$ inches. Unfortunately, the pigments used to color the concrete will fade. Like concrete blocks and pavers, the bricks have a slightly rough, pitted surface.

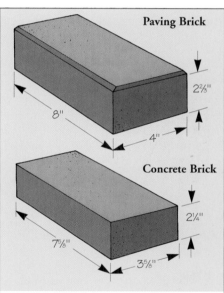

Paving Brick

2⅔"

8"

4"

Concrete Brick

2¼"

7⅞"

3⅝"

Types of brick. For walks, the best bricks are pavers with chamfered edges; face brick is the next best choice, followed by concrete brick.

Durability. Most clay bricks are manufactured to withstand the weather. The most expensive grade, SX paving bricks, will withstand severe weathering, such as freeze-thaw conditions in cold climates, and are recommended for outdoor walks and patios. MX paving bricks will withstand moderate weather conditions, including rain and mild frost. Before you start your project, consult your local building department for the brick types that are suitable for your particular area and project.

Bricks are also rated for hardness. The hardest, Type I, is rarely used in residential applications. Type II is suitable for residential driveways and entry walks, and Type III is adequate for low-traffic garden walks and patios.

Estimating brick amounts.
Pavers designed to be used with mortar joints are usually referred to by their nominal size—the actual size plus the width of a mortar joint. Pavers designed for swept-sand joints usually have spacer nubs that leave space for the sand. Whether or not you are using joints, it will take an average of 4.5 bricks to cover a square foot. For example, a 12-foot-by-20-foot patio is 240 square feet. Multiply 240x4.5 bricks to find you need 1,080 bricks. Order 5 to 10 percent extra to allow for miscuts, breakage, and future repairs.

Certain brick patterns, such as herringbone and basketweave, require a brick type whose length is exactly twice its width, if the bricks will be set without mortar joints. A standard modular brick works well for these patterns—it has a nominal size of 2⅔ inches thick, 4 inches wide, and 8 inches long.

Split pavers are half the thickness of a standard brick and are useful when headroom is limited, such as in an enclosed porch. Soap bricks are half the width of a standard brick. Soaps are sometimes used as border bricks for walks or to create special patterns within the paving area.

Cutting bricks. If your walk requires a few cut bricks, you can cut them with a brick chisel, or brickset, and small sledgehammer. To cut a brick with a chisel, first mark the cut line with a piece of chalk or grease pencil. With a hammer and brickset, tap all four sides of the brick to score it along the cut line; then center the brickset over the line and strike the chisel sharply. If you need to cut a large number of bricks or want to make more precise cuts, you can rent a masonry saw or a mechanical cut-

ter, called a guillotine, at a tool rental shop. For more on cutting bricks, see "Cutting Bricks," page 82.

Brick Patterns

Bricks require careful layout to avoid misaligned joints or partial bricks along the edges of the walk. Before you lay the bricks, do a dry run to spot any potential layout problems.

Jack on jack. Also called a stack bond, this pattern is the simplest to lay and the least interesting. Starting at one end of the walk, place a single

brick in one corner, then place remaining bricks in stair-step fashion, in the sequence shown. If possible, plan the walk width to avoid cut bricks. If you can't do this, cut the bricks you'll need to the same size, all at once with a masonry saw. Place cut bricks along the least conspicuous edge of the walk, such as against a building or along an overhanging plant border.

Running bond. This is the most popular brick pattern and is easy to lay out. Also, the pattern visually minimizes any minor variations in brick sizes. Place the first course of bricks

Brick Patterns

Among the popular brick patterns shown, some are more difficult to lay than others, but all require careful planning.

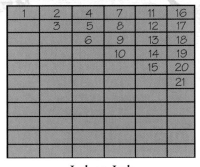

Jack-on-Jack

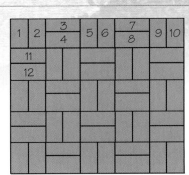

Basket Weave

Running Bond

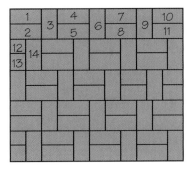

Half-Basket Weave

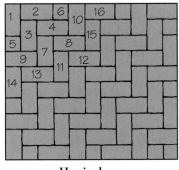

Herringbone

Ladder Weave

end to end across the walk. Start the second course with a half brick, followed by whole bricks placed end to end so that joints fall midway between bricks as shown.

Herringbone. This pattern looks best on wide walks. On walks 3 feet wide or less, the pattern may appear confusing. As with the running-bond design, a herringbone pattern requires partial bricks along the walk edges and ends, which are best cut in advance on a masonry saw. Starting at one corner, place full bricks in the step pattern shown, using half bricks to fill in along the edges. Use a framing square to align bricks meeting at right angles.

Weaves. Basket-weave designs look best when you use modular bricks on which the nominal width is exactly half the length. To make a simple two-brick basket weave, lay two bricks side by side to form a square in one corner of the walk. Working across the walk, lay a second square of two bricks at right angles to the first. Alternate the direction of each square until you reach the other side of the walk. Install the second course by laying two bricks at right angles to the square above it. Continue in this manner to create the pattern shown. Start the half-basket weave as shown, beginning the second course with bats. The ladder weave is similar to the jack-on-jack pattern.

Adobe Blocks

With its earthy tan color characteristic of southwestern and early California architecture, adobe lends a warm, natural feel to the garden. Because traditional adobe is not waterproof, it's used mostly in warm, arid climates. Modern adobe paving blocks, however, are nearly as waterproof as clay bricks. Adobe paving blocks come in a variety of square and rectangular sizes. Consider using small, brick-size units for walks; large blocks may be out of scale in the landscape. Most adobe block is produced in the Southwest and California, where it is inexpensive compared with standard clay brick. Elsewhere, shipping costs make adobe more expensive.

Installation. When laid on a sand-and-gravel base, modern adobe blocks will hold up nearly as well as brick pavers. The blocks usually have rough edges, so they are laid with open joints that are filled with sand or compacted earth.

Installation. Lay adobe on a gravel-and-sand bed, as you would brick. (Follow the instructions in "Laying Paving Units in Sand," page 125.) The sand bed should be perfectly smooth and pitched slightly across its width to shed water. Set the bricks with wide (3/4- to 1-inch) joints to compensate for the irregularity of the brick edges and to provide sufficient drainage. Pack the joints with sand or well-draining soil. Do not use mortar, which can stain the adobe. Jack on jack and running bond are two popular patterns.

Stone

Natural stone walks lend a sense of permanence to the landscape and blend with almost any decor. Stone comes in a variety of colors, shapes, and sizes. The most common types used for walks and patios are split along natural fissure lines to produce a slender, flat stone. Such stones include slate, quartzite, and sandstone. These and many other types of split, or "cleft," stones are available as flagstones and dimensioned paving stones, but you'll usually be limited to what's available in your area.

Ashlar. Ashlar is cut to square or rectangular shapes either in random or uniform sizes to present a more formal appearance. Typically, such stones are laid in a coursed pattern.

Flagstone. Flagstones—usually slate, limestone, or sandstone slabs—come in random shapes and sizes and are fitted together like a jigsaw puzzle in a random pattern. Generally, flagstones are less expensive than ashlar.

Fieldstone. As their name implies, fieldstones are rocks collected from fields, dry creek bottoms, and similar sources. Most fieldstones have a fairly smooth, weathered surface, but their irregular shape makes them difficult to lay in walks. If you have access to a free source of stone (and a means of transporting it to the building site), pick relatively thin, flat stones with smooth surfaces.

Rubble. Rubble is usually the least expensive stone you can buy at rock yards and patio suppliers. It consists of irregularly shaped stones, usually with sharper edges than fieldstone. Rubble may have been blasted from construction sites, or it may be broken pieces left over from cutting quarried stones. At construction sites, rubble is sometimes free for the hauling. Depending on the type, size, and shape of the stones (and their cost), it may or may not be worth your time and energy to haul them home and try to set them into a walk. Consider your walk requirements carefully before choosing rubble or fieldstone.

Installation tips. Stones for dry-laid walks should be at least 1½ inches thick, as thinner stones may break. With stones of consistent thickness, the sand bed is usually 2 inches thick. Stones of varying thickness should be laid on a thicker sand bed. Remove sand as necessary to create a level walk surface. Along walk edges, use larger stones, which aren't so easily dislodged.

Stonework is backbreaking work, so you should not try to do too much in one day or feel pressured to get the job done quickly. Also, it's a good idea to enlist the aid of a strong helper. Even modest-size paving stones can weigh 50 pounds or more.

Estimating amounts. Quarries and patio suppliers sell natural stone either by the ton or by the cubic yard. Because of the spaces between stones and thickness variations, stones sold by weight or by volume may not cover what they are slated to cover. You'll need to rely on the experience of the supplier to calculate your needs. Generally, it's best to order 20 to 25 percent more than you think you need to allow for cutting and breakage. Some suppliers will let you return any unused stones. You can also use any extras in other parts of the yard for stepping stones or plant borders.

Interlocking Pavers

Interlocking pavers are modular concrete units manufactured to fit in a tight pattern. Available in a variety of sizes and shapes, most pavers are 2⅜ to 2½ inches thick, about the same as a standard brick. One type, called a grass paver, has an open-grid shape for planting grass or other groundcover. Grass pavers provide a durable, natural-looking walk surface, and the turf itself helps hold the pavers in place.

For all pavers, check manufacturer's literature for coverage estimates, and buy a few extra for replacement purposes.

Installation. Interlocking pavers are usually butted together and finished

with swept-sand joints. Some pavers have small tabs on one side and one end to ensure consistent joint spacing. Laying pavers is much the same job as laying bricks on a sand bed, but check the manufacturer's instructions. (See "Laying Paving Units in Sand," page 125.) Where soil conditions and climate permit, pavers may be laid directly on well-tamped soil. Depending on the shape of the paver, you may end up with voids or chinks along the edges of the walk. Some manufacturers make special edging pieces to fill the chinks and create a straight edge. Otherwise, you'll have to cut the pavers or fill the voids with mortar to make straight edges.

Concrete Patio Blocks

Concrete patio blocks are thinner (usually only 1 inch thick) and therefore less expensive than concrete bricks and interlocking pavers. Patio blocks come in a variety of shapes and colors; the standard size is a 1-foot square that is 1 inch thick. The surface texture is similar to that of concrete building blocks used in foundations, although exposed aggregate surfaces are also common and much more attractive. Like all molded concrete products, there is little size variation in a given run of concrete patio blocks, and their nominal size is the same as their actual size. Therefore, calculating the number of blocks you need is simply a matter of dividing the total walk area by the area of a single unit. Order 10 percent extra, however, because concrete patio blocks are prone to accidental breakage and don't always split cleanly when you cut them.

Installation. Patio blocks should be set on a highly compacted and well-drained sand-over-gravel base, but you should expect some shifting, sinking, and even breakage due to stress or severe weather conditions. Because concrete patio blocks are only 1 inch thick, there's less area for sand to create an interlocking joint than with concrete bricks or interlocking pavers. To provide a better interlock between the patio blocks, space

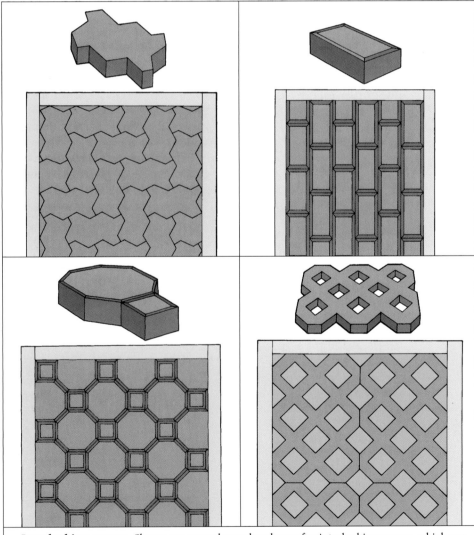

Interlocking pavers. Shown are several popular shapes for interlocking pavers, which are designed to be laid in a tight pattern with swept-sand joints. Grass pavers (bottom, right) have openings that you can plant in.

Installation. Mix mortar and sand for the joints between patio blocks. Pack the dry mixture between the joints, compact it with a mini-tamper, then wet it.

them ½ inch apart and mix the jointing sand with portland cement in a 1:1 ratio. Sweep the dry mixture into the joints, pack it with a thin wood tamper, then wet it and let it dry for two or three days before using the walk.

SETTING STONE DIRECTLY ON THE GROUND

Mostly because it is impractical to construct a sand base for thick, irregularly shaped stones, they may be set directly in stable, well-drained soil that isn't subject to frost heave. These walks have topsoil joints, so they are not as formal or as smooth as walks with sand or mortar joints.

Suitable Materials

When setting stone directly on the ground, you'll get the best results using flat stones with a fairly consistent thickness. Another requirement is that the paving be heavy enough so that it can't be dislodged easily. Stones more than 1½ inches thick—including flagstones, fieldstones, and rubble with at least one flat side—and precast concrete stepping stones are good choices.

Most precast concrete stepping stones are 2 inches thick, in square or round shapes, with an exposed-aggregate surface. Others are poured into molds to simulate natural stones; these are referred to as "cultured" stone. You can buy round stones up to 24 inches

in diameter; square stones range from 12 to 48 inches. Space smaller stones 18 to 20 inches apart to accommodate an average stride. Larger stones (2 feet square or larger) can be butted together on firm, tamped soil or sand to form a solid walkway. With these large stepping stones, no mortar or edging materials are necessary. If the stones sink or shift, use a prybar to lever them up and place more dirt or sand underneath.

Laying Stone in the Ground

This section describes how to construct a stone walk without a gravel-and-sand subbase and without edgings. Setting stones directly in the ground so that they are stable requires some fussing with digging and filling. Select a good mix of large and small stones; fill spaces between large stones with small stones.

1. Outline the walk. Lay out the edges of the walk, using stakes and string for straight walks or a rope or garden hose for curved walks, as described in "Plotting Curves," page 110. Mark the ground with sand or flour, and remove the sod or loose topsoil within the walk area. Tamp the bottom of the excavation.

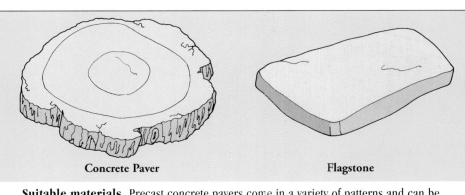

Suitable materials. Precast concrete pavers come in a variety of patterns and can be laid directly on the ground. Flagstone, fieldstone, and rubble can also be set directly on the ground.

Concrete Paver   Flagstone

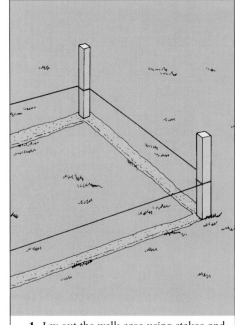

1. Lay out the walk area using stakes and string. Sprinkle sand or flour to mark the ground directly below the strings.

Cutting Stone

Cutting stone is not particularly hard, but it takes practice. Plan on wasting several pieces as you learn the process. When cutting stones, wear safety glasses, heavy gloves, and long sleeves to protect yourself from flying chips.

1. Score the Stone. After marking the stone with a piece of chalk, position the stone on a solid spot on the ground or on a wood prop. Then hold the chisel in place on the line and lightly tap it with a hammer. As you tap, move the chisel along to score the marked line. Turn the stone over and do the same thing on the other side.

2. Break the Stone. In most cases, the stone will break along the second scored line as you tap it. If it doesn't, turn the stone back over and continue tapping on the first side, deepening the groove until the stone breaks. The trick is to hit the stone just hard enough to score it, rather than trying to split it with several hard blows. In some cases, the stone may not break exactly where you want it to; in other cases, it may break into several smaller pieces. If so, set the pieces aside and use them to fill between larger stones.

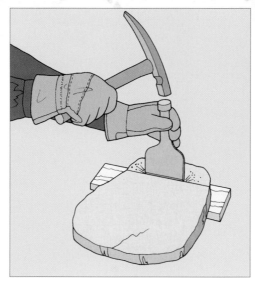 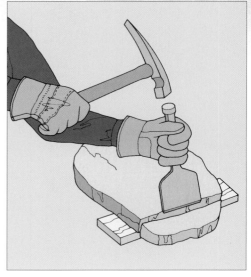

2. Position the stones. Starting at one end of the walk, select and lay out enough stones to cover about 3 or 4 feet of walkway. Arrange the stones in a pleasing pattern; try not to group similar sizes and colors. Use smaller stones to fill in between larger ones. Leave ½-inch spaces between stones.

3. Set the first stone. Leave one cornerstone in place, but remove those immediately surrounding it. Cut around the stone with a shovel or trowel to mark the outline. Set the stone aside, dig out the area where it will be placed so that the stone rests 1 to 1½ inches above ground level; then set the stone back in position

2. After removing the grass and topsoil, place several feet of the stone walk in the desired pattern.

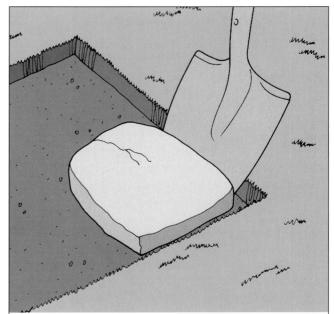

3. Take away the stones surrounding the cornerstone, and with a shovel or trowel, mark the stone's outline in the ground. Remove the cornerstone and dig a hole so that the stone is no more than 1½ inches above grade level.

4. After setting several stones, check them for level. When the walk is complete, pack the joints with topsoil.

and check it for level. If the stone rocks back and forth, remove it and dig out more dirt until it sits firmly. If the soil is very hard or rocky and the stone still won't bed properly, dig a slightly deeper hole and backfill with several inches of damp sand to provide a firm base.

4. Set remaining stones. Position the remaining stones in the same manner, leaving at least ½ inch between each stone. Check frequently with a level and straightedge to make sure all the stones are at the same height. Fill the crevices between the stones with soil and tamp firmly with a ½-inch-thick piece of wood. Spaces between the stones can be planted with groundcover. If the spaces are more than 2 inches deep or contain pockets or voids beneath the stones, fill the joints with sand, topped with 1 to 2 inches of fine, tamped soil.

WALKS ON A GRAVEL-AND-SAND SUBBASE

Most walks last longer and fare the elements better when built on a sub-base consisting of 2 inches of sand over 4 inches of gravel.

The best gravel for the job is compactible gravel, because you can tamp it to form a well-drained, firm subbase. Crushed limestone with ¾ inch or smaller stones is ideal for this application. Avoid smooth river-run or pea gravel. When you buy the stone, figure on using 1 cubic yard for every 75 square feet of walk area.

A bed of builder's sand is placed on top of the gravel base. The sand helps drain water away from the pavement and makes a smooth, level base that supports individual paving units.

When ordering builder's sand, figure on using 1 cubic yard for every 150 square feet of walk area.

Although joints between paving units can be filled with topsoil or mortar, most often dry-laid walks have joints filled with mason's sand. This sand is finer than the builder's sand used for bedding the pavement. The amount of mason's sand needed depends on the size of the joints. For a standard brick walk, you will need a few cubic feet for every 100 square feet of walk area.

Plotting and Excavating the Subbase

Begin by determining the exact width of the walk. On a flat surface, such as a driveway, lay down several courses of the paving pattern you've chosen. Joints should be ⅛ inch or less for sand or ½ inch for topsoil. Measure across the pattern to determine the exact width of the walk. Then cut a piece of wood to that length and use it to check the spacing between the edging or temporary forms when you install them. The following explains how to lay out the path in step-by-step detail.

1. Locate the edges of the walk. At each end of the walk, drive two 1x2 stakes at least 2 feet into the

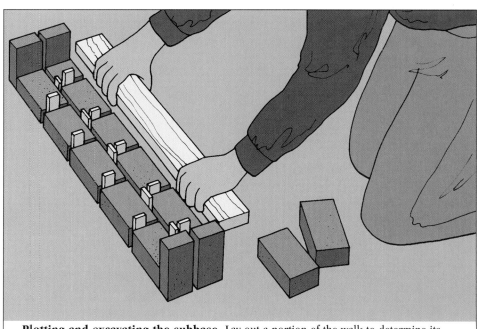

Plotting and excavating the subbase. Lay out a portion of the walk to determine its actual width.

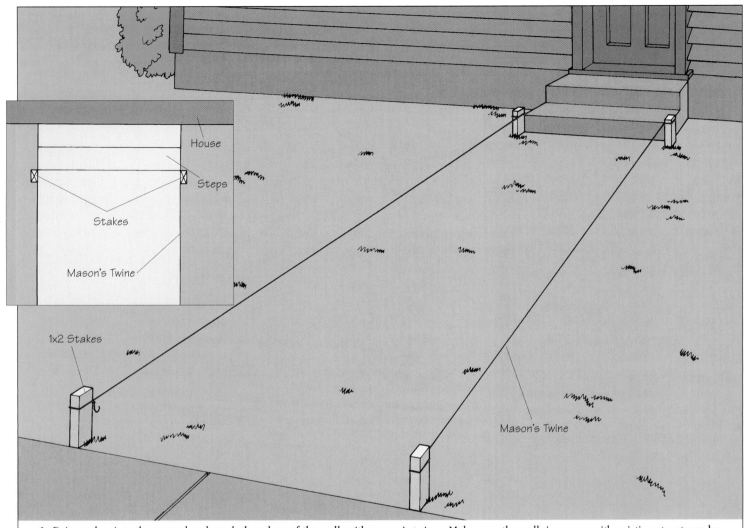

1. Drive stakes into the ground and mark the edges of the walk with mason's twine. Make sure the walk is square with existing structures by using the 3-4-5 triangulation method.

ground to indicate the edges of the walk, and attach strings. Check to make sure that the strings are the same distance apart at both ends. If the walk leads straight to an entry, make sure the lines are perpendicular to the house by using the 3-4-5 triangulation method, explained in "Finding a Square Corner with the 3-4-5 Method," page 46.

2. Establish the walk's height.
Mark one stake at each end to indicate the walk's height. In most cases, this will be about 1 inch above ground level.

A poured-concrete walk or dry-laid walk with irregularly shaped paving materials, such as flagstones, should be pitched ¼ inch per foot along its width. Mark the walk height on one stake, then use a level to transfer this mark to the opposite stake. Adjust

2. Adjust the strings to mark the height of the walk. Transfer the height from one side of the walk to the other, making adjustments for the pitch of the walk, if necessary.

the second mark up or down to establish the pitch and attach the strings to the stakes.

If drainage is a problem, slope the walk along its length as well. Use a line level to level the strings between the stakes. Measure down the stakes at the far end of the walk to get a ¼-inch-per-foot slope, and attach the strings at this point. (If the walk abuts a sidewalk, the low end of the walk should be level with it.) If the slope between the house and sidewalk is more than about 2 inches per foot, steps may be required. (For information on plotting slopes, see "Determining a Slope for Directing Water Away from Your Site," page 24.)

3. Mark the ground. Mark the location of the walk edges on the ground by sprinkling flour or sand over the strings. Mark the string locations on the stakes, and remove the strings so that they won't interfere when you dig the walk. Make sure the string marks are clear because you will reattach the strings later.

4. Excavate the site. Use a pickax and shovel to dig a trench about 1 foot wider than the walk so that you have room to install edging. While digging, check the depth frequently by measuring down from your layout strings. The trench needs to accommodate a 4-inch gravel bed and whatever edging you will put on top of it. Use a hand tamper or power tamper to compact the soil in the bottom of the excavation.

Laying Paving Units in Sand

Have the correct amounts of compactible gravel, builder's sand, and the paving material on hand. You will also need topsoil for backfill (and, if you desire, for joints) and fine mason's sand for swept-sand joints. You begin by partially filling the excavation with compactible gravel. Then you install the edgings and add more gravel. Next comes the sand bed and finally the pavement. The following text explains these steps in detail.

3. Sprinkle flour or sand over the string to transfer its location to the ground.

4. Dig a trench wider than the walk and tamp the bottom to create a firm surface.

1. Place the gravel. Spread at least 4 inches of compactible gravel in the excavation, tamp it, level it with a rake, then tamp again. Retie the string to the layout stakes at the point that marks the top of the walk. Continue adding gravel until an edging set on top of the gravel is level with the layout strings. If you are not installing edging, add and tamp gravel until the distance between it and the strings equals 2 inches plus the thickness of the paving material.

2. Set the stakes to hold the forms.

If the walk requires forms, drive 2x3 stakes near the ends of the walk excavation and every 2 feet along it. Position the stakes to create a walk the width of the strings: If the stakes are for permanent two-by edging, use pressure-treated 2x3s and drive the stakes so the outer edge is flush with the layout strings and so that the stake is a few inches below the finished walk surface. Drive stakes for temporary forms so their inner edge is outside of the layout lines by the thickness of the form. Align brick edging with the help of a temporary form set outside the strings. Add the thickness of the form to the thickness of the edging to get the location of the stakes.

If the walk has a ribbon of concrete for an edging, drive two rows of stakes to hold the forms for each edging. The outer face of one row should be inside the layout string by the width of the form. Set the inner face of the second row of stakes outside the layout string by the width of the edging plus the thickness of the form.

3. Install the forms.

Using galvanized nails or deck screws, fasten the stakes to temporary two-by forms or to permanent pressure-treated two-by edging. For concrete edgings, use 2x8 forms that extend below grade. Check the width of the forms with a piece of wood cut to the width of the walk. Use the layout strings to help you keep the boards straight and to make sure that the edging conforms to the desired pitch of the walk.

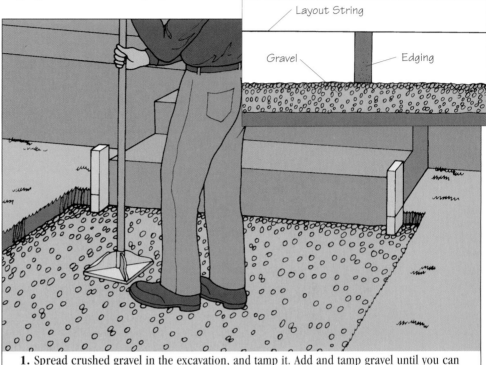

1. Spread crushed gravel in the excavation, and tamp it. Add and tamp gravel until you can set edging on it at finished height.

Distance equals thickness of two forms plus edging.

2. Set stakes to hold the forms. The inset drawing shows stake positions for concrete edging.

3. Screw or nail 2-by lumber forms to the stakes. Use the layout strings as guides for keeping the forms level and straight.

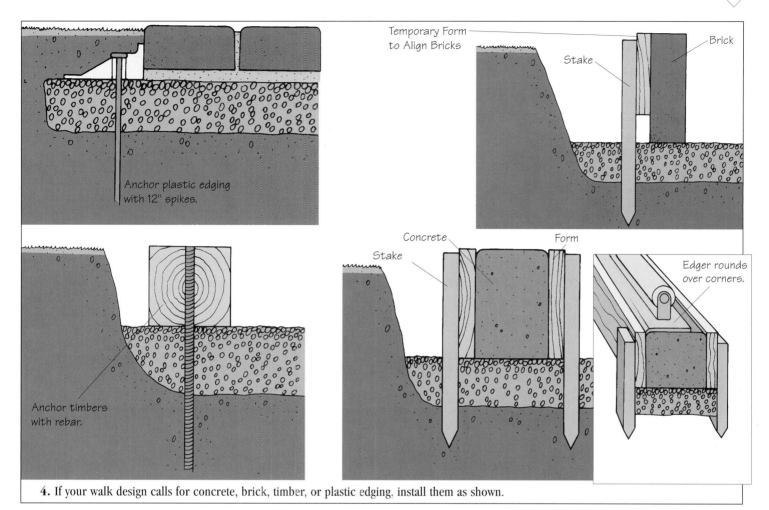

Anchor plastic edging with 12" spikes.

Temporary Form to Align Bricks

Stake

Brick

Anchor timbers with rebar.

Stake

Concrete

Form

Edger rounds over corners.

4. If your walk design calls for concrete, brick, timber, or plastic edging, install them as shown.

4. Set the edging. Place the edging material on the gravel, against the forms or aligned with the layout strings. Add sand or gravel as needed to bring the edging to the proper height. Pack the sand around brick or block edging to hold it in place. Drive rebar spikes through landscape ties to anchor them to the ground. Use 12-inch galvanized spikes to hold plastic edging in place. Check the spacing between edgings with the board you cut to measure walk width. (See "Plotting and Excavating the Subbase," page 123.)

For concrete edgings, pour the concrete in the forms, screed the tops, and trowel them smooth. Use an edger to round over the edges, and when the concrete has set, remove the forms. You also can bed brick or dimensioned stone in the wet concrete.

5. Add more gravel. Unless you used plastic edgings, rake out, compact, and level gravel between the

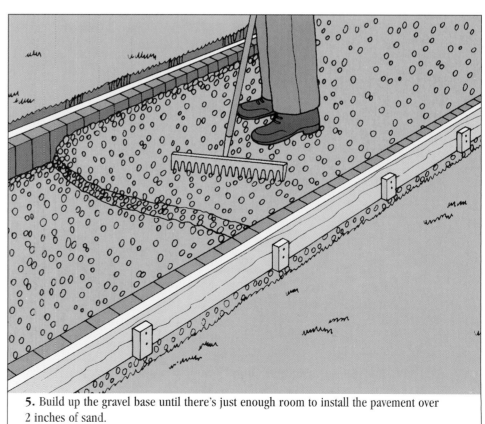

5. Build up the gravel base until there's just enough room to install the pavement over 2 inches of sand.

edgings until there's just enough space to place the paving material on 2 inches of sand. To help prevent weed growth, place landscape fabric on top of the compactible gravel. Cover plastic edging once the walk is complete.

6. Spread the sand.
Shovel builder's sand evenly over the crushed gravel, and spread it with a rake. With a hose set on fine spray, thoroughly dampen the sand. Fill in any low spots, dampen the filled areas, then tamp the sand firmly. Repeat the process, building up the sand so that the pavers, stones, or bricks will be ¼ to ½ inch higher than the intended walk height, to allow for settling.

7. Screed the sand.
While the sand is still moist, pull a notched 1x6 screed board in a zigzag motion along the edging to knock down any high spots in the sand bed and fill in low spots. After screeding, dampen the sand again with a fine mist.

8. Set the paving material.
Working from one corner against an edging or string, carefully place the pavement in the desired pattern. Avoid displacing the sand beneath. To help maintain straight brick or paver courses, mark the walk layout on the forms or edgings and stretch a string across the marks. Leave a space of 1/16 to 1/8 inch between the paving units for the jointing sand. If you're setting dimensioned stone, arrange the pattern to produce joints of a consistent width (½ to ¾ inch). Joints between irregular flagstones will vary, but try to keep a minimum width of ½ inch and a maximum of 1 inch

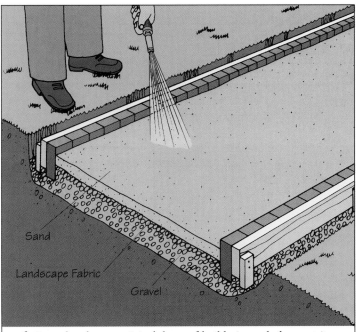

Sand

Landscape Fabric

Gravel

6. Spread and tamp a 2-inch layer of builder's sand; then wet it, fill in any low spots, and wet it again.

7. Smooth and level the damp sand by pulling a notched 2x6 screed board along the edging. Pull toward you in a zigzag motion.

8. Begin setting the pavement at one corner of the walk. Use a level to make sure that all the units are the same height. For formal patterns, mark the course layout on the forms, and use a string to lay straight courses.

9. After laying about 5 feet of walk, place a short 2x6 board on the pavement and tap the board with a mallet to set the pavement into the sand.

10. Spread a thin layer of mason's sand over a section of the walk, then sweep the sand into the joints with a stiff broom.

between stones. Check frequently with a level to make sure all units are the same height. Remove any that don't conform or that aren't stable, adding or removing sand as necessary.

9. Bed the pavement. After setting several square feet of pavement, lay a 16-inch length of 1x6 on the walk and tap over the entire surface with a hammer or mallet to bed the pavement into the sand. If individual units are slightly tilted or too high, tap them gently into place with a rubber mallet. Avoid standing or kneeling on the sand base or previously laid pavement. If you must kneel on the pavement, lay down a piece of ½-inch plywood to distribute your weight.

10. Fill the joints. The joints can be filled with sand, topsoil, or mortar. If you choose sand, then spread a thin layer of dry mason's sand evenly over a 5- or 6-foot section of paved walk. With a stiff broom, sweep the sand into the cracks between the pavers. Sweep in all directions to fill all the joints completely. Sweep excess sand into a pile, and scoop it into a bucket for future use. Then lightly spray the walk with water to pack down the sand and wash it off the surface. Do not use a heavy spray or you will dislodge sand from the joints. Allow the

11. When the walk is complete, dismantle and remove temporary forms. Shovel gravel along the walk to support the edging, then complete the fill with soil.

surface to dry, then repeat the process until all the joints are completely filled in and compacted.

Topsoil or mortar should be used in joints that are wider than ½ inch thick. To fill the joints with topsoil or mortar, lightly hose off the entire walk surface. When all standing water in the joints has disappeared, you can either pack the joints with topsoil and plant grass or a groundcover, or you can mortar the joints, using the

method described in "Dry Mortar Method," page 144.

11. Remove the forms and backfill the walk edges. When the walk is complete, carefully pull up any temporary forms and shovel gravel along the outside of the edging. Tamp it and fill with a few inches of topsoil. Be sure to cover any permanent stakes. If you used plastic edge restraints, simply cover them with topsoil, and seed or sod the filled-in area.

CHAPTER 12

HARD MORTAR-BED WALKS

The most durable type of paved-walk construction involves setting the pavement in a mortar bed over a concrete base. The concrete base keeps the paving units from sinking, buckling, and shifting, and the mortar bed holds the pavement to the concrete. Almost any hard-walk paving material that can be set in sand can be set in mortar. In addition, you can set other materials that would crack if set on a sand bed. These materials include brick and concrete pavers less than 1¼ inches thick, stone less than 1½ inches thick, and all tile.

Mortar-bed walks are well suited to mortared joints because the rigid concrete base minimizes cracking due to ground movement. Joints between these materials may also be filled with sand or soil.

CONSTRUCTION MATERIALS

As with dry-laid walks, mortar-bed walks should be set on a firm, well drained subbase. Depending on soil conditions, this subbase could be firmly tamped soil, but usually the subbase consists of tamped gravel. A concrete base is placed on the gravel, mortar is spread over the concrete, and the pavement is then bedded in the mortar.

Mortared stone and brick walks are both more formal and more durable than walks set on a sand bed. A concrete bed under the walk provides support for the walk and keeps it from cracking as the ground shifts.

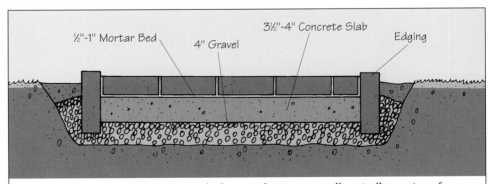

Construction Materials. A mortar-bed, or rigid pavement, walk typically consists of a concrete base over a tamped gravel subbase. The mortar bed bonds the pavement to the concrete. Edging is optional.

Mortared walks are more difficult and expensive to build than dry-laid walks; however, there's less upkeep as long as the concrete base is structurally sound. You can build a mortar-bed walk over either a new concrete base or an existing concrete walk.

Placing a New Slab

A new concrete base should be set low enough so that the finished walk surface will be about 1 inch above grade level. Normally, the concrete is placed on a 4-inch gravel base. The concrete base should be as wide as the finished walk; lay out a few courses of the paving material on a flat surface (with properly spaced joints) to check the walk width. Place the concrete, and apply a rough-floated or broomed surface to ensure good mortar adhesion. Once the concrete has cured, simply pave over the slab.

Edging isn't necessary, although you can add it for aesthetic purposes. If you want to add it, adjust the depth and width of the excavation accordingly. (For details of adjusting the width of the walk, see Step 2 of "Laying Paving Units in Sand," page 125.) You can also install the edging after the walk is complete; for more information, see "Simple Edging," page 143.

Using an existing walk. You can lay unit masonry over an existing concrete walk, provided the surface is level and stable. Small holes should be patched and leveled with a concrete-patching material. Although the mortar bed will compensate for any minor defects or irregularities in the walk, any cracking or buckling indicates unstable soil, a weak slab, or both. Do not attempt to pave over such walks. Replace them with a new, stable one.

If headroom is limited, consider using stone, ceramic tiles, or split pavers half the thickness of a standard brick.

It's important to clean the surface of an existing walk thoroughly. Remove grease or wax with a commercial driveway cleaner or a solution of

Using an existing walk. Clean existing walks, patch any minor holes, and treat a painted or a slick-troweled surface with muriatic acid and water. Wear gloves and eye protection.

1 part trisodium phosphate (TSP) to 5 parts water. Scrub briskly with a push broom or heavy bristle brush, rinse, and allow to dry. If the walk has been painted or has a slick finish, prepare the surface by brushing on a solution of muriatic acid and water using a push broom or by applying a coat of concrete bonder using a roller. Wear gloves and goggles when using muriatic acid.

Mortar Mixes

For most mortar-bed walk projects, it's more convenient to buy ready-mixed mortar, sold by the bag at building suppliers, than to mix your own. The mortar to use, called Type M, is noted for its high compressive strength and water resistance. Type M mortar consists of 1 part portland cement, ¼ part hydrated lime, and 3 parts sand. Local building codes may specify different proportions, depending on your climate. Also, local patio and masonry suppliers can advise you on the best mix for your particular area and application. Lime can stain certain kinds of stone. If your walk will be stone, buy a lime-free mortar mix or substitute fireclay for lime.

Follow the directions on the bag when mixing mortar. The amount of water required depends on the composition of the dry mixture, the width of the mortar joints or mortar bed, the absorption rate of the materials used, and the weather. Because of these many variables, you may have to do some experimentation to achieve the proper mix for your project. Use a wet mix if you are working with brick and concrete patio blocks because they tend to absorb more water than stone and tile, which require a dry, or stiff, mix.

Tile and gauged stone are either set on a dry bed of mortar, which you wet later, or on latex-portland cement. You can make latex-portland cement mortar by combining the appropriate amount of liquid latex additive to portland cement and sand.

Estimating mortar amounts. The quantity of mortar you will need for the mortar bed depends on the size of the walk and the paving material. Generally, large, heavy, or irregularly shaped materials, such as flagstones, require thicker beds than thin, and uniform materials, such as split pavers. For estimating purposes, order one 80-pound bag of mortar for every 15 square feet of walk.

The mortar you need to fill the joints depends on the size and number of joints and the size of the paving material. Also, consider the depth of the joints. With 2¼-inch-thick bricks, one 80-pound bag of mortar will fill joints for about 160 standard bricks spaced ⅜ inch apart or about 110 standard bricks spaced ½ inch apart.

Tools for working with mortar.
To mix mortar, you'll need a mortar hoe; contractor's wheelbarrow; and a mortar box or flat, clean surface, such as a 4- by 4-foot piece of plywood. If you will be mixing a lot of mortar, it's

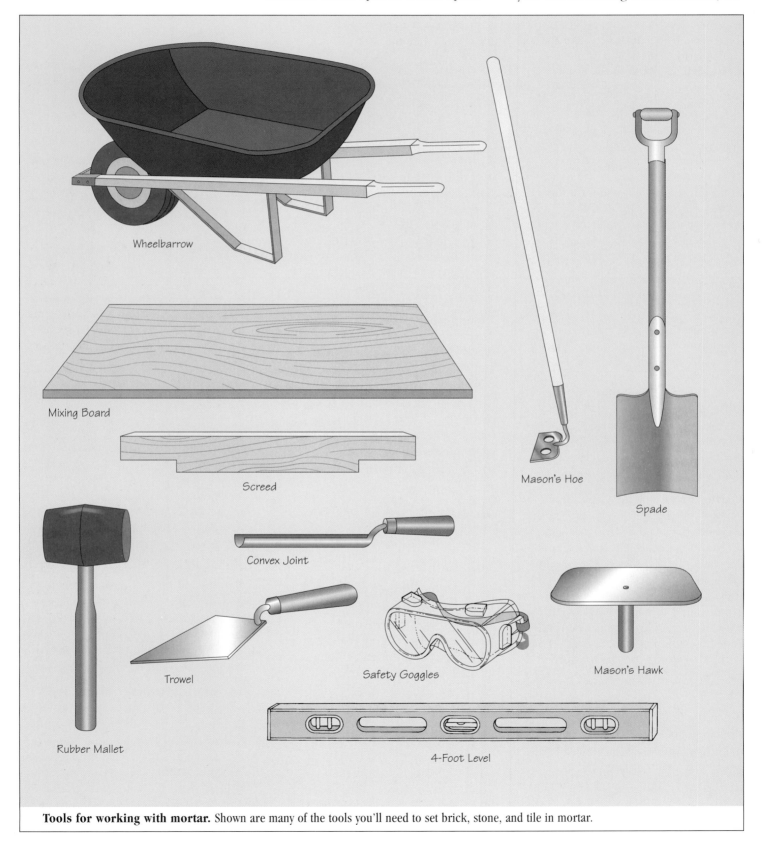

Wheelbarrow

Mixing Board

Screed

Mason's Hoe

Spade

Rubber Mallet

Convex Joint

Trowel

Safety Goggles

Mason's Hawk

4-Foot Level

Tools for working with mortar. Shown are many of the tools you'll need to set brick, stone, and tile in mortar.

best to rent a power mixer. Because mortar sets up quickly (usually within 1 hour), you'll be mixing only small amounts at a time (usually 3 cubic feet or less for mortar beds and ½ to 1 cubic foot for joints, depending on how fast you work). For more on mixing mortar, see "Mortar," page 52. To carry small amounts of wet mortar to the work area, you can use a mason's hawk or you can make a mortar board from a piece of plywood cut to a convenient size, such as 12 by 12 inches. You will also need several screed boards, to level gravel, concrete, or the mortar bed. The mortar screed board is a piece of 2x6 cut a few inches longer than the walk is wide. Both ends are notched; the depth of the notches usually equals the thickness of the paving material. The others are straight pieces of wood. (For details on making a screed board, see "Screed Board," page 117.)

Paving materials. Whether they come from a stone yard or your backyard, stones tend to be covered with

dirt, dust, and grit. Wash the stones with clear water, because any residue clinging to them will draw moisture from the mortar, weakening the bond. Before setting porous stones, such as sandstone, dampen them so that they don't suck moisture out of the mortar mix. Denser stones, such as Rocky Mountain quartzite, may be set dry.

Because most face brick absorbs moisture quite readily too, it should be wetted down before setting. Otherwise the bricks will suck moisture out of the mortar base, resulting in a poor bond. You can check the absorbency of the bricks you're setting by putting 20 drops of water in one spot on the brick. Wait 90 seconds. If the water disappears, spray all of the bricks with a garden hose before you mix the mortar. Continue spraying until water runs out from the brick pile. By the time you get the mortar mixed, the surface water should have evaporated from the bricks, leaving them slightly damp to the touch. Bricks that don't absorb water quickly, such as sealed paver bricks, may be set dry.

PREPARING A NEW CONCRETE BED

Before you set up the forms and pour the concrete, excavate the site to provide room for a gravel base, a concrete slab, and the paving material. Begin by outlining the walk with stakes and string as described in "Plotting and Excavating the Subbase," page 123. Then excavate to a depth that will accommodate a 4-inch gravel base and 1½ inches of concrete and mortar, and that will place the top of the paving material 1 inch above grade. Remove soil 6 inches beyond each side of the proposed walk to allow room for installing the forms. Tamp the soil firmly to compact it.

1. Install the forms. The wet concrete is held in place by 2x4 forms, which are removed after the concrete dries. Cut the form boards to length. Align the inside edges of the formboards with the layout strings and attach the boards to 2x4 stakes with duplex (double-headed) nails or

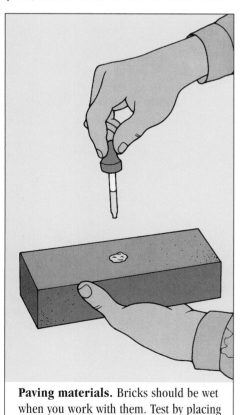

Paving materials. Bricks should be wet when you work with them. Test by placing 20 drops of water in one spot on the brick. Wait 90 seconds; if the water disappears, hose down the whole pile of bricks.

1. Place forms around the perimeter of the concrete base to hold the concrete in place once it's poured.

2. Once the forms are in place, fill the bed with gravel, tamp it in place, and screed it.

3-inch galvanized deck screws. Because wet concrete can exert quite a bit of pressure on the forms, space the stakes no more than 4 feet apart and cut them long enough to be driven at least 18 inches into firm ground. Make sure the stakes don't protrude above the forms. If more than one form board is needed for either side of the walk, splice the board ends together with a short length of 1x4, as shown. At each end of the walk, nail an end form between the side forms and stake each corner securely, as shown.

2. Add the gravel. After the forms are placed, spread the gravel evenly in 1-inch layers, tamping each layer firmly before adding the next. Be careful not to knock the forms out of alignment while tamping. Allow some of the gravel to run under the form boards and keep adding gravel until it's ½ inch below the bottom of the formboards. Rake or screed the gravel smooth and level. (To make a screed, cut a length of 2x4 or 2x6 to fit loosely between the forms.) Brush a commercial form-release agent on the inside of the forms, so that the forms won't stick to the concrete.

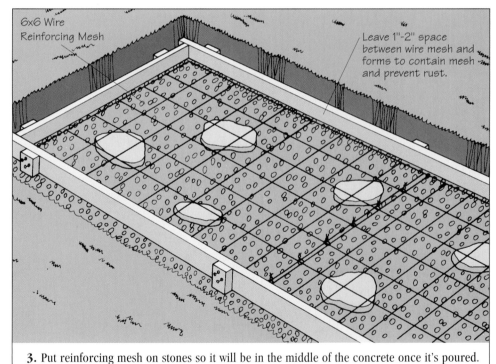

6x6 Wire Reinforcing Mesh

Leave 1"-2" space between wire mesh and forms to contain mesh and prevent rust.

3. Put reinforcing mesh on stones so it will be in the middle of the concrete once it's poured.

3. Add the wire mesh. The concrete must be reinforced with wire reinforcing mesh that has 6- by 6-inch openings. Cut it with heavy wire cutters, bolt cutters, or large fencing pliers. (You can flatten the unrolled mesh by walking on it.) If more than one piece is required, overlap the pieces by 6 inches and tie them together with wire. Place stones or pieces of brick under the wire mesh to raise it about 2 inches above the gravel or roughly in the middle of the finished slab. Avoid walking on the mesh once you've placed it.

Curved Forms

You can build curved forms using strips of ⅜-inch bending plywood. This wood bends easily because the grain in all the plies runs in the same direction. Cut the plywood into strips equal to the thickness of the slab, and screw the strips to stakes set up along the curve of the walk. (For information on laying out a curved walk, see "Plotting Curves," page 110.) Space the stakes 18 to 24 inches apart. If you want permanent curved edging, you can make a series of saw cuts, or kerfs, in a two-by to increase its flexibility. Space the kerfs evenly about 1 inch apart, and cut them about 1 inch deep.

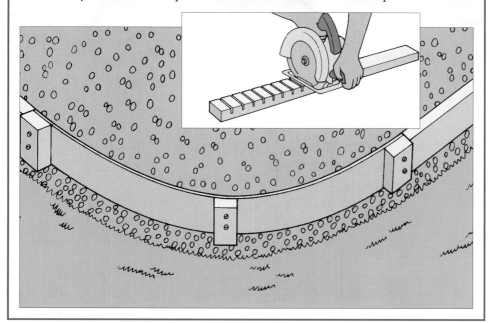

Pouring the Bed

Once you've set up the forms and added the base materials, thoroughly hose down the gravel the day before you pour the concrete. If any settling occurs, add more gravel, tamp it, and rescreed it. The base is now ready to support the concrete.

If you're mixing and pouring the concrete by yourself, you can work at your leisure, mixing, pouring, and finishing one section of the walk at a time. To make working by yourself easier, put together a movable stop board like the one shown. Divide the total length of the walk into equal sections, then mark the sections on the form boards. Position the stop board at the end of the first section, secure it with temporary stakes, and pour the concrete up to the board. After finishing the concrete surface, remove the stop board. You can pour the next section right up to the one you just finished or even leave the job for a few days and pick up where you left off.

Expansion strips. Concrete expands and contracts with the weather, so you need to set expansion strips along the walk every so often. Expansion strips (available at masonry suppliers) consist of a compressible fibrous material that you place between concrete sections.

If the walk butts against an existing structure, such as a house foundation, steps, or another walk, you must place an expansion strip between the walk and the existing structure. Cut the material to length with a utility knife, and set it against an existing section of walk before placing more concrete. If the walk is longer than about 40 feet, you'll need to install expansion strips every 8 to 10 feet along the walk (or as required by code), even if you're doing the walk all at once. In this case, set an expansion strip against a stop board, bring the concrete up to the expansion strip, then pour concrete on the other side of the stop board. Remove the stop and push the concrete against the expansion strip. Do not cover the top of the strip with concrete. When the concrete has cured, you can caulk the top of the strip to keep water out.

Pouring the bed. If you're working alone, put a temporary stop in your forms. Pour and finish the concrete up to the stop. Move the stop, and make a new pour. Use the stop especially if you'll have to quit for a few days in the middle of the job.

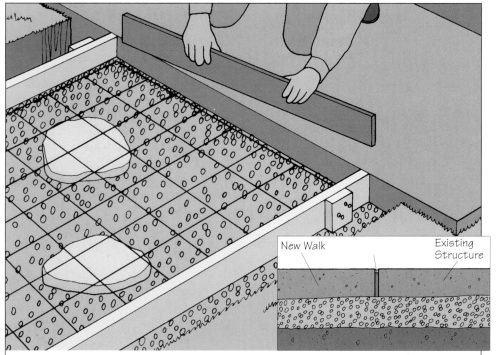

Expansion strips. Put an expansion strip between existing structures and the new walk. The strip expands and compresses as the walk changes size with fluctuations in temperature. You'll also need strips every 8 to 10 feet along the walk.

New Walk

Existing Structure

1. Dump concrete into adjoining piles inside the forms.

Pouring the Concrete

Because time is limited when you work with concrete, it's important to eliminate potential problems. Provide access for the concrete truck or wheelbarrows by laying down planks or plywood to bridge rough spots. If you think that wheelbarrow traffic might dislodge the form boards, build a ramp over them. Check the forms to be sure they are level, spaced correctly, and fastened firmly to the stakes. If the forms will be permanent, protect the top edges with masking tape.

1. Begin the pour. At the end of the walk farthest from the source of the concrete, start placing the material in the forms. If you're using a wheelbarrow to transport the concrete, do not overfill it. Dump the concrete in mounds that extend about ½ inch above the top of the forms. Avoid dumping loads of concrete on top of each other or in separate piles; the loads should be dumped against each other.

2. Spread the concrete. Use a hoe or rake to spread the concrete evenly into the forms, chopping it with the hoe to remove any air pockets. Use the back of the hoe to tamp the concrete into corners and along the edges of the form. If necessary, use a shovel to lift concrete from high spots to fill voids or low spots. After spreading, the concrete fill should be even with, or slightly above, the top edges of the form.

3. Position the mesh. As you pour and spread the concrete, use a hooked prybar, claw hammer, or sturdy rake to pull up the reinforcing mesh so that it remains in the center of the pour. Where necessary, add concrete and tamp to fill any voids under the mesh.

4. Screed the surface. As soon as you've filled 4 or 5 feet of walkway, use a screed board to strike off excess concrete. Select a straight 2x4 approximately 1 foot longer than the width of the forms. Starting at the back end of the pour, place the screed board firmly on the form boards and pull it toward you in a

2. Spread the concrete with a hoe or rake. Fill low spots by shoveling concrete into them.

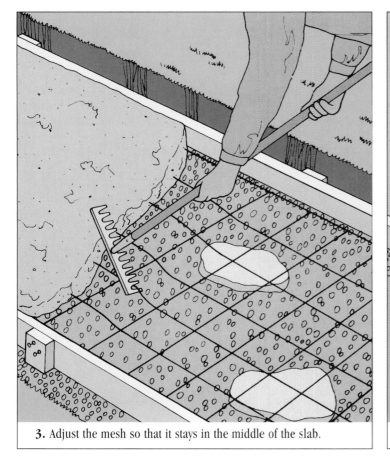

3. Adjust the mesh so that it stays in the middle of the slab.

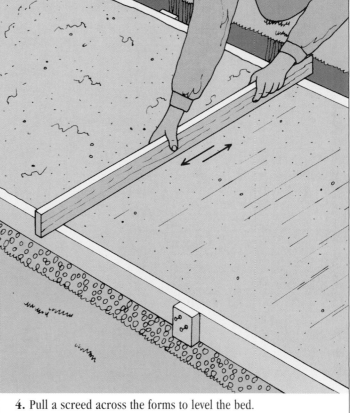

4. Pull a screed across the forms to level the bed.

side-to-side sawing motion. Fill any hollow spots with more concrete, and rescreed, always pulling the screed toward the unscreeded area. Use a hoe to pull away any concrete that builds up in front of the screed board. Do not reuse any concrete that spills outside the forms, because it will be contaminated with soil.

Finishing the Surface

Concrete beds need either a rough-floated or broomed surface to ensure good mortar adhesion. You'll give the bed an initial floating and edging, then play a waiting game before finishing the surface. The amount of waiting time depends on climatic conditions—wind, humidity, temperature—and the type of mix used. As a general rule, you can start finishing the concrete as soon as the water sheen disappears from the surface and the concrete is hard enough to make a thumbprint about ¼ inch deep. If you start too soon, you'll notice excess water bleeding to the surface, which will weaken the slab. If you wait too long, the concrete won't smooth out at all, and you'll be stuck with the surface you have.

1. Rough-float the surface. Right after screeding the surface, float the concrete to level it and embed any aggregate below the surface. For most walks, floating is done with a darby, although very wide walks will require a bull float, which has a long handle so that you can reach the middle of the slab. Swing the darby in an arcing motion along the length of the walk. As you work, tilt the leading edge of the tool slightly upward to avoid digging into the wet concrete. Do not apply too much pressure. Also, do not overwork the surface. When water starts to appear on the surface, you are done. If too much water rises to the surface, remove it by dragging a garden hose or heavy rope over the walk, directing the water over the sides of the forms.

2. Edge the slab. Immediately after floating the concrete with the darby,

1. Work a darby in arcs across the surface to further level it. Tilt the leading edge up, so it doesn't catch in the work.

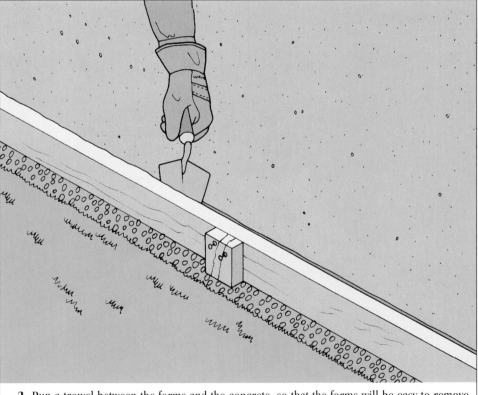

2. Run a trowel between the forms and the concrete, so that the forms will be easy to remove.

insert a pointed trowel between the forms and the concrete and slide the tool along the forms to separate them from the concrete. Repeat the edging process after each smoothing operation below.

3. Apply the finish. Once the concrete is "thumbprint hard," you can rough-trowel the surface by making one or two passes with a wood float. If desired, you can run a broom across the surface to create a rougher surface for the mortar.

4. Let the slab cure. Allow the slab to set for 4 or 5 hours, then dampen it with a fine mist from a garden hose. (If the water pressure is too high, you will wash out the finish.) Keep the slab moist for at least 1 week either by spraying it several

times a day or by wetting the slab once and covering it with polyethylene sheeting to prevent moisture evaporation. Check the slab several times a day to make sure it remains wet. You can also use a commercial spray-on film, available at masonry

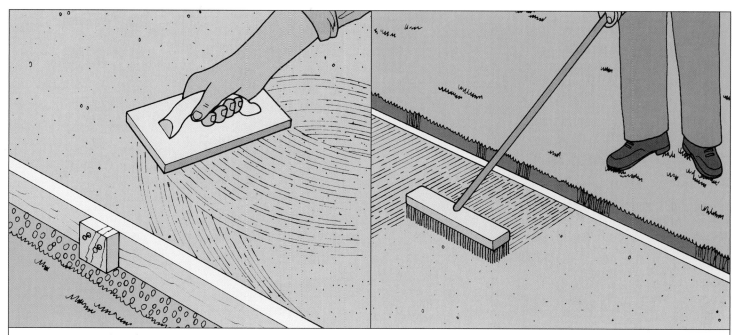

3. Create a rough surface on the slab by working it with a wood float. For a rougher surface that holds mortar even better, you can float the slab then pull a broom across it.

4. Concrete must be kept wet to harden properly. Hose it down and cover it with plastic sheeting.

suppliers, to avoid having to keep the slab wet. If the temperature drops below 50 degrees, continue curing for another 3 to 7 days. If you expect freezing weather, cover the slab with 6 to 12 inches of straw or hay and a tarp or plastic sheet. After about 10 days, strip off the forms and back-fill along the edges with soil or gravel.

SETTING A MORTAR-BED WALK

Once the concrete bed has cured, you can begin setting the mortar bed on it. It's best to make a trial run to make sure the paver material works out to the width anticipated.

Lay out enough paving material to cover about a 3-foot section of the concrete slab. To space bricks, use ⅜- or ½-inch wood strips and determine the size and number of cut bricks necessary. Between irregular stones, joints should be between ½ and 1½ inches wide. Joints for dimensioned stones should be no more than 1 inch wide. If you need to cut any stones, use the technique described in "Cutting Stones" on page 122. Place large stones along the walk edges—they aren't as easily dislodged as small stones.

1. Set up the forms. Set the paving material aside in order, so that you can replace it in the same pattern. Install temporary 2x4 forms on either side (but not on top of) the concrete slab. Set one side to a height that equals the thickness of the mortar bed and pavement. Set the other side higher to pitch the walk for water runoff. The pitch should equal ⅛ inch per foot of width.

2. Prepare the mortar bed. Hose down a few feet of the slab to wet it. Mix enough mortar to cover a small section, and pour the mortar into the forms. Use a wetter mix for brick and a drier mix for heavy paving materials, such as flagstones. The mortar bed should be at least ½ inch thick for bricks and dimensioned stone and at least 1 inch thick for paving of varying thickness, such

Setting a mortar-bed walk. Before you put mortar on the concrete slab, chose and position the paving stones that will make up the walk.

1. Remove the stones or bricks and set forms around the edge of the slab to hold the mortar and bricks or stones.

as flagstone. Use a 2x6 screed board with notched ends to level the mortar. The notched ends ride on the temporary forms as you pull the screed board in a zigzag motion. As your working speed increases, you can mix and screed mortar to cover larger areas.

If you are setting flagstones, furrow the screeded mortar bed with the edge of your trowel, as shown. This helps ensure even mortar coverage under the stones and allows some of the mortar to squeeze out into the joints, making a better bond.

3. Set the pavement. Starting at one corner, gently set the paving units into the mortar bed with a slight twisting motion. Use wood spacers to establish the joint widths. If you're setting bricks with sand joints, butt each brick carefully against

Furrow the mortar bed with a trowel.

2. Pour mortar into the forms, and then level it with a screed.

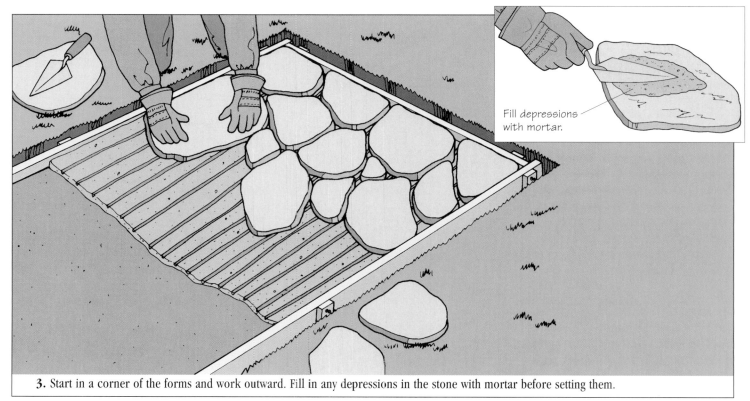

Fill depressions with mortar.

3. Start in a corner of the forms and work outward. Fill in any depressions in the stone with mortar before setting them.

its neighbor to keep mortar from squeezing up between the joints. If you are using stone, fill any depressions or hollows on the underside with mortar before setting. If the stones vary in thickness, set the thickest stones first; then set thinner ones to the same height by adding mortar beneath them.

4. Bed the pavement. Bed bricks in the mortar with a firm tap from a trowel handle. To bed stones, use a rubber mallet. Use a level to make sure all units are at the same height. If one is too low, too high, or out of level, gently pry it up with a prybar and add or remove mortar as needed.

5. Fill the joints with mortar. Mix a batch of mortar that is thin enough to pour, but not too soupy or watery. If you are mixing your own ingredients, combine 1 part cement to 3 parts sand. Scoop some mortar into a coffee can, bend the can rim slightly to form a spout, and pour the mortar into the joints. Work carefully to avoid getting mortar on the walk surface.

6. Finish the joints. Use a trowel to strike the mortar flush to the surface and remove any excess mortar. Continue filling and striking, until all joints are filled, including any gaps between the edge stones and the forms. Before the mortar hardens completely, you can tool the joints with a piece of dowel or jointing tool to produce a slightly concave surface. Avoid making deep, recessed joints, which will trap dirt and water and make a rougher walking surface. Several hours after tooling, brush off any mortar crumbs with a whisk broom, then lightly scrub the walk surface with a damp sponge or wet burlap sack to remove any mortar smears. Once the mortar has set (about one week), any remaining mortar haze can be removed by applying a light solution of TSP (½ cup per gallon of water) and scrubbing with a stiff brush or broom. Rinse thoroughly with clear water.

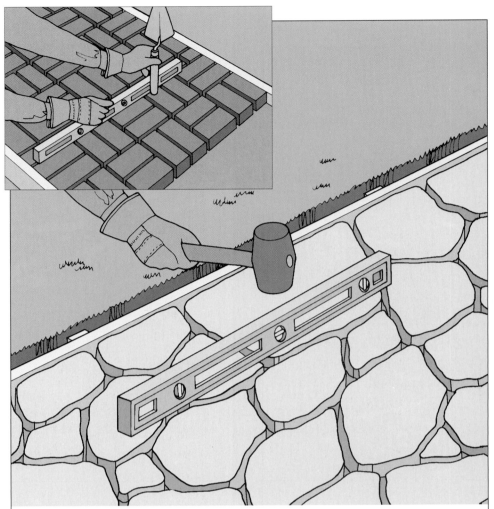

4. Bed stones by striking them with a rubber mallet. Bed bricks by striking them with the heel of your trowel.

5. Pour a thin mortar mixture between the stones or bricks.

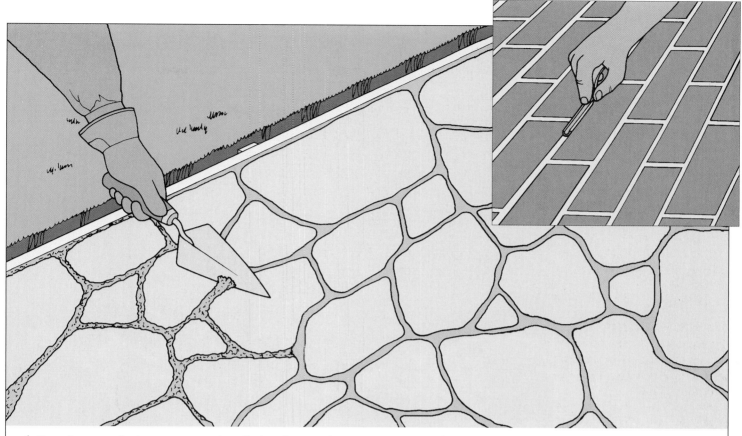

6. Once the mortar begins to set up, strike it flush with a trowel, removing any excess from the walk surface. If you choose, tool the joints with a convex jointer.

After the mortar joints have cured thoroughly, remove the forms and backfill the edges of the walk with a few inches of gravel and a layer of topsoil.

Simple edging. For mortared walks, you can install a simple edging of bricks or patio blocks by standing them on end, directly in the ground or on a gravel base. After laying the walk, dig a narrow trench around the perimeter to a depth that enables you to sink the edging material flush with the walk. Position the edging in the trench, level the tops, and firmly pack soil around the outside. You can lay the bricks diagonally, on end, or on their edges. If you're setting the bricks on edge, set the first brick on end so that it won't be dislodged easily. If the edging bricks will be set in a mortar bed, you can lay them at the same time you do the paving bricks.

Simple edging. After the walk is complete, dig a trench deep enough to bury at least two-thirds of the edging material. Set the edging level; then pack soil against it.

Dry Mortar Method

Rather than mixing a batch of mortar and pouring it into the joints, many stonemasons use a dry-mortar method to save time and labor. If you live in a warm climate, where freeze-thaw conditions are not a concern, you can use this method to fill joints between bricks, blocks, or stones. Here's how to proceed.

1. Mix and spread the mortar. After cleaning the walk surface, mix 1 part portland cement with 3 parts sand, or use bags of premixed mortar. Spread the dry mortar evenly over the walk area, then sweep it into the joints with a stiff broom or stiff-bristle brush.

2. Pack mortar in the joints. Use a short piece of wood to pack the dry mixture firmly into the joints. Sweep in

more dry mix, if necessary, and continue packing the joints until they are flush with the surrounding paving.

3. Moisten the joints. Set the nozzle on a garden hose to spray fine mist and dampen the mortar. Gently soak the joints, being careful not to flush the mortar out. Don't allow pools of water to form. Over the next hour, keep the surface moist by periodically misting with a hose.

4. Finish joints and clean off excess. When the mortar hardens slightly, you either can tool concave joints with a convex jointer or strike the joints flush with a trowel. When the mortar dries, clean the excess off the stones with a damp piece of burlap.

1.

2.

3.

4.

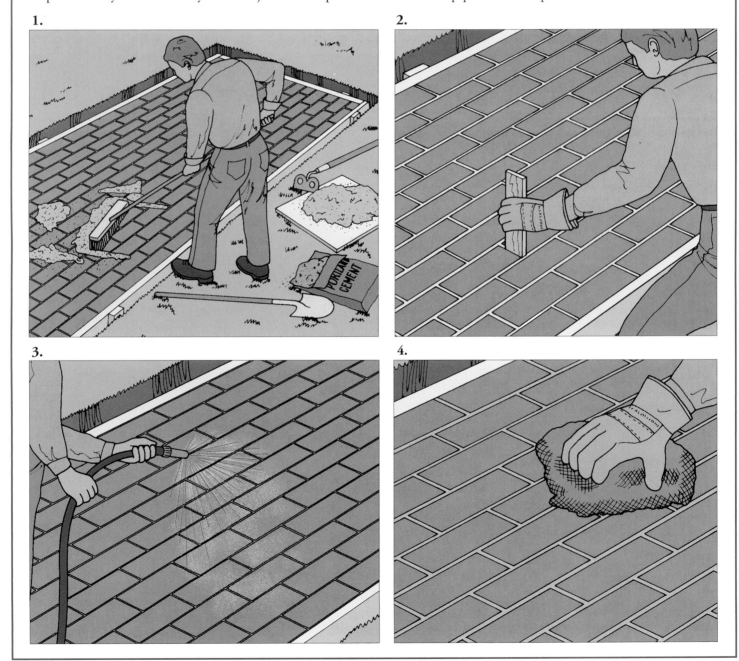

CERAMIC AND STONE TILE

Tile—either stone or ceramic—lends a formal look to a walk and often is used to make an indoor-outdoor connection. Tile is expensive, however, and many kinds aren't suited for outdoor use. Generally, climatic conditions in your area will dictate which outdoor tiles will be carried at local tile dealers, stone yards, and patio suppliers.

Unless you're tiling an existing concrete walk, choose the tile first, then lay out the walk based on the tile size. Most tile dealers will loan you a few samples for this purpose. Sizes for square tiles range from 4 inches to 24 inches; other shapes include rectangles, hexagons, octagons, and curved ogee profiles. Ceramic floor tiles usually look best with mortared joints spaced ⅜ to ½ inch apart. Stone tiles can be either butted together with swept-sand joints or spaced for mortared joints.

Although most ceramic and stone tiles are extremely dense, they are also brittle and thin (⅜ to ¾ inch thick), so they require a perfectly smooth, flat, and sturdy concrete base. Tiles are set in special thin-set cement tile adhesive. Consult the tile dealer or manufacturer for the appropriate type of adhesive for your particular project.

Suitable Types of Tile

In most outdoor situations, you'll want a tile that doesn't absorb too much water—one that can go through the freeze-thaw cycle without cracking. You'll also want tiles that won't become slippery when wet. Some tile manufacturers use a labeling system devised by the International Standards Organization that makes it clear which tiles are best. A snowflake on the box indicates that the tile is freeze-thaw resistant. A footprint means the tile stands up well to foot traffic, and a hand means the tile is for walls only. Without the labels, however, it's very hard to tell from the box whether a given tile is good for outdoor use.

Fortunately, some categories of tile have proven themselves for outdoor use. Unglazed quarry tile, unglazed pavers, and gauged stone are all tiles that work well outdoors.

Unglazed quarry tile. This category includes any hard, red-bodied ceramic floor tile of consistent dimensions, not less than ⅜ inch thick. Most are vitreous (glossy in appearance) or semivitreous. The tile body (called the bisque) is usually a deep brick red, although pigments may be added to produce other colors, usually earth tones or pastels.

Unglazed pavers. All tiles that are not classified as quarry tiles are called unglazed pavers, although the terms are sometimes used interchangeably. Pavers range from impervious porcelain varieties to nonvitreous clay. Use the densest you can find. These pavers are usually uniform in size and dimension and come in a wide variety of colors and surface textures.

Cement-bodied tile. As the name implies, these tiles are made of cement. Extruded cement-bodied tiles are extremely dense and offer strong resistance to wear. These tiles are made for a wide variety of applications. Tiles made for outdoor use are treated with a sealer that must be reapplied periodically.

Gauged stone. Slate, marble, and granite come as gauged stone tiles. They are cut to precise shapes (squares or rectangles) and sizes, and they're ground to uniform thickness. The surface may be left natural or machine-polished to a high sheen. Set much like ceramic tile, gauged stone is extremely expensive and is used for interior floors, walls, and countertops. However, you can use it to make an indoor-outdoor connection, such as extending a stone floor in a foyer out to a front porch. For outdoor use, avoid stones with smooth, slick surfaces.

Cutting tiles. If you have a lot of tiles to cut, it's best to rent a tile saw. If you need to cut only a few tiles, follow these instructions: Equip a hacksaw with a carbide-grit blade, then cut a groove in the face of the tile about ¹⁄₁₆ inch deep along the cut line. (Very thick tiles may require a second cut on the backside to make

Cutting tiles. Mark where you want to cut, and make a shallow groove along the line with a carbide-grit blade in a hacksaw. Snap the tile in two by placing it on a wood dowel and pressing down.

a clean snap.) Place the tile over a wood dowel or length of heavy insulated wire and press down sharply on either side to snap the tile. Gauged stones can be cut on a tile saw, or you can use the method described in "Cutting Stone," page 122.

Setting Tiles in Mortar

Setting tiles and gauged stone in mortar over a concrete walk is done pretty much the same way as are bricks or patio blocks. Square tiles can be laid in a jack-on-jack or running bond pattern. These tiles also can be laid diagonally. Fill in the edges with triangular pieces that you cut using the score-and-snap method described above.

1. Prepare the surface. Existing concrete walks should be cleaned thoroughly to remove all grease, oil, wax, and other contaminants. Use a solution of 1 cup TSP to 1 gallon of water. Small holes should be patched and leveled with a concrete patching material. Treat slick-troweled or painted surfaces with muriatic acid or concrete bonder.

2. Prepare and apply the mortar. Tile and gauged stone are laid in a either dry-set mortar or latex–portland cement. Check with the tile manufacturer for the appropriate product and application requirements. Dry set the tile as explained in "Dry Mortar Method," page 144. To set a wet coat of mortar, first apply a ¼-inch bond coat of mortar over the entire walk with a flat trowel and allow it to dry. Then apply a second coat with a ½-inch notched trowel, on which you'll set the tile. Ideally, the mortar should be applied on a warm, mild day (about 65°) and out of direct sunlight to prevent the mortar from setting up too quickly. Spread only as much mortar as you can cover with tile before the mortar sets up—in about a half hour.

3. Lay the tiles. Starting at one end of the walk, lay the tiles in the chosen pattern, with open (⅜- or ½-inch) joints. To ensure even joints, make a spacer

1. Use a solution of trisodium phosphate and water to clean a pre-existing concrete surface and a concrete patching material to patch any small holes.

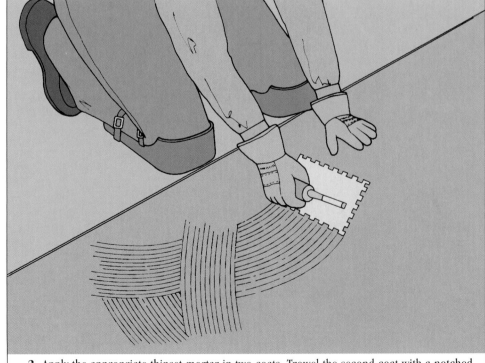

2. Apply the appropriate thinset-mortar in two coats. Trowel the second coat with a notched trowel to create a better bedding surface for the tile.

stick by nailing 4-inch lengths of wood lath to a piece of 1x4. Position the pieces of lath on the 1x4 so that they fit in the joints between two tiles, as shown. Use a 4-foot level or 2-foot level placed atop a straightedge to make sure all the tiles are even.

4. Bed the tiles. Use a rubber mallet or a hammer and wood block to bed the tiles into the mortar. Tap lightly over the center of each tile. Recheck the tiles for alignment and level.

5. Mortar the joints. Prepare a mortar mixture of 3 parts sand to 1 part portland cement, or use a premixed bagged mortar. Add water until the mix is easy to pour but not too soupy. To pour the mortar, use a large can with a bent rim to form a spout, as shown. Pour a bead of mortar to fill all joints, being careful not to let mortar splash onto the tile surface.

6. Tool the joints. After the mortar sets up (which takes about 15 to 20 minutes), remove any excess mortar with a flat trowel and wipe off the tile surface with a coarse, damp cloth. Then tool the joints. Most installations look best with a slightly concave joint, which you can make with a jointing tool or a short length of dowel or copper tubing. After striking the joints with a trowel, clean the tile surface again to remove mortar smears. Dried mortar film or haze remaining on the surface can be removed with a commercial tile cleaner. After the mortar joints are thoroughly dry (which can sometimes take two to six weeks of warm weather), you can apply a clear tile sealer to protect the tile from stains and weather. Consult your tile dealer for the appropriate product to use in exterior applications.

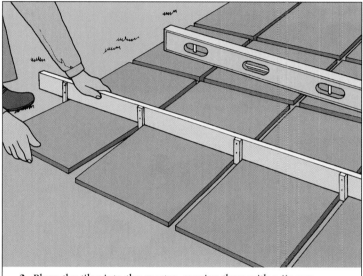

3. Place the tiles into the mortar, spacing them with a jig you make from scraps.

4. After setting a few feet of walk, tap the center of each tile with a rubber mallet or a hammer and board to fix the tile in place. Make sure the tiles are level.

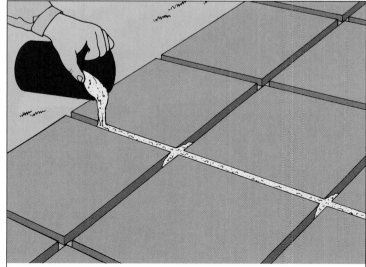

5. Mix a thin batch of mortar, then pour it from a coffee can into the joints. Mortar will stain some tiles, so try not to get any on the walk surface.

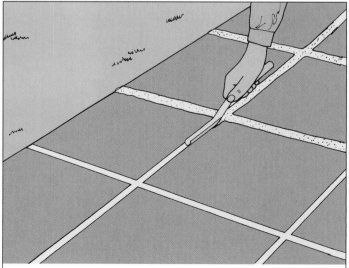

6. Once the mortar begins to harden, strike it flush to the walk surface with a trowel. Then tool the joints with a convex jointer, if desired.

BUILDING STEPS

If the ground level of your walk changes dramatically or if your patio is terraced into the side of a hill, steps or ramps need to be part of your design. While both require a little thought, some math, and careful layout, you'll find that actual construction is simple.

Exterior steps are generally less steep than interior steps: The step itself is wider, and the rise between steps is smaller, making the steps easier to navigate in bad weather. The exact design of your steps or ramp will depend on the terrain, but all steps have certain things in common.

Step width. Steps must be wide enough to accommodate the traffic they have to handle. Steps 4 feet wide are usually adequate for one person to stroll comfortably. Two people walking abreast need a walk 5 to 6 feet wide. Steps in the middle of walks should be the same width as the walk.

Steps leading to entries, decks, and patios should be wide enough to complement the scale of their surroundings. Build narrow steps for a small patio: They'll look proportionate and will easily handle the traffic. A large patio, on the other hand, may call for steps wider than strictly necessary. The extra width helps accommodate the occasional crowd

Brick steps are traditional in gardens and walks. Depending on your needs, you can also make steps from concrete, pavers, or wood.

and helps keep the steps in scale with the surroundings.

Tread/riser relationships. All steps have two critically important dimensions. The tread depth is measured from the front to the back of the tread—the part of the step on which you walk. Technically, tread depth is called the unit run. The height of the individual step is equally important and is called the unit rise. Typically, the higher the unit rise, the shallower the tread. As a rule of thumb for exterior steps, the combined length of one tread and two rises should be 25 to 27 inches.

The maximum rise between any two steps should be the amount most people are comfortable stepping up—between 5 and 7 inches. This leaves a tread depth of between 15 and 17 inches, a distance equal to the space between the toe of one foot and the toe of the other in the average person's step. Many landscape designers believe that the best tread/riser proportion for garden steps is a 15-inch tread with a 6-inch riser.

Landings. Where a flight of steps is at right angles to a walk or driveway, there should be at least a 3-foot landing between the steps and the walk or drive. If a door or gate opens toward a landing or porch, the landing should be the width of the door plus at least 3 feet. Landings should be the same width as the treads.

Finding the Run and Rise

Before you can figure tread/rise relationships, you need to compute the total rise and the total run. The total rise is the height between the lowest and highest levels of the stairs. The run is the horizontal distance from one end of the stairs to the other.

If the steps run from a walk to a patio or deck, you get the rise by measuring the height of the structure. If the steps go up a hillside, drive a tall stake into the ground at what will be the bottom of the stairs and a short stake at the top of the stairs. Each stake should be plumb, and the tops should be at about the same height. Tie a string to

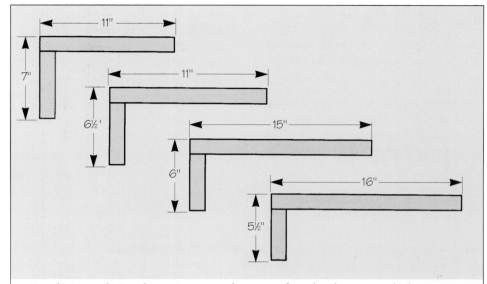

Tread/riser relationships. Certain combinations of tread and riser provide the most comfortable steps. As a rule of thumb, 25 to 27 inches as the combined length of one tread and two risers is the most comfortable.

the upper stake at ground level, then tie the string to the lower stake. Level the string with a line level, and measure the distance at the tall stake from the ground to the string: This distance equals the rise—the combined height of each step.

To find the run, simply measure the horizontal distance between the stakes.

Determining tread and riser sizes. Once you know the rise and run, you can figure out the tread and unit rise. To determine the unit rise, divide the total rise by the potential number of steps. Remember, the ideal unit rise is between 5 and 7 inches. If your answer is outside this range, adjust the number of steps. If, for

example, the total rise is 39 inches and you have 5 steps in mind, you'd need a riser height of 7.8 inches—too big for outdoor use. Six steps, however, would give you a riser height of 6½ inches (39÷6=6.5), well within the right range.

Once you know the unit rise, calculate tread depth. Remember that as a rule of thumb the tread depth plus twice the unit rise should be somewhere between 25 and 27 inches. Twice the riser height in our example is 13 inches; subtracting that from 25 and then from 27 tells you that the treads should be somewhere between 12 and 14 inches deep (25–13=12; 27–13=14). Choose the depth that will give you the proper run.

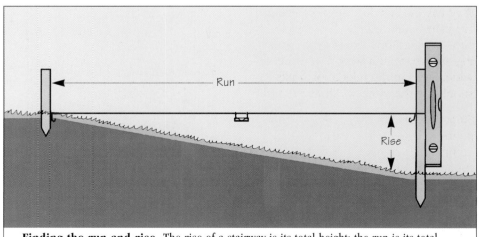

Finding the run and rise. The rise of a stairway is its total height; the run is its total length. Find them by driving stakes, stretching a level string, and measuring.

If the rise and run won't work out to something that fits the formula, you usually have flexibility about where the top and the bottom of the steps will be located. If necessary you can adjust the total run to create a stairway that has a comfortable rise and run ratio.

WOOD STEPS

On steep or irregular slopes or severe grade changes, raised steps can often bridge the grade change with little or no excavation or grading required. On gentle slopes, you can outline each step by laying landscape timbers directly on the ground and filling the spaces between them with smooth stones, bricks, poured concrete, or other suitable walk materials.

Steps on Grade

The steps shown here are supported by a notched wooden stringer to which the treads are nailed. The stringer lays directly on the same type of sand-and-gravel base that supports the rest of the walk. Concrete footings at each end of the steps anchor them in place.

Since the steps will be installed on grade, you can simply measure the

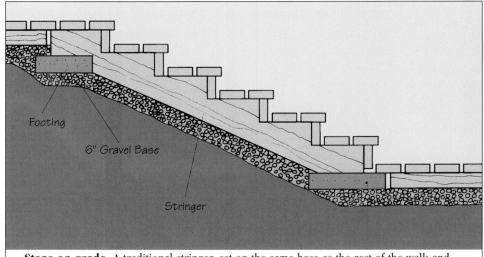

Steps on grade. A traditional stringer, set on the same base as the rest of the walk and held in place by concrete footings, makes a durable stairway.

slope along the ground to determine the length of the stringers. Calculate the total run and rise of the slope, as described in "Finding the Run and Rise," page 149. Calculate the individual tread and riser sizes, as described in "Determining Tread and Riser Sizes," also on page 149.

1. Lay out and excavate for the steps. Drive a stake at each of the four corners of the steps and connect them with string to locate the steps on the ground.

To build a support for the bottom end of the stringers, excavate a 10-inch-deep trench that extends about 6 inches beyond the sides of the steps. Fill the trench with a 6-inch layer of gravel,

and tamp it. Then install a 2x4 form, fill the trench with concrete, and level the concrete by pulling a screed across the forms. Before the concrete dries, insert anchor bolts with hex-head nuts to hold steel framing angles. The space between the framing angles should equal the space between the stringers. Install a second footing to support the top end of the stringers. If you're building a concrete walk or patio at the bottom of the steps, either one can serve as a footing. Install the hardware when you pour the concrete. For more on concrete work, see "Mixing by Hand," page 44.

2. Lay out the stringers. Stringers are usually made from 2x12 stock. Lay out a single stringer with a framing

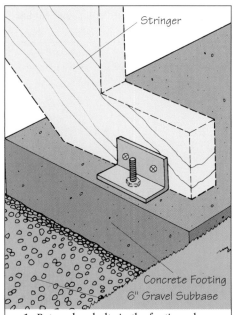

1. Put anchor bolts in the footing when it's still wet, and attach the stairs to the footing with a framing angle.

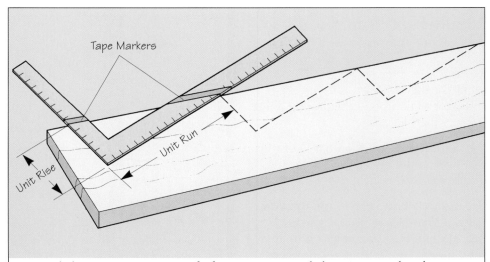

2. Mark the unit rise on one arm of a framing square. Mark the unit run on the other arm, and lay out the notches that will support the steps.

square before making any cuts. After you cut the first stringer, use it as a pattern for the second.

Begin your layout with your framing square. With tape, mark the length of a riser on the outside of one arm. With another piece of tape, mark the width of the tread on the outside of the other arm.

Put the framing square at the top end of the stringer board, as shown. With a pencil, mark a tread and the first riser.

3. Mark the rest of the steps.

Reposition the square, as shown. First, position the tape indicating the tread rise on the edge of the board at the top of the first step. Then position the tape indicating the tread width with the edge of the board. Draw lines along the square to mark the riser and tread. Repeat, working your way down the steps.

4. Mark the end of the stringer.

Extend the line for the top riser, as shown, to mark the top end of the stringer.

As laid out, the bottom step will be larger than the others by the thickness of the stair tread. Measure up a tread thickness from the existing layout line and draw a new line. Cut along this line and the line you drew to mark the bottom of the stringer.

5. Cut the stringers.

Cut along the layout lines with a circular saw, but do not cut past the line for the adjoining riser or tread. Finish the cuts with a hand saw. Use the first stringer as a template to mark the second stringer, and cut it out. If necessary notch the stringer to fit around the footing at the top of the hill.

Attach the top and the bottom of the stringer to the bolts in the concrete with angle brackets.

6. Attach the risers and treads.

Add at least 1 inch to the width of the tread to create a tread that overhangs the one below it. Cut the treads from two-by lumber. Nail or screw the treads in place with 10d galvanized nails or 3-inch deck screws. Predrill

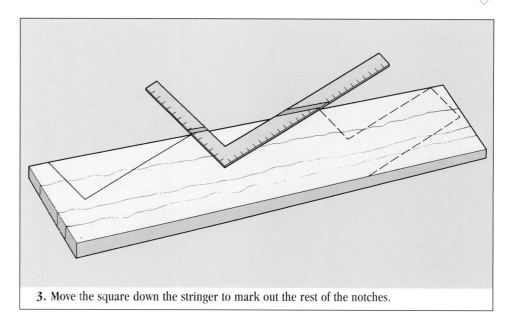

3. Move the square down the stringer to mark out the rest of the notches.

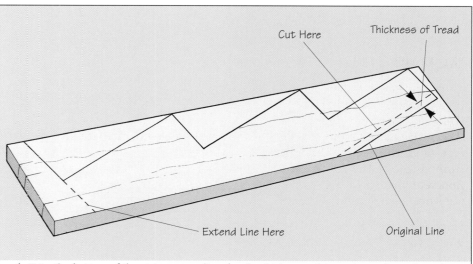

Cut Here   Thickness of Tread

Extend Line Here   Original Line

4. Trim the bottom of the stringer to adjust for the thickness of the stair treads, and cut the top of the stringer to fit in place.

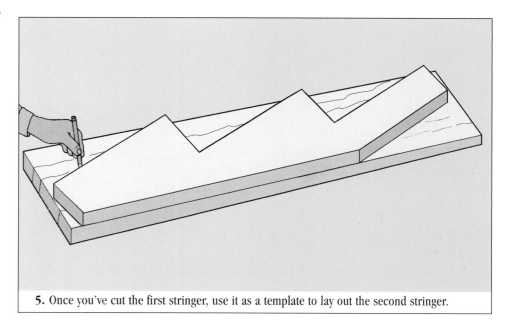

5. Once you've cut the first stringer, use it as a template to lay out the second stringer.

6. Nail the risers and treads to the stringer.

nail and screw holes to avoid splitting the wood. Leave a ¼- to ½-inch space between treads to facilitate drainage and to allow for wood expansion in wet weather.

Landscape Steps

If your steps will be along a grade, you often can build them directly on the ground without a stringer. The steps shown here are carved out of a hillside and built up with landscape timbers and brick. They will work well on a hillside where the run equals 24 to about 32 inches per foot of rise. On steeper or shallower hills, you can adjust the run to solve some problems. You can also make the treads deeper than the 15 or so inches usually called for. If you do, increase the tread by about 17 inches, the amount of the

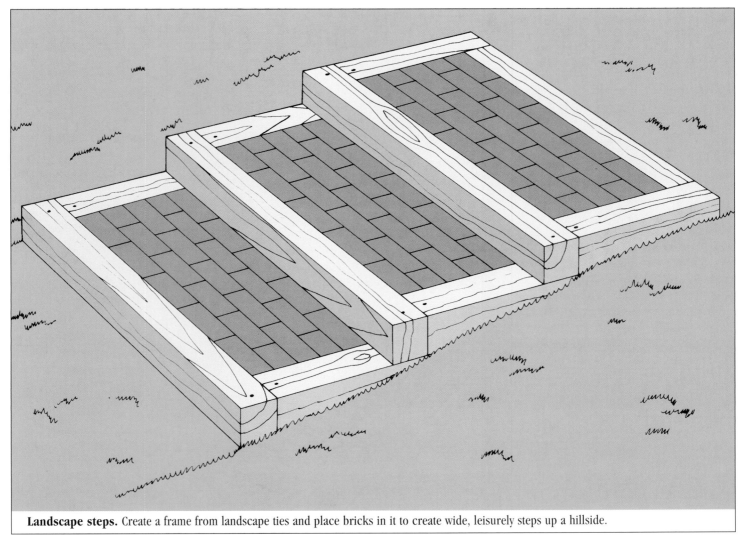

Landscape steps. Create a frame from landscape ties and place bricks in it to create wide, leisurely steps up a hillside.

average person's step. There are limits to what will work without excessive regrading, however, so measure your rise and run, and map out the steps on a sheet of graph paper before you begin work.

The steps shown here are made from landscape ties and brick. There are three ties per step—one serves as a riser, the other two serve as side timbers that contain the brick tread. The side timbers extend far enough into the hill to allow parts of the next step to sit on them.

To build these steps, you place the ties and excavate between them. Then you place a bed of gravel and sand between the ties to support a brick surface. Design your steps so that the space between the side timbers is a multiple of the brick width and length, and allow for another $\frac{1}{16}$ to $\frac{1}{8}$ inch between bricks. This will allow you to lay the bricks without having to cut any to fit.

1. Compute the rise and run of each step. First, measure the overall rise and run of your steps as described in "Finding the Run and Rise," page 149. The riser height is determined by the thickness of a landscape tie—6 inches. Divide the rise by 6 and round off to the nearest whole number to determine the number of steps. Divide the run by the number of steps to determine tread depth. For a comfortable stairway, the tread should be between 13 and 15 inches deep.

2. Stake out the stairs. Drive short stakes at each corner of the stairway and stretch string between them to outline the stairs. Sprinkle sand or flour on the ground along the string to mark the stair path directly on the ground.

3. Excavate the first step. Start at the bottom of the stairs. Dig a trench for the first riser, which should be little more than a shallow groove in the ground. Dig trenches for the side timbers, which need to be long enough to extend 6 inches past the riser of the next step. Check to make sure the trenches are level.

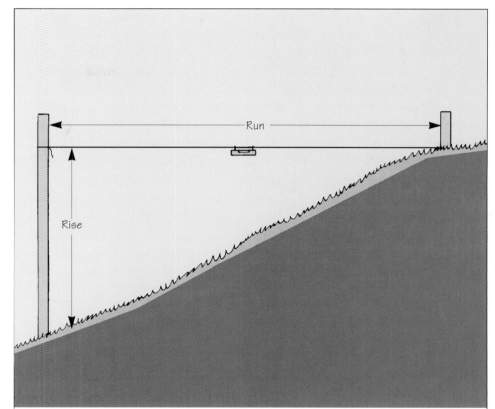

1. Use stakes and string to compute the overall rise and run. The number of steps will be the rise, divided by the height of a landscape tie (6 inches).

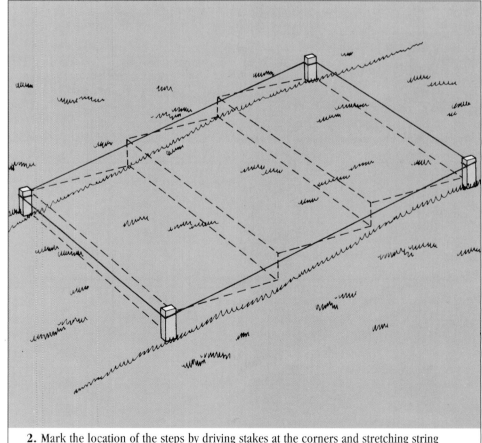

2. Mark the location of the steps by driving stakes at the corners and stretching string between them.

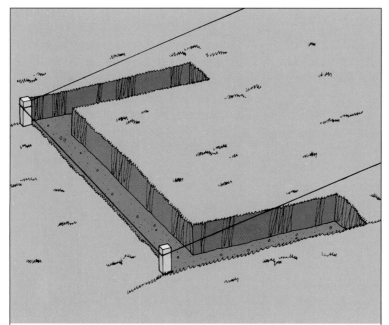

3. Dig trenches for the first risers and for side timbers that go back into the hillside. The side timbers need to be long enough to support the next riser and to extend 6 inches beyond it.

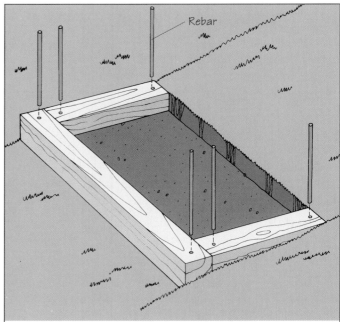

Rebar

4. Drive 18-inch lengths of rebar through the cut timbers to anchor them into the ground.

4. Cut the timbers. Cut the riser to length. Measure and cut the side timbers to length. Bore ½-inch holes 2½ inches from each end of all three timbers. Put the riser in place, and remove and add soil as needed to level it. Anchor it to the ground by driving 18-inch lengths of #4 (½-inch) rebar through the holes and into the ground.

Set the side timbers in place, and level and anchor them, too. Shovel out the soil between the sides to create a surface that is roughly level with the bottom of the timbers. You'll create the final grade when you add gravel and sand.

5. Build the next step. Dig a trench for the next riser, and trench back into the hill for the sides, as before.

Set the riser roughly in place. Measure from the front of the first riser to locate the second riser precisely. The riser is attached to the side timbers below it with 12-inch galvanized spikes. Drill a pilot hole about 5 inches into the riser, and spike the riser to the side timbers below it.

Place the side timbers, drill pilot holes, and spike the timbers to those below. Excavate between the sides,

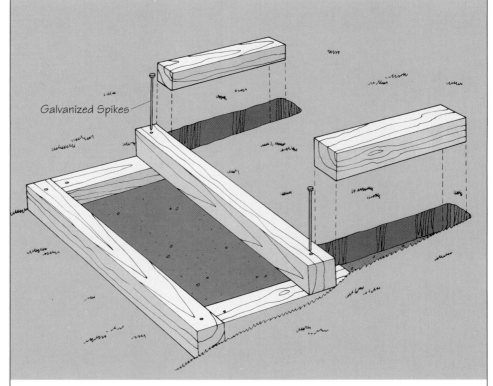

Galvanized Spikes

5. Trench for the next riser and side timbers. Spike the riser to the side timbers below it. Each set of side timbers sits on the one below, and the two are spiked together.

as before. Continue up the hillside in this fashion.

When you install the top step, cut the side timbers 6 inches shorter than the ones on the lower steps—these timbers do not need the extra length,

as no further stairs will be resting on them.

6. Backfill with gravel and sand. When installed, the bricks sit on a bed of gravel and sand roughly 4 inches deep. Pour the gravel in the openings between the timbers, tamp, and pour in more until you've laid a bed roughly 2 inches deep. Pour in sand, tamp, and add sand and tamp again. Continue until a brick set on the bed is level with the top of the riser.

Level the bed with a screed as shown. Rest the notches of the screed on the side timbers, and drag it across the bed to level it. Add sand to low spots if necessary. Remove excess sand as needed.

7. Install the bricks. Place bricks on the sand. Depending on the design of your steps, the bricks can be parallel to either the riser or the side timbers. Leave ⅟₁₆- to ⅛-inch joints between the bricks. If necessary, cut bricks to fit, as described in "Cutting Bricks," page 82.

On the top step, lay the bricks, then trench behind them for a timber that will enclose the back of the step. Cut the timber, and anchor it in place, as shown in step 4, with 18-inch lengths of rebar.

After setting the bricks, lay a 16-inch length of 1x6 on the walk, and tap over the entire surface with a hammer or mallet to bed the bricks into the

sand. If individual bricks are slightly tilted or too high, tap them into place with a rubber mallet.

8. Fill the joints. Spread a thin layer of dry mason's sand evenly over each step. With a stiff broom, sweep the sand into the cracks between the

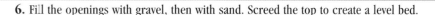
Screed Detail

bricks. Sweep in all directions to fill each joint completely. Sweep excess sand into a pile, and scoop it into a bucket for future use. Then lightly spray the walk with water to pack down the sand and wash it off the surface. Do not use a heavy spray or you will dislodge sand from the joints. Allow the surface to dry, then repeat the process until all the joints are completely filled and compacted.

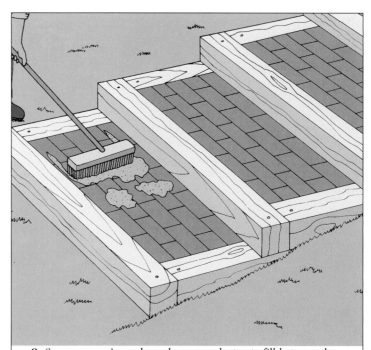

6. Fill the openings with gravel, then with sand. Screed the top to create a level bed.

7. Place bricks on the sand in the pattern of your choice. Bed the bricks by laying a length of 1x6 on the walk, and tap over the entire surface with a hammer.

8. Sweep mason's sand evenly over each step to fill between the bricks.

CONCRETE STEPS

Concrete steps are durable and work well as garden steps to traverse slopes in the landscape. The broomed surface described here provides good traction even when the steps are wet.

When building concrete steps, you dig a flat-bottomed trench into the hillside and line it with gravel. You then build a step-shaped form that molds the concrete into one long stairway.

Concrete garden steps require a footing at the bottom. If there are more than three steps, you'll need a footing at the top as well. The footing should be at least 2 feet deep, or in areas where freezing occurs, six inches below the frost line. Pour the footing before the steps, and stick reinforcing bars in it that extend up to tie the steps to the foundation. For more on foundations, see Chapter 4, "Wall Footings," beginning on page 41.

1. Determine the total run. Drive a stake in the ground at the top of the grade, about where you want the top of the steps to be. Hook your tape measure over the stake and pull the tape out until you reach the bottom of the grade. Stop at an even number if you can—say, 8 feet. Drive a longer stake into the ground at this point. Use a level to check that the stake is plumb.

2. Determine the total rise. Tie string to the uphill stake. Mason's twine is best. Make sure the string is attached to the uphill stake at ground level. Stretch the string tautly to the downhill stake, and put a line level on it. Adjust the string at the downhill side until it is level. When it is, mark where the string crosses the downhill stake. Now measure from the ground to the mark to get the total rise.

3. Determine the unit rise and run. As mentioned earlier, the ideal riser height (unit rise) for outdoor stairs is 6 inches. If, for example, the total rise is 30 inches, you need five steps ($30 \div 6 = 5$). Dividing the total run of 96 inches by five steps gives you a tread depth (unit run) of 19.2 inches. That's too deep for a comfortable stride.

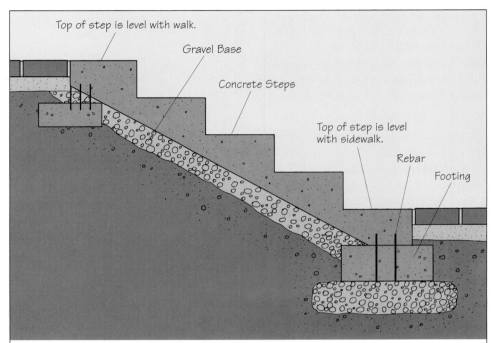

Concrete steps. The bottom trench for concrete steps is flat, and the forms that support the pour create the stepped top.

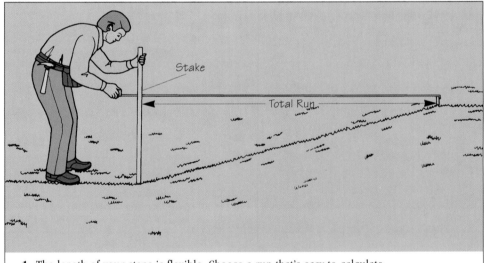

1. The length of your steps is flexible. Choose a run that's easy to calculate.

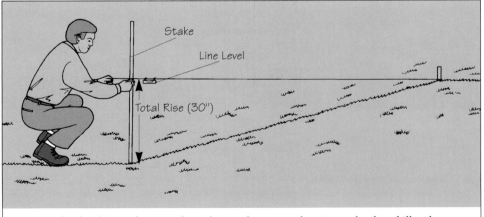

2. Stretch a level string between the stakes, and measure the rise on the downhill stake.

See what happens if you try six steps: 96 inches divided by six steps equals 16 inches for the unit run, well within the acceptable range. With a total rise of 30 inches, six steps would give you 5-inch risers; 5 inches is a small riser, but still within the acceptable range. For more information, see "Tread/Riser Relationships," page 149.

4. Calculate the side-form lengths.

Make your side forms from 2x12s. Here's a quick-and-easy way to use your framing square and tape measure to determine how long the boards need to be.

Using a scale of 1 inch equals 1 foot, measure from the framing square's blade to its tongue to find the length of the form board. The example stairway has a total run of 96 inches—8 feet—so start measuring from the 8-inch mark on the blade. The example stairway's total rise is 30 inches—2½ feet—so measure up to the 2½-inch mark on the square's tongue. The measurement on the tape measure is about 8½ inches. Since lumber is sold in 2-foot increments, you know you need to purchase two 10-foot 2x12s for your side forms.

5. Lay out and cut the side forms.

Place one of the 2x12s on a pair of sawhorses, and lay out the treads, risers, and top step full-scale. In the illustration, this layout is shown with dotted lines. Lay out these lines lightly; they won't be final cutting lines. For more on layout see "Lay Out the Stringers," page 150.

For drainage, the treads should slope downhill about ¼ inch per foot. The example steps have a run of 16 inches, so slope each tread about ⁵⁄₁₆ inch. Also, it's a good idea to slant the risers in about 1 inch to prevent stubbed toes. To make the slant adjustment, measure in 1 inch from the tread and riser intersections, as shown in the illustration. Then measure up ⁵⁄₁₆ inch for the slope adjustment. Use a circular saw to cut out the first form, then use the first form as a template to lay out the second form. Cut out the second form.

6. Excavate the site and set the forms.

The concrete will need to be poured to a depth of 6 inches below

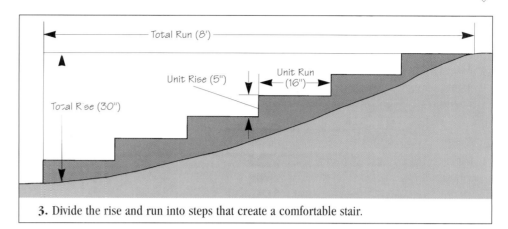

3. Divide the rise and run into steps that create a comfortable stair.

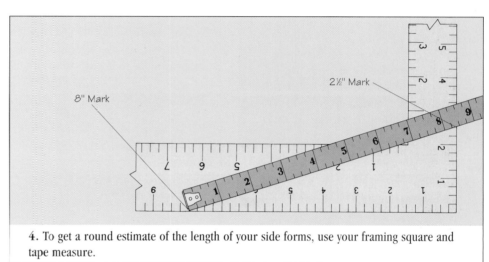

4. To get a round estimate of the length of your side forms, use your framing square and tape measure.

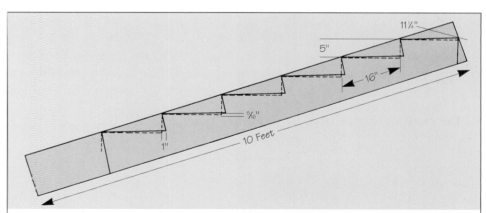

5. Lay out the unit rises and runs on the side forms as indicated by the dotted lines. Adjust the layout for tread slope and riser slant.

Garden Steps to Span Long Distances

In outdoor construction, you may want to intersperse the steps with sections of sidewalk if there are a number of grade changes in the landscape. If you do this, try to make the sidewalk sections an uneven number of paces long. Of course, pace length varies according to each person's height and walking style, but 17 inches is a good average. So make the sidewalks 17 inches, 51 inches, or 85 inches long, if you can. This way walkers will alternate between left and right feet when stepping up, making the walk feel more natural and comfortable.

grade. Excavate to that depth. You may need to excavate deep enough for a gravel base under the concrete—check your local codes. For a brick stairway add the combined thickness of the brick and mortar bed.

The excavation need not be level at the bottom. It should follow the slope of the natural landscape. Make the excavation about 12 inches wider and 12 inches longer than the steps to give you room to assemble the forms.

Set the side forms into the excavation. Make sure the forms are plumb at the top of the steps, as indicated in the illustration. Cut enough 24-inch-long 2x4 stakes to space them every 2 or 3 feet. Pound the stakes into the ground, and secure them to the form boards with 8d double-headed nails.

Cut two end form boards to 3 inches longer than the final step width. Nail one to each end of the side form boards with 10d double-headed nails.

7. Install the riser forms and bracing. Rip two-by stock to equal the rise of the steps. For this example, rip 2x6s to 5 inches wide. When you make the rip cuts, set the blade of your saw to 45 degrees to create bevels. Place the bevel to the outside at the bottom, so you can reach the entire tread when you pour and finish the concrete. Cut the riser forms to the width of the final steps plus 3 inches for the width of the side forms.

Nail the riser forms across the side forms. To brace the form, lay a 2x6 up the stairs, centered side to side, as shown. Attach the brace to a stake against the outside of the bottom end form with 8d double-headed nails. Cut cleats with ends angled at 45 degrees. Place a cleat against each riser form, and nail it to the brace. Toenail the cleat to the risers. Toenail the brace to the uphill end of the form with no cleat. To keep concrete from sticking to the forms after you pour it, coat the forms with a commercially available liquid called a release agent.

8. Place the reinforcing mesh. To provide added strength for your steps and to prevent cracking, place

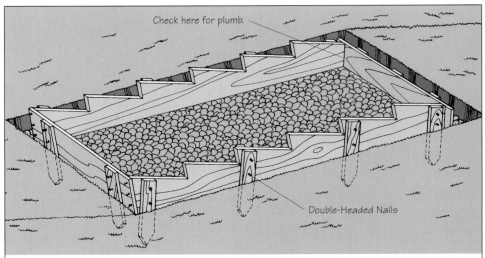

6. Dig to a depth of 6 inches plus 4 inches for the gravel base, following the frame. Then support the forms with stakes fastened with double-headed nails.

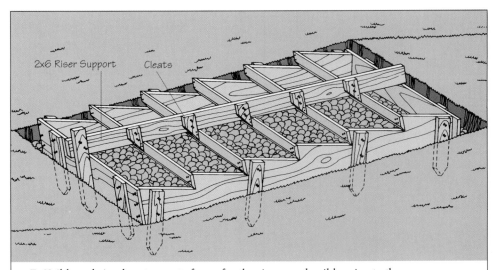

7. Nail boards in place to create forms for the risers, and nail bracing to them.

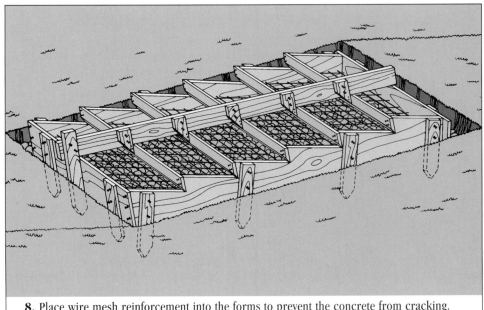

8. Place wire mesh reinforcement into the forms to prevent the concrete from cracking.

wire mesh reinforcement in the form. Reinforcing mesh must be completely embedded in the concrete. Use small stones, bricks, or pieces of broken concrete or concrete block to support the mesh so that it will be in the middle of the pour. Allow 2 inches between the edges of the mesh and the edges of the form. Overlap the pieces of mesh by 6 inches, and tie them together with wire.

Before you start mixing the concrete, check the formwork for correct size and depth. Once you're sure that everything is in its proper place, spray the inside surfaces of the forms, the rubble fill if any, and the soil subgrade with water from a garden hose. This will keep them from drawing moisture from the concrete, possibly resulting in a poor surface. Moistening the forms and soil is especially important on a warm, windy day.

9. Place the concrete.

Mix your concrete as near the job site as you can, or have the delivery truck park as close as possible. If you're lucky, the delivery truck's chute extensions will reach your form and you won't have to cart the concrete. Otherwise, move the concrete from the mixing area or from the truck to the project site with a wheelbarrow. Lay 2x12s across lawn areas to protect them from the weight of the wheelbarrow.

Start dumping the concrete in the bottom step, making sure to fill the form completely. Fill the next step, using a shovel if you are transporting with a wheelbarrow. Tamp the concrete with a shovel to fill in corners and remove air voids. Tap the outside of the form boards lightly with a hammer to settle the concrete around the perimeter of the forms.

As you place the concrete, lift up the wire reinforcing mesh with a hammer claw to make sure it is totally embedded. Continue transporting and dumping the concrete until the form is full.

10. Strike the concrete level.

Once you have filled the form with concrete, you can remove the middle brace. The danger of the forms bulging is greatest as the concrete is being

9. Pour concrete in the forms beginning with the bottom step.

10. Use a 2x4 to screed the surface of the concrete level with the top of the form.

flung down into the form. Begin to strike off, or screed, the surface of the concrete level with the top of the form. To do this, drag a straight 2x4 that is slightly wider than the steps along the top of the form. Press both ends down on the form. Fill any hollow areas with a shovel, then level them.

11. Smooth the surface.

Smooth the surface of the concrete for the first time with a darby or a float. Make large sweeping arcs, being careful not to gouge the surface. Do not do anything else until the water sheen is gone from the surface. The waiting time depends on the temperature, wind, and humidity, as well as the type of cement used.

12. Separate and form the edges.
Next, use the point of a small trowel to cut the top inch or so of concrete away from the face of the form, so concrete won't chip off when the form is removed. Then use an edger to round the edges so they will be attractive and resistant to damage. Run the edger back and forth to smooth the surface, being careful not to gouge the concrete.

13. Float, trowel, and broom the surface.
Use a wooden float to smooth the surface and bring a cement paste to the top of the concrete of the treads and risers. Hold the float nearly flat, and move it in wide sweeping motions. Be sure to smooth over any marks or gouges. If water comes to the surface when you begin the floating, stop and wait a while before trying again. Go back over the edges with the edger to touch up after floating. Be sure to float the risers and sidewalls of the steps. You can purchase a right-angled edging tool, which helps in smoothing the inside cove where the riser meets the tread.

For brick steps, pull a damp broom along the floated surface to create a rough surface for the mortar bed. Pull the broom across each step in one motion, perpendicular to the direction of traffic.

Cure the concrete. After the concrete has cured for a day, carefully remove the forms. Do not pry or hammer against the concrete itself.

Cover the steps with a 6-mil sheet of plastic, and keep the steps moist for seven days to allow it to cure properly. The concrete will continue to cure slowly for another month until it reaches full strength, but if you are going to apply brick, you can do so after the first week.

BRICK STEPS

Mortared brick steps sit on a concrete base that keeps the bricks and joints from cracking as the ground moves with the weather. To build brick steps, follow the directions for build-

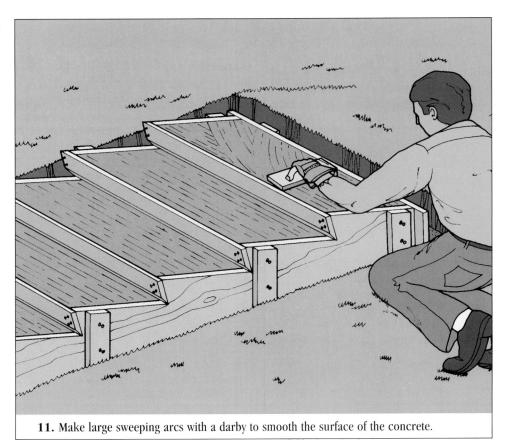

11. Make large sweeping arcs with a darby to smooth the surface of the concrete.

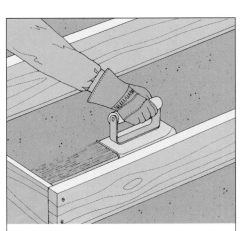

12. Use an edger to create and round edges that will be safe, attractive, and resistant to damage.

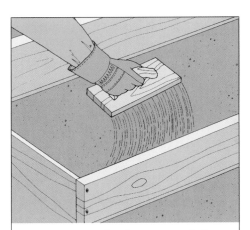

13. Use a wooden float to smooth the surface and bring a cement paste to the top.

ing concrete steps, but add to your excavation depth the height of the bricks plus ½ inch for the mortar bed that holds the bricks on the concrete.

In laying out your steps, consider the size of the bricks so that each step will be made of whole units. The illustration shows four different ways of creating brick risers and treads by using different brick thicknesses (1½ or 2¼ inches), laying the bricks

flat, setting them on edge, and varying the mortar joint thickness (⅜ to ½ inch). These options give you some flexibility in achieving the exact riser height you need so that the risers add up to the correct overall height. The exposed length of the brick shown produces a tread of 12 inches.

Tread design. A tread width that is a multiple of 8 inches will accommodate the use of whole bricks. (Two 3⅝-inch-wide bricks laid flat

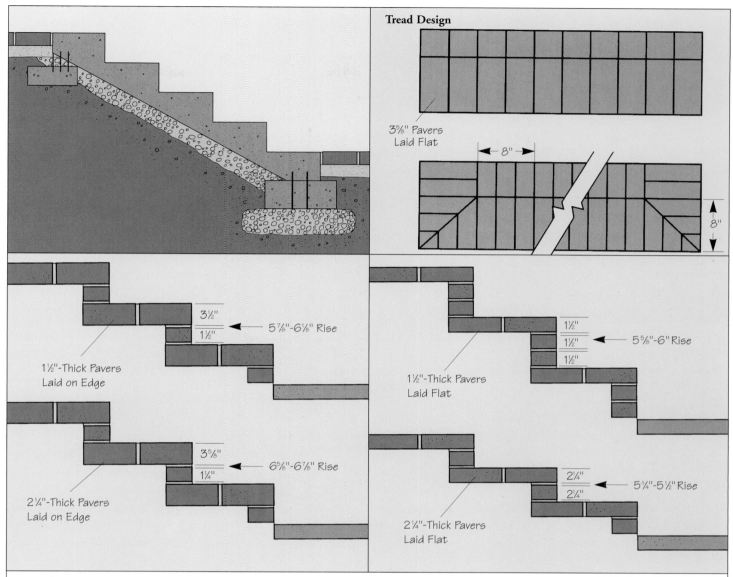

Tread Design

3⅝" Pavers Laid Flat

8"

8"

1½"-Thick Pavers Laid on Edge

3½"
1½"
5⅞"-6½" Rise

2¼"-Thick Pavers Laid on Edge

3⅝"
1¼"
6⅝"-6⅞" Rise

1½"-Thick Pavers Laid Flat

1½"
1½"
1½"
5⅝"-6" Rise

2¼"-Thick Pavers Laid Flat

2¼"
2¼"
5¼"-5½" Rise

Brick steps. Brick steps are supported by a concrete base (top left). Lay out the treads to take advantage of the standard 8-inch length of a brick (top right). The four patterns shown create a comfortable rise and run while using brick efficiently.

plus two ⅜-inch mortar joints equals 8 inches.) Three 2¼-inch-thick pavers laid on edge plus three ⅜-inch mortar joints makes a unit that is also nominally 8 inches (rounded up from 7⅞ inches). If you draw a plan of the treads, you will be able to figure the number of paving bricks you'll need.

Once you've built the concrete base for the brick steps, the project is simply a matter of laying the bricks in the correct pattern and keeping the joints a consistent size.

1. Test-fit the units. To check the size of the base and the spacing of the pavers, lay out the units without mortar on at least two steps.

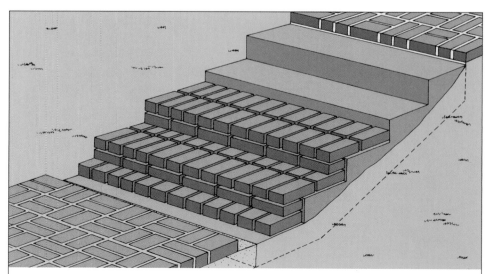

1. Do a test run. Lay out the bricks on the steps to check the size of the base and the spacing of the pavers.

2. Clean the surface and lay a ½-inch-thick mortar bed, working on one tread at a time.

3. Spread mortar on the sides of the bricks, and set them in the mortar bed.

4. When the mortar is thumbprint hard, use a rounded jointer to tool the mortar joints.

metal trowel; score the surface with a notched trowel.

3. Set the brick. Spread mortar on the sides of the bricks with a trowel, and place them on the mortar setting bed, forming joints that are about ⅜ inch wide. Cut off excess mortar with the edge of the trowel. Check the surface with a level, and tap the units gently with the trowel handle, if necessary, to bed them in the mortar.

4. Tool the joints. The joints are ready for tooling when the mortar is "thumbprint" hard, meaning that you can press your thumb against the mortar and leave a print impression without the mortar sticking to your thumb. Using a rounded jointer, tool the short joints first, then the long joints to produce a concave-shaped joint. Then finish the remaining steps. Mortar the next tread, and lay the brick as previously discussed until you finish the top step.

Clean the steps. After the steps have set for about a week, brush the surface with a stiff natural- or synthetic-bristle brush—or a wire brush—to remove mortar drips and dust. Use a plastic or wooden scraper and a brush to remove large mortar splatters.

If necessary, clean the completed project with a diluted solution of muriatic acid (mixed 1:10 with water). Don't use muriatic acid on white, cream, buff, gray, or brown brick, because it can leave ugly green or brown stains—check with the brick manufacturer or distributor. Before applying an acidic cleaning solution, thoroughly wet the pavers with a garden hose. Wearing rubber gloves, apply the acid solution carefully with a special acid brush (made with polystyrene bristles, available from masonry suppliers). Scrub lightly, then thoroughly rinse with a garden hose. Be extremely careful when working with acid to avoid burns. Don't use metal tools or buckets because the acid will corrode them. Use plastic. To avoid dangerous splashes, always pour the water in the bucket first, then add the acid.

Adjust the width of the mortar joints as necessary to get the best fit.

2. Install the mortar bed. The mortar bed holds the bricks in place and helps to compensate for minor irregularities in the concrete surface. Clean off the concrete surface, then start with the bottom step and mortar one tread at a time. Apply a bed of Type M or Type S ready-mix mortar. (For more information, see "Mortar Mixes," beginning on page 131.) Make the mortar bed about ½ inch thick. Place the mortar, then smooth the surface with the flat side of a rectangular

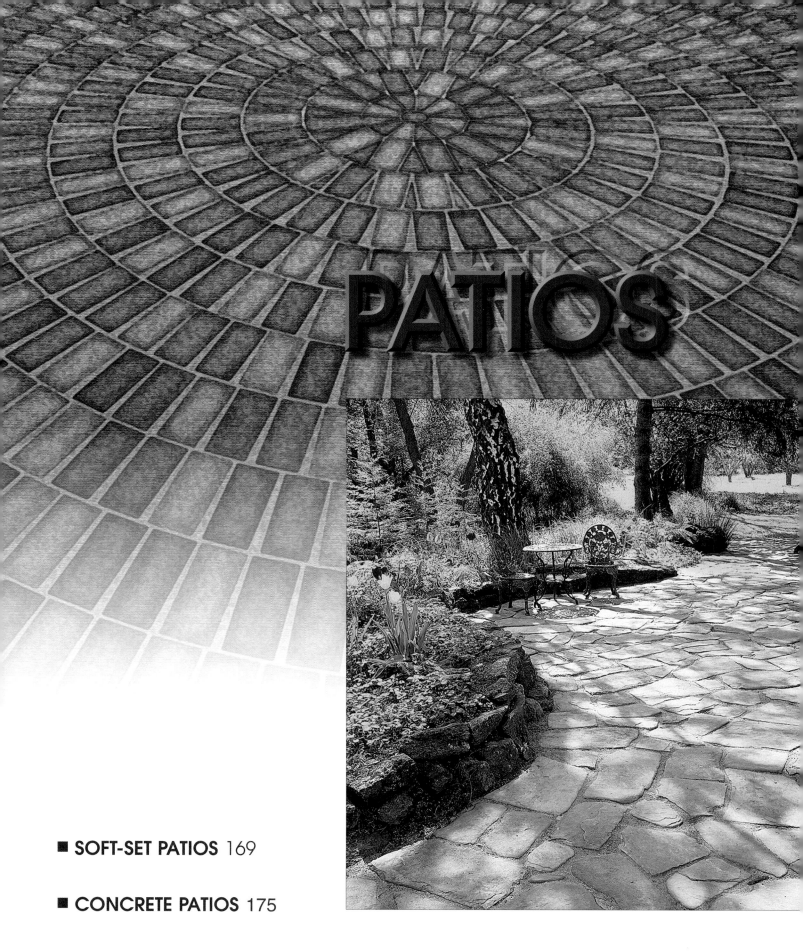

PATIOS

A brick patio in a herringbone pattern makes an elegant statement, whether it is set in a suburban garden (top) or an urban backyard (bottom). Laying pavers out on a sand-and-gravel base (right) is the simplest way to make a patio.

A flagstone patio blends well with plants and works well whenever you want to create a relaxed, natural space.

The patio and steps in this yard (below) match the chimney that dominates the back of the house, tying the two together and providing smooth transition between the house and yard.

A patio doesn't have to be flat. This patio steps from the house down into the yard, creating a place to sit and a place to gather. The rough texture of the stone works well in a wooded environment.

The concrete patio around this pool may not be as elegant as stone, but it provides a flat, slip-resistant surface that is safer and easier on bare feet.

The flagstone above has been milled to create flat, regular stones that are easy to lay but still have a natural feel. Piecing together irregular flagstones (bottom left) or an intricate brick pattern (bottom right) takes a good deal longer, but the patio that results is worth the effort.

SOFT-SET PATIOS

A well-designed patio adds more to the value of your home than it costs to build. The patio can be anything from a simple small pad outside the back door to a large expanse wrapping around a corner of the house.

Typically, however, a patio is about one-third the size of the house—larger perhaps than any room in the house. A 1,500-square-foot house, for example, might sport a 500-square-foot patio, one perhaps measuring 20 by 25 feet.

Site your patio to protect it from the hottest sun and coldest wind. Moreover, consider the terrain. You want your patio in an area that is well drained, and at the same time, you want to make sure you're not blocking

Patios like this one are set over sand or gravel bases. They do not require mortar and can be designed in a number of bond patterns.

or disrupting the existing drainage. To keep it from flooding, a patio is usually built an inch or so above ground level. To keep rain and snow out of the house, the patio should slope away from the house at a rate of ¼ inch per foot and should meet the house 1 to 3 inches below the house floor. For more on planning, see "Working with the Land," page 22.

Patios are much like walks, in that you can lay them over one of two kinds of bases. The simplest is a sand-and-gravel base, which will support flagstone, brick, or interlocking pavers. Mortared brick and stone patios, on the other hand, sit in a mortar bed on top of a concrete pad laid slightly below grade.

The easiest patio you can build uses concrete block, brick, flagstone, or adobe block laid on a sand-and-gravel subbase. Pavers and flagstone of various sizes, shapes, colors, and textures come in a variety of patterns, but anything thinner than 1¼ inches may crack with use.

The secret of success in dry-laid paving is a proper subbase, which minimizes settlement. The subbase consists of a 4-inch layer of gravel, topped off with an easy-to-smooth sand layer. On poorly drained soils and in very cold climates, the drainage base should be 6 inches thick. In some soils and in areas where the ground doesn't freeze and thaw, you may be able to do without the gravel entirely. Check with your local building office.

Edging. Edging holds the patio surface in place and keeps the individual pavers from moving. If the patio is built at ground level, the earth can serve as an edging. But to discourage flooding, you may want to build your patio slightly higher than grade and put an edging around it. The simplest type of edging is rot-resistant or pressure-treated wood. A harder-to-install but attractive edging uses pavers set on edge or on end in surrounding trenches. The pavers hold best if they're laid in mortar. A paver patio can also be edged with a cast-in-place concrete curb. (See "Concrete Edging," page 105.)

Because cutting paving units is hard work, it's best to avoid a design that requires partial pavers. The easiest way to do this is called the open-field method in which you begin by edging the patio only on two adjacent sides, such as the north and east. The other two sides—south and west—are left open until all pavers have been laid. The open-field method works best with rectangular paver patterns, such as basket weave or stack bond. Other patterns, such as herringbone, require a lot of trimming, no matter what edging technique you use. For directions on laying various patterns, see "Brick Patterns," page 118.

When ordering pavers, allow at least 5 to 10 percent extra for waste.

A Paver Patio over a Sand-and-Gravel Bed

Concrete pavers, available at home-improvement centers, can be used to make a simple, attractive patio. Pavers usually have a tab system that helps you space the blocks accurately without measuring. Concrete pavers are available in a variety of patterns, and installation will vary slightly from brand to brand and pattern to pattern. Concrete paving blocks, however, can be laid over a sand-and-gravel bed. The basic principles for building a paver patio are given below, but be sure to follow the manufacturer's directions as well.

You can also build a brick patio by following the directions below; for more information on brick, see "Laying a Soft-Set Brick Patio," page 174.

1. Lay out the patio. Use wood 1x2 stakes and string lines to outline your patio. Begin by driving two stakes near the house wall at the patio edges. Set up batter boards at the outer corners. Stretch mason's twine along what will be the perimeter of your patio. (Mason's twine stretches less than string.) Level the twine by hanging a line level at midspan.

Check to make sure the layout is square using the 3-4-5 triangle method. Measure from one stake 3 feet along the house, then 4 feet along the line. The corner is square if the diagonal between the two points measures 5 feet. If the corner is not square, slide the string along the batter boards until it is, and mark the location of the string on the board. For more on the 3-4-5 method, see "Finding a Square with the 3-4-5 Method," page 46.

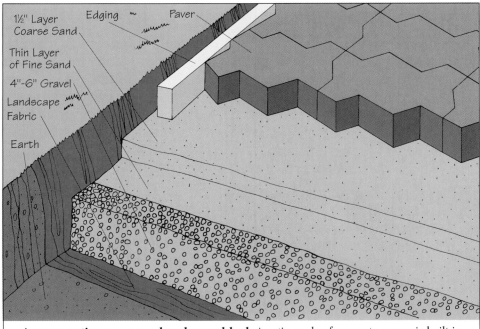

1½" Layer Coarse Sand
Edging
Paver
Thin Layer of Fine Sand
4"-6" Gravel
Landscape Fabric
Earth

A paver patio over a sand-and-gravel bed. A patio made of concrete pavers is built in several layers.

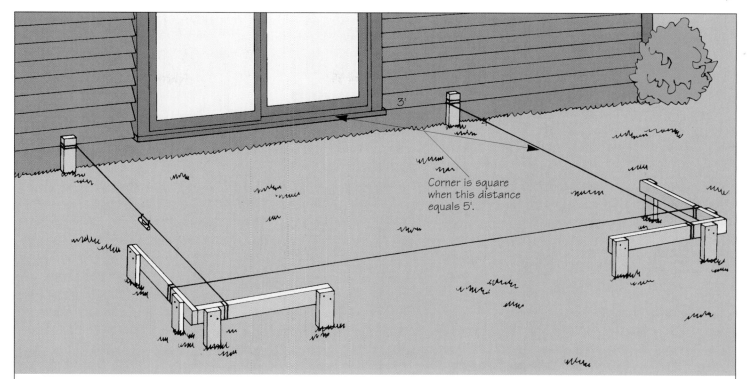

Corner is square
when this distance
equals 5'.

3'

1. Place stakes at the house and erect batter boards at the outer corners. Run string lines between them to outline the patio. Square it with the 3-4-5 method.

Square the second line that meets the house, then square the remaining side of the patio.

When all the sides are placed properly, make a saw cut where each string line crosses its batter board. If you need to remove the strings during subsequent work, you can pop them back in the cuts without having to remeasure.

2. Plot the slope. To drain well, the patio should slope away from the house ¼ inch per foot. Adjust your level string lines to reflect this. If, for example, the patio is 12 feet wide, the edge nearest the house needs to be 3 inches higher than the far end (12 feet times ¼ inch per foot equals 3 inches). In this case, you would slide the string 3 inches up the stake nearest the house. Compute the slope for your patio, and mark the new location with a saw cut. Slide the string up into the cut.

Sprinkle sand or flour over the strings to transfer the layout to the ground. Where the strings cross to mark the corner of the patio, suspend a plumb bob from the line, and mark the corner with a nail struck through a piece of paper into the ground.

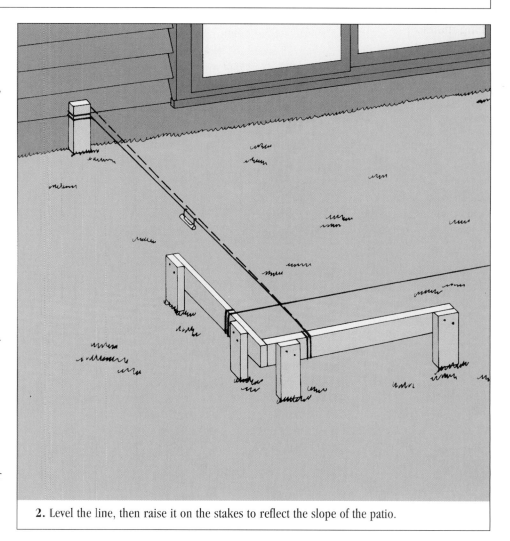

2. Level the line, then raise it on the stakes to reflect the slope of the patio.

3. Excavate the soil. Begin by digging out the sod and all organic material. Then dig deep enough to allow for the depth of the pavers, plus a 1½-inch sand subbase, plus 4 to 6 inches of gravel. (Check with your local building department to find out the required depth.)

To determine the depth of the excavation, first figure out the total thickness of the finished patio. If the pavers sit on 1½ inches of sand, for example, and the required gravel subbase is 4 inches, the combined thickness is 7 inches (1½+1½+4=7). If you wanted to have the surface 1 inch above grade, the depth of the excavation at the end farthest from the house would be 6 inches—7 inches for the patio thickness minus 1 inch for the elevation. In this case, you dig a hole 6 inches deep at the batter boards. To slope the bed, measure from the bottom of the string to the bottom of the hole. Keep the bottom of the excavation roughly this distance from the string.

Compact the soil by tamping it, and roll landscape fabric out over the tamped dirt. Overlap the fabric at least 6 inches at the seams. The fabric discourages plant growth and pre-vents soil from infiltrating the gravel. If soil gets into the gravel base, it can no longer function as a drainage base.

4. Place the edging. Choose an edging option from one of those shown. If you removed the strings in the course of placing the gravel, retie them. Dig a deeper trench around the perimeter of the excavation, as needed, to hold the edging. Measure

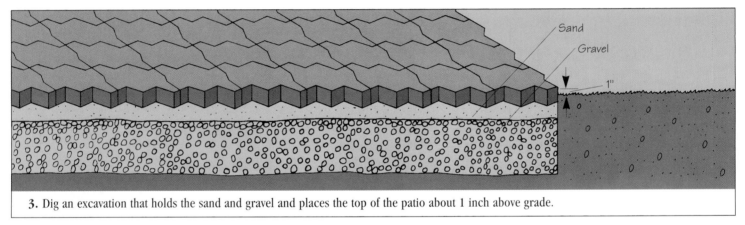

3. Dig an excavation that holds the sand and gravel and places the top of the patio about 1 inch above grade.

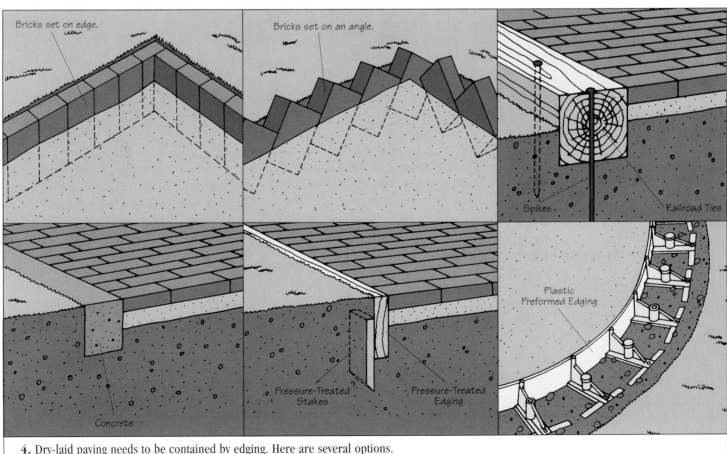

4. Dry-laid paving needs to be contained by edging. Here are several options.

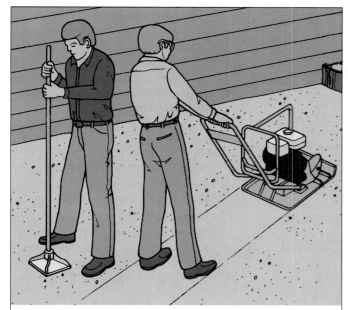

5. Line the dig with gravel, and tamp it in place.

6. Spread sand over the gravel to create a layer 1½ inches deep. Lay 1½-inch outer-diameter pipes on both sides of the patio and guide a screed along them to level the subbase.

down from the layout lines periodically to make sure the trench will put your edging at the desired height—at or just below the finished elevation of the pavers.

Install edging on two sides—one of which should be the house wall. Set the edging flush with or slightly below what will be the surface of the patio. Fill in around the edging with sand.

5. Lay the gravel base. Lay a
4- to 6-inch layer of gravel as required by code. Spread the gravel about 1 foot beyond the edges of the patio on all sides.

Tamp the gravel down. For large spaces, like a patio, consider renting a mechanical tamper.

6. Spread and level the sand.
Spread a thin layer of fine sand over the gravel base to keep the coarser sand from choking the gravel. Then spread a coarse concrete sand over the gravel to create a layer 1½ inches deep. To level the bed, place pipes with a 1½-inch outer diameter along the edges of the patio. Push the pipes down into the sand until the top of the pipe is at the proper grade, as measured from the strings.

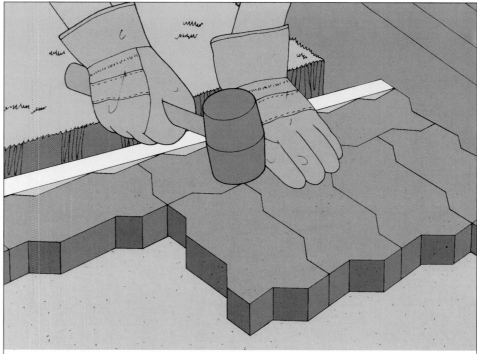

7. Start in a corner, and place pavers throughout the entire patio area. Set each paver firmly with several taps of a rubber mallet.

Level the sand by laying a 2x4 across the pipes and sliding it along the pipes.

7. Lay the pavers. Starting in a
corner, begin laying pavers on the smooth sand. Tap each one several times with a rubber mallet to set it firmly on the sand. Avoid twisting the units into place, as that disturbs the

sand subbase. The exact order in which you lay the blocks will depend on the pattern they create and the way they are designed. Check the manufacturer's directions as you work.

Most block pavers have built-in spacers to create a minimum joint width. If you're working with ones

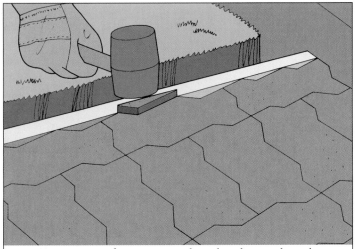

8. Trim pavers to fit in openings along the edges, and put them in place.

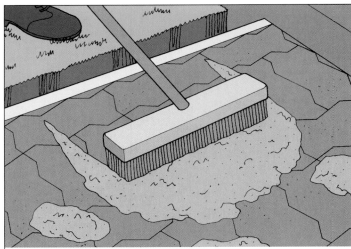

9. Sweep fine, dry sand into the joints between paving units to keep dirt out, discourage weeds, and lock the pavers into a solid layer.

that don't, space them to create ¹⁄₁₆- to ⅛-inch joints. If your work requires you to stand or kneel in the subbase, lay down a sheet of plywood to keep from disturbing the smooth sand. Continue laying pavers to the outer edges of the patio.

8. Complete the edging. If you're working with rectangular pavers, install the outer edging snugly against the pavers. If you're working with irregular units, install the edging with space to spare, then cut units to fill the spaces.

To trim a concrete paver, mark it, place it in sand, then score it by striking it with the chisel end of a mason's hammer. (You can also use a heavy hammer and a cold chisel.) Score all the way around the paver, and repeat, striking progressively harder until the paver breaks on the score line. Bricks are cut the same way or by using a brick chisel and hammer, as explained in "Cutting Bricks," page 82. For cutting flagstones, see "Cutting Stones," page 122. Wear eye protection while cutting pavers, bricks, or flagstone.

9. Fill the joints. Complete the patio by sweeping fine, dry mortar sand into the joints between units and around the edges. Sanding may need to be repeated several times to completely fill the joints. When you can sweep sand across the patio and end with the same pile you began with, joint-filling is finished.

Laying a Soft-Set Brick Patio

Pavers are not the only material that can be laid over a sand-and-gravel bed. Bricks laid on sand make an excellent patio. Because there is no mortar involved, you can take your time to build intricate patterns, combining parallel and diagonal lines. The simplest patterns to lay are running bond, stacked bond, and basket weave, where the bricks run parallel to the patio edges. Patterns like herringbone, where the units run diagonally, require cutting each brick at the edge of the patio. Consider renting a masonry saw for patterns that require this much cutting. For more on paving patterns, see "Brick Patterns," page 118.

Excavate and lay the brick the same way you'd lay block pavers. Most patterns are easiest to lay if you lay two courses at a time. Lay the initial bricks in the courses, leaving a ¹⁄₁₆- to ⅛-inch gap between bricks. Align the rest of the bricks with the help of a string. Wrap the string around a loose brick, and set it at one end of the course. Wrap the string around a second brick at the other end of the course, and align the string with the edges of the bricks you've laid. Follow the string as you set the bricks on the sand, tapping them with the trowel handle to level them. Don't push or twist bricks into the sand—bricks should rest on top of the subbase.

For most mortarless paving patterns, you'll need a paving brick that is exactly twice as long as it is wide. For good wear and weathering, get Class SX brick.

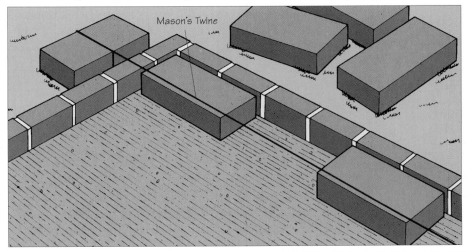

Mason's Twine

CONCRETE PATIOS

When most homeowners think of a patio, they think of concrete. Concrete forms a hard, even, stonelike surface that requires little maintenance. Reasonably easy to build and long lasting, it's the basic home patio. A concrete slab can also become the base for a brick, stone, or tile patio.

For a small patio—80 square feet or less—you can buy a prepackaged concrete mix and mix it in a wheelbarrow. For a larger patio, you can purchase the separate ingredients—portland cement, sand, and gravel—and mix them yourself. (For more on mixing concrete see "Mixing Concrete," page 43.) Perhaps the most practical method is to have ready-mix concrete delivered by truck to the job site. Ready-mix is sold by the cubic yard, and every 100 square feet of 4-inch-thick patio requires roughly 1.23 cubic yards. A 450-square-foot patio would require 4.5x1.23 cubic yards—just over 5½ cubic yards of ready-mix. Add 10 percent for spillage.

Consider ordering air-entrained mix. Air-entrained concrete contains billions of microscopic air bubbles in the hardened slab that act as safety valves to prevent damage caused by freezing and thawing.

To order ready-mix, call your dealer at least a day ahead of time. Tell him when you want delivery—the day,

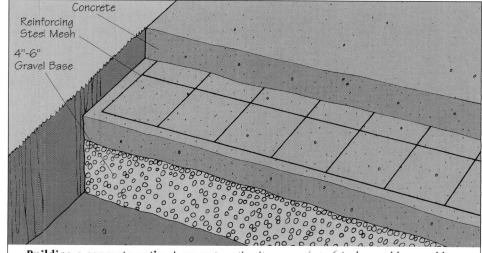

Concrete creates a durable, simple patio that is virtually maintenance free. A concrete pad is also required to support mortared brick, stone, and tile patios.

Building a concrete patio. A concrete patio sits over a 4- to 6-inch gravel base and has steel mesh running through it as reinforcement.

time, place and number of cubic yards. Tell the supplier exactly what you're using the concrete for, so you'll get the right mix. Typically, you'll want a mix with

- ¾-inch maximum-size coarse aggregate (stones).

- A minimum of six 94-pound bags of portland cement in each cubic yard—for good finishing.

- A maximum slump of 5 inches for hand methods of finishing—slump is a measure of workability.

- From 5 to 7 percent entrained air by volume in a severe climate, and from 3 to 4½ percent in a nonfreezing climate—to aid in finishing.

- A 28-day compressive strength of at least 4,000 pounds per square inch (psi). Compressive strength is a good measure of the strength and durability you'll have in the hardened concrete; a 3,500-psi compressive strength is sufficient for a nonfreezing climate.

If you order ready-mix this way, it should arrive ready to use without adding any water to make it workable. In fact, you should avoid adding water, as that cuts down on the strength and durability of your patio.

If the truck mixer cannot safely back up and dump into your patio forms, you can have the ready-mix pumped through a hose to the construction site. The hose can be routed through a gate, over a fence, or wherever necessary to reach from street to patio. If you think you'll need to have the concrete pumped to the site, be sure to discuss this with the supplier.

On concreting day have two or more strong helpers on hand when the truck mixer arrives. If the ready-mix will be brought in from the street by wheelbarrow, have an additional two helpers to man the wheelbarrows. Each worker should have work gloves and eye protection. At least one worker—who may have to wade into the mix while placing it—will need rubber boots. Once the concrete is poured, you'll need time to screed (flatten) it and to work the surface several times to create the finish you desire.

Making a Concrete Patio

Building a concrete patio is much like building a concrete walk. You first need to lay out and excavate the area. The concrete is usually poured over a 4- to 6-inch gravel base that you lay next. (The drainage base may be omitted if your soil is sandy and well-drained or if you live in a mild climate without a frost line. Check with your local building department) Once the base is prepared, you set the forms, pour the concrete, and work it with a series of tools to create the desired surface. Here's how to proceed with construction from excavation to pour.

1. Lay out the patio. Lay out the perimeter of the patio by stretching strings from stakes driven at the house to batter boards at the far end of the patio. Check to make sure the layout is square with the 3-4-5 triangle method. See "Finding a Square Corner with the 3-4-5 Method, page 46. The patio needs to slope ¼ inch per foot for drainage. Set level strings, and adjust to get the proper slope. For more on adjusting the strings, see Step 1 of "A Paver Patio over a Sand-and-Gravel Bed," page 170.

2. Excavate for the patio. Dig out the sod and all organic material. Dig deep enough to accommodate a slab 4 inches thick plus any required gravel drainage base. Measure down from the string lines to slope the excavation for proper drainage. Dig a few inches beyond the edges of the slab to allow room for the concrete forms.

Fill the excavation with any gravel required and tamp the gravel in place.

3. Build the forms. Next, position 2x4 forms around the edge of the patio, cutting them to length as necessary. Because 2x4s are actually ½ inch narrower than 4 inches, prop them up on scraps of ½-inch plywood so you can have a slab that is a full 4 inches thick.

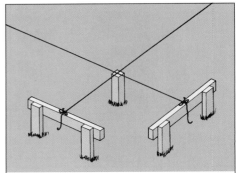

1. Lay out the area you will dig and square it with the 3-4-5 triangle method.

2. Dig to a depth that will accommodate the slab plus any base materials. Excavate about 8 to 10 inches wider than the layout lines to provide room for constructing the formwork.

Splice forms together with a 1x4 and decking screws.

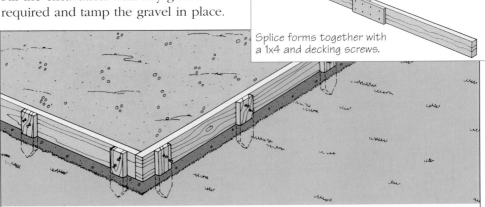

3. Proper formwork has stakes every 3 to 4 feet and is perpendicular to the subgrade. Where two sections of forms meet, splice them together with a 1x4 cleat.

Pouring Large Patios

If your patio is large, you may want to pour it in sections. If so, you'll have to have the proper formwork. One alternative is to put in permanent forms that define the sections, and then leave them in the finished patio as decorative elements. Be sure to use a rot-resistant or pressure-treated wood. Drive galvanized 16d nails every 16 inches on alternate sides. Drive the nails about halfway into the boards, and leave the rest of the nail exposed. This ties the permanent forms to the concrete and keeps them from sinking down below the slab when the patio is finished.

The second alternative is to create a construction joint. Construction joints are installed wherever a concrete pour is interrupted for more than thirty minutes or stopped at the end of the day. Within the formwork, the section being poured is closed off with a temporary stop board. The section is poured, screeded, edged and floated. The next day, you remove the stop board and continue with the pour. Construction joints can act as control joints when placed accordingly.

For slabs that are only 4 inches thick, a straightedged butt joint is adequate, but for thicker slabs, a keyed tongue-and-groove joint may be used to help transfer loads between adjoining sections of concrete. The tongue-and-groove construction allows the slab surface to remain level, but the sections can expand and contract independently.

A tongue-and-groove joint is shaped by attaching a wood, metal, or molded plastic beveled form along the middle of the temporary stop board. The edge of the pour takes this beveled shape. The subsequent pour takes an inverse shape. An oil coating prevents a bond between the pours. After the second pour has set, tool a control joint above the construction joint.

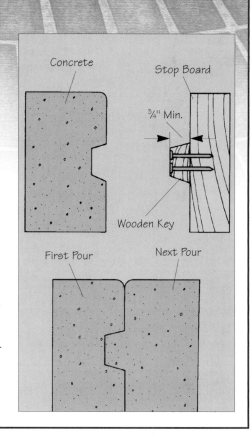

Concrete Stop Board ¾" Min. Wooden Key

First Pour Next Pour

Align the inside edges of the form boards with the layout strings. On the outside edges, drive stakes into the ground, and attach them to the forms with 3-inch deck screws or duplex (double-headed) nails. Because wet concrete can exert quite a bit of pressure on forms, space the stakes no more than 4 feet apart, and cut them long enough to be driven at least 18 inches into firm ground. Make sure the stakes don't protrude above the forms. If more than one form board is needed to create the desired length, splice the board ends together with a short length of 1x4. Stake each corner securely, as shown.

You'll be using the forms later to level the patio, so check your work as you go by measuring down from the strings to make sure the forms follow the required slope.

If desired, the forms can be left in place as edging or dividers, provided they are made of a nonrotting wood. If you're going to leave the forms in place, drive galvanized 16d nails partially into the slab side of the form.

This will tie the forms to the concrete once it's poured. Space the nails about 16 inches apart about 2 inches below the top. If you intend to remove the forms, coat the insides of the forms with a form-release agent.

To create curved patio edges, lay them out with a garden hose and form them with saw-kerfed 2x4s or with ¼-inch plywood with its face grain running vertically. Really tight

curves can be formed with ⅛-inch hardboard or sheet metal, well staked. (For more on curved work, see "Curved Forms," page 135.)

4. Add wire mesh reinforcement.
The concrete must be reinforced with #6 wire reinforcing mesh that has 6-inch by 6-inch openings. Cut it with heavy wire cutters, bolt cutters, or large fencing pliers. (You can flatten the unrolled mesh by

4. Lay mesh on bricks so that it will fall in the middle of the concrete slab. The mesh reinforces the concrete, which is otherwise likely to crack.

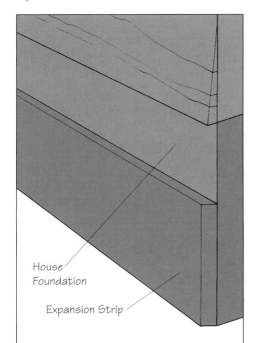

House Foundation

Expansion Strip

5. Expansion strips isolate the new concrete from existing foundations and sidewalks and prevent cracking as the concrete expands and contracts with the weather.

6. Begin the pour by placing concrete in the far corners of the forms. Spread the concrete with a hoe.

7. Remove trapped air from the wet concrete by working it with a spade, rake, or hoe. This is especially important near corners and edges, which are prone to breaking.

walking on it.) If more than one piece is required, overlap the pieces 6 inches, and tie them together with wire. Place stones or pieces of brick under the wire mesh to raise it about 2 inches above the gravel, so it will fall roughly in the middle of the finished slab. Avoid walking on the mesh once you've placed it.

5. Place expansion strips. If the patio butts against an existing structure, such as a house foundation, steps, or a walk, you must also place an expansion strip between the patio and the existing structure.

Expansion strips (available at masonry suppliers) consist of a soft, compressible fibrous material. Buy the strips in ½- by 4-inch by 8- to 10-foot lengths. Cut the material to length with a utility knife, and attach the strips to the existing structure with construction adhesive from a caulking gun.

6. Pour the concrete. Before the ready-mix arrives, sprinkle the subgrade with water, leaving it damp but puddle free. If you'll be hauling concrete from the truck to the patio with

wheelbarrows, build ramps to get over the forms by placing two-bys on concrete blocks. Transport fresh ready-mix as smoothly and gently as possible in a wheelbarrow with pneumatic tires to keep the ingredients from separating. Dump the concrete directly against the forms or against previously placed concrete. This helps consolidate the two loads, making the

patio stronger. Don't dump and drag concrete into place, as that separates the ingredients. Overfill the forms slightly.

7. Tamp out air bubbles. During the pour, you must remove air bubbles from the concrete by moving a shovel, hoe, or 2x4 up and down through the pour. This is especially important near the edges and corners. Do not overdo it, though! If you over-work the concrete, the water will separate and rise to the top, a condition called segregation, which weakens the concrete. Further settle the concrete against the perimeters by tapping the outside of the forms with a hammer.

8. Screed the surface. Start finishing the patio by screeding the surface to make it flat. Use a 2x4 1 or 2 feet longer than the distance between forms as the screed. If necessary, have a partner work from one side of the pour while you work from the other. Lay the screed across the forms, and slide it back and forth as you move it, keeping a little concrete ahead of it. If too much concrete builds up, shovel the excess away. Add more concrete to low spots with a spade as necessary. Then back up and strike off the low spot again.

Screed the surface twice. The first time, tilt the 2x4 forward to cut off the concrete. Strike off for several feet, lift the screed off, back up, and make a second pass. On the second pass, tilt the screed backward a little so it compresses the surface. Striking off should leave the slab even with no high spots and no low spots.

9. Float the surface smooth.
Immediately give the fresh slab a preliminary surfacing using either a darby or a bull float. The purpose of bull floating or darbying is to push stones just below the surface, level out ridges, and fill in depressions left by the screed. A bull float has a long handle so that you can reach quite a distance, making it especially good for finishing a patio. Push the bull float with the leading edge raised to keep it from tearing the surface. Then pull it back with the surface flat for maximum smoothing. Overlap the passes somewhat.

If you use a darby, move it flat along the surface in an arc, adding a saw-like motion. On a second pass, lift the leading edge of the darby to fill any holes left by the first pass.

To finish the inner portions that the darby won't reach, you'll have to

8. Guide a screed along the edging or along pipes to level the pour.

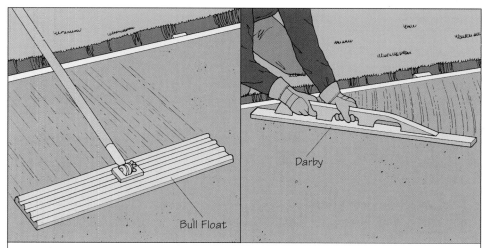

Bull Float

Darby

9. A large pour is smoothed with a bull float, while a smaller one is floated with a darby.

get out onto the slab with the help of a pair of knee boards. Make knee boards of ½-inch plywood with 2x2 end braces/handles. While finishing, you can support yourself by resting one hand on a float.

Avoid overworking the concrete, as that makes the surface less durable. Work until water begins to form on the surface of the pour. The water brings a fine coat of sand and cement with it, and too much will weaken the top layer of the pour.

When you're done floating, run a trowel around the perimeter of the

pour, between the pad and the form. This cuts the pad away from the form, and keeps it from chipping when you remove the form.

10. Edge the pad. The edge of a concrete pad should be rounded over slightly, to keep it from chipping during normal wear. It's done with a tool called an edger.

Put the blade of the edger in the space between the pad and the forms, and rest the surface of the edger on the pad. Move the edger back and forth, with the leading edge raised to prevent gouging. (Some edgers have a

10. Edging rounds the edge of the slab to prevent chipping and gives the pour a finished look.

11. Control joints purposely weaken the slab at regular intervals so that any cracks will fall in the joint rather than on the surface of the patio. Guide the jointer against a long plank.

rolled up leading edge and don't need to be lifted.) Work your way around the perimeter of the slab.

11. Cut the control joints.

Control joints are the grooves you see on sidewalks roughly every 3 feet. They're designed to control cracking as the slab hardens and are cut with a jointing tool. Get one with a ½-inch radius cutter that is 1 inch deep. Guide the tool along a straight board that rests on the forms and stretches across the pad. (If you're pouring the pad as a subbase for a brick or stone patio, control joints are not necessary.)

Control jointing should divide the patio into panels no larger than 8 feet square. A 16- by 24-foot patio, for example, would be jointed into six panels with one control joint 8 feet from the longer edge and a control joint 8 feet from each of the shorter edges. To be effective, control joints must be at least one-fourth the slab thickness—1 inch deep on a patio slab. Mark the forms to show where the joints will meet the edge of your patio.

The width-to-length ratio of the panels you create by jointing should be no greater than 1:1½; a 5 by 7½-foot panel is fine, but 5 by 8 feet is too long. Any unusual shapes that stick out from the rest of a patio need to be jointed off so that random cracks don't form.

If you've designed a patio that has interior wooden forms that stay in place, these forms serve as control

12. Follow edging and jointing immediately by floating. Carry an extra float and use it to support yourself as you work.

joints, as long as the maximum size of your panel is 8 feet square. Larger panels will require control joints.

12. Float the surface. Wait until the water sheen has left the surface of the concrete. Test the surface by standing on it. If your foot leaves a depression of no more than ¼ inch, the concrete is ready for a final floating.

The best hand float to use—especially for air-entrained concrete—is a magnesium float. Float by moving the tool flat against the surface in sweeping arcs, adding a slight sawing motion. Cut off any bumps, fill holes, and level the ridges as you go. Work from the edges first, then use a pair of knee boards to get out onto the slab.

If you stop working the surface at this point, it is likely to be rough and uneven. Edge, joint, and float a second time. This not only makes the surface smoother, it further compresses the concrete at the surface, making it stronger and more durable.

13. Let the pad cure. To gain maximum strength and durability, your concrete patio should be cured for five to seven days. The longer the better. The most practical methods of curing are by spraying on a curing compound or by spreading 6-mil polyethylene sheeting over the slab and weighing it down with sand. Do not use curing compound on a slab that is to be covered with bricks or stones. After curing, allow the slab to air dry completely before being exposed to any de-icers.

13. Concrete cures, rather than dries. For a strong surface, keep the patio damp while it cures. Cover it with plastic and sprinkle it with water occasionally for five to seven days.

A Broomed Surface

Running a broom over the top of a wet concrete pad creates a slip-resistant surface that is a good idea on almost any patio. If the pad you are pouring is to be a subbase for brick or stone, brooming provides a good surface for mortar to cling to. You can create the surface with almost any broom, but a soft-bristle push broom works best. (Concrete suppliers sell a concrete broom made especially for creating broomed surfaces.)

To broom a surface, pour the pad as you normally would: Float, edge, joint, and float again. Then trowel the surface, preferably with a well worn 4- by 14-inch concrete-finishing steel trowel. (A worn trowel is less likely to dig in.)

The concrete is ready to be troweled once the water sheen left by floating leaves the surface and when you can work without bringing any water to the surface. Hold the trowel flat on the surface and move it in sweeping, half-overlapping arcs. If necessary, use knee boards to get out onto the surface.

For a rough-textured broomed surface, broom immediately after steel troweling. For a finer texture, wait longer. Experiment on small sections near the edge. Trowel out any mistakes, and choose the timing that produces the texture you like.

Dampen the bristles before applying the broom to the surface. Move it in wavy, overlapping lines across the patio. For the best results, pull the broom across the surface in a direction that is perpendicular to the general direction of foot traffic.

FLAGSTONE, BRICK, AND TILE PATIOS

The most elegant-looking patios are made of flagstone, brick, or tile, and are mortared together. These patios wear and weather well, and are quite durable. Like mortared walks, mortared patios sit on a concrete slab to provide support and prevent cracking. Pouring a slab and applying the brick, stone, or tile, is a serious time commitment. You can often shortcut the process by applying stone or brick over an existing concrete patio.

If you'd like to build a stone or brick patio from the ground up, pour a slab as described in "Making a Concrete Patio," page 176. Dig and lay the base so that pad elevation will place the pavers at the desired height. Then follow the directions below.

Covering an existing concrete patio. The concrete base slab may be new or old, but it must be clean; sound; and free of oil, grease, and loose materials such as dust, paint, and efflorescence. Clean the slab thoroughly with a solution of 1 part muriatic acid to 9 parts water. This is a strong acid: For safety's sake, pour the water first, then the acid. Wear heavy rubber gloves, long sleeves, goggles, and a vapor respirator. Apply the solution with a stiff-bristle brush. Rinse thoroughly with clean water.

A scaled surface that is structurally sound presents no problem because the new surface will cover it. If the slab has settled unevenly, in most cases it can be corrected by installing the units on a thick, corrective layer of mortar. Every crack and joint in the old slab, however, must coincide with a joint in the new paving. Otherwise, movement across the crack or joint will damage the new paving.

Cover all joints and cracks in the base slab with something to hold the mortar—½- by ½-inch sticky-back weather stripping will work. Follow the cracks faithfully.

Paving raises the elevation of a slab—make sure you have room for what you're planning. It wouldn't do to

This tiled patio makes an elegant statement in a well manicured backyard. The mortared surface is rigid and would crack if the ground underneath shifted. A concrete pad set slightly below grade provides a foundation that prevents cracking.

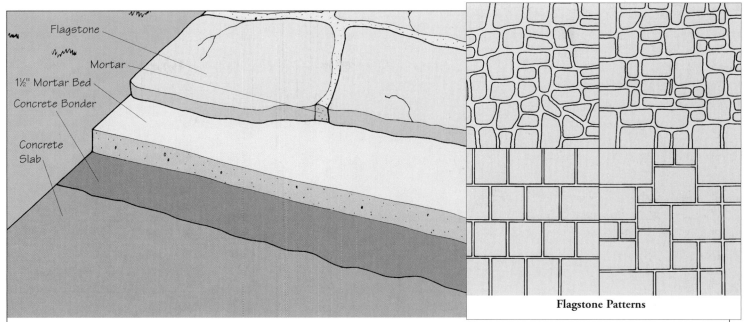

Flagstone Patterns

Covering an existing concrete patio. Upgrade an existing patio by putting mortar and flagstone or other paving units on the old concrete surface. A thin coat of paintlike concrete bonder helps the mortar adhere to the slab.

have your patio end up higher than the house floor, for example. In fact, to prevent flooding, make sure that there is at least a 1-inch drop from the threshold to the new patio surface.

Flagstone Patios

Flagstone is not a type of stone, but a style of cutting stone. It falls into two classifications: sawed flagging and natural-bed flagging. Sawed flagging is regular, almost like manufactured pavers, and it lays quickly. Natural-bed flagging is rough-textured and requires some thought as to fitting the units into your pattern.

The stone itself may be slate, argillite, or bluestone. Slate and argillite flagstone is thin and is available in rectangles with either cleft or ground surfaces. Bluestone flagging is available both in sawed sizes and natural-cleft random patterns. Most stone is sold by the ton. Check with your dealer.

Cutting and shaping flagstone.
You'll often have to trim flagstone to fit it against an edge or another stone. Use a pencil or crayon to mark the pieces of stone that need to be trimmed for a better fit. For small sections, trim the pieces off with a brick hammer. Cut larger pieces to fit by

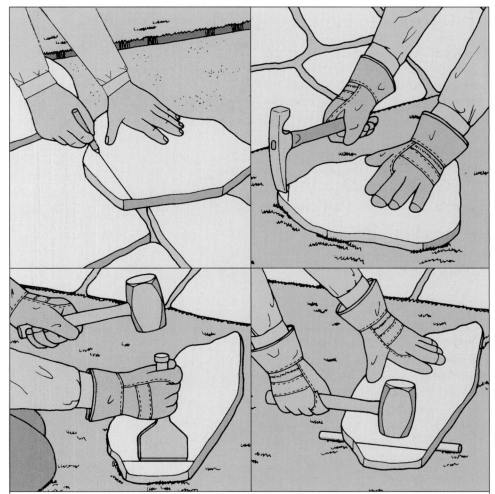

Cutting and shaping flagstone. Hold the stone to be cut over those already in place, and mark the cutting line (top left). Small sections can be nicked off with a mason's hammer (top right). For large cuts, score along the line with a chisel (above left). Split the stone along the scored line by placing it over a section of pipe and gently striking it with a hammer (above right).

placing the stone on the ground and scoring along the line with a brickset. Prop the scored flagstone on a board or pipe, and tap off the unwanted piece with a hammer.

1. Fit the irregular stones.

Cutting and fitting irregular stones can be time-consuming, and it's something you don't want to do once you've mixed the mortar. Cut and fit stones for a portion of the patio ahead of time. Lay out a section of around 30 square feet. For a formal look, trim the stone to align with the edges of the pad. For a more random look, leave the edges in their original shapes.

For irregular stone, choose pieces or cut them to fit neatly together. Aim to lay the stones with 1-inch joints. This takes a bit of trimming with cleft stone, and there is no need to be concerned if the joints are wider or narrower in spots. Trim the stone to follow the joints and cracks in the base slab. Once you've cut the stones, move them off the slab, keeping them in the same relative positions. Put the stones back on the patio one at a time once the mortar is in place.

Milled, rectangular flagstones won't need to be trimmed, except perhaps at cracks and the edges of the patio.

2. Coat the surface with a bonder.
A smooth concrete surface should be painted with a commercially made concrete bonder before the mortar is applied. Use the bonder full strength according to the directions on the container, spreading it over the slab with a brush or roller. (Bonder may be mixed into the mortar, too, following directions.) Coat a section that is about 10 square feet—you'll need to place the mortar while the bonder is still wet.

3. Lay the mortar bed.
The stone is set on a bed of mortar made from portland cement and fine (mortar) sand, usually in 1:4 proportions. Buy the ingredients as a ready-mix mortar, or mix the sand and cement together with a hoe. Then mix in water until the mixture has the consistency of damp sand. Mix no more than you

1. Before laying mortar, fit individual stones in place along a section of the patio.

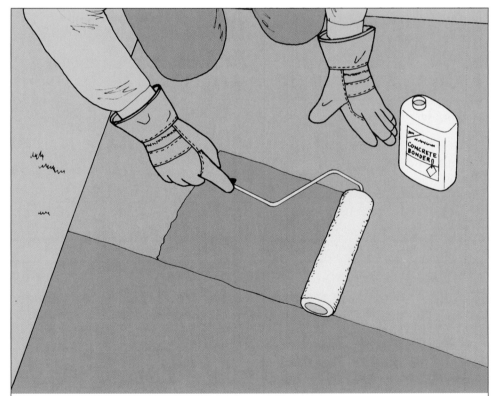

2. Coat the surface with a concrete bonder to increase adhesion between the pad and the mortar.

can use in one hour. If you're using bags, one 60-pound bag is plenty. If you're mixing your own, mix about ½ cubic foot. Adjust the amount as experience dictates.

Spread no more than 10 square feet of mortar at a time. While the bonder is still wet, spread fresh mortar over the slab to a thickness of 1½ inches. Strike off the mortar to form a flat bed. If you installed edging, guide a screed across it to level the bed. If there's no edging, lay a pair of pipes with a 1½-inch outside diameter on each side of the bed. Guide the screed across them to level the bed.

Scrape off mortar over joints and cracks in the base slab so they can be readily seen and won't get paved over. Cover the cracks with a closed-cell foam strip sold as "backer rods." This keeps them from filling in during subsequent work.

4. Lay the pavers. Starting in one corner, lay the first paving unit. Work along the edge toward the opposite side.

Tap each stone into the mortar with a rubber mallet, and check it with a level. Correct out-of-level stones by adding a little mortar or scraping some out. Lay down plywood as a work surface so that you won't stand directly on freshly laid flagstones.

When several flagstones have been laid, lift each one up in turn and paint the bottom with a thick-cream slurry of portland cement and water. Reset the stone and tap it back into place. (This is unique to stone and helps provide a stronger bond. You need not lift and reset brick.)

Lay the units one row at a time, fitting the stones and laying the mortar one small section at a time. Continue laying mortar and stone until you've finished the patio.

5. Grout the joints. Let the mortar bed set overnight so that the units are firmly in place.

You can mix your own joint grout or purchase a commercial grout in a choice of colors. If you're mixing your own grout, use 1 part portland cement to 2 parts mortar sand for stone.

Place the grout between the stones with a margin trowel, which has a rectangular blade about 1 inch wide or with a small pointed trowel shaped like a bricklayer's trowel. Build the joint level with the face of the stone, compress it, and build the joint level with the face of the stone again. Avoid getting grout on the face of the stone. Do not grout over joints and cracks in the base slab. Leave them open. Once the grout

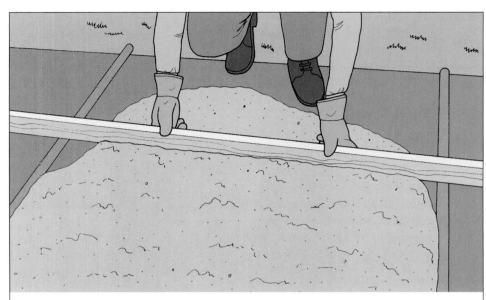

3. Put a 10-foot-square section of mortar on the pad, and screed it flat by guiding a two-by across pipes temporarily laid in place.

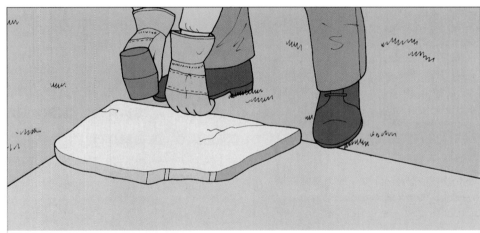

4. Lay flagstone carefully in the smooth layer of mortar, starting in one corner and working in rows. Tap each stone down firmly with a rubber mallet to seat it.

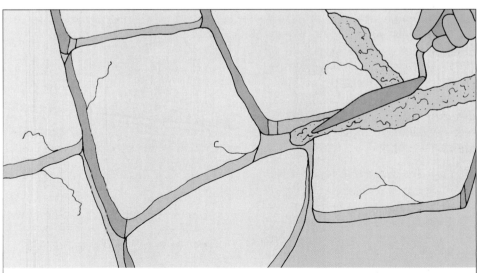

5. Place grout between the joints with either a pointing or a margin trowel. Immediately clean grout from the flagstones using a damp sponge, cleaning the stones but not the joints.

reaches its initial set, compact and shape the joint by pulling a jointing tool across it. The grout is ready to work when it holds the impression you make by pressing your thumb into it. A ¾-inch copper tube makes a good jointing tool.

About 5 or 6 hours after grouting, rub any excess grout from the stone with a dry cloth. Then with a clean, wet sponge, wipe each unit toward the joints. Do not sponge onto the joints, however, as that will only pick up more grout. When the surface is dry, caulk the open joints over cracks in the base slab with a silicone rubber caulk.

Concrete grout and mortar should not be allowed to dry too rapidly, so keep the pavement moist for at least three days—longer if practical—by frequent sprinkling or covering with a 6-mil polyethylene sheet. Check with your dealer about a non-yellowing protective coating to enhance the beauty of your patio.

Tiling a Patio

Ceramic patio tiles create a formal look unlike any other tiling material. Tiles used outdoors not only must be low in water absorption to resist damage from freezing and thawing but should have a surface that does not get slippery when wet. The tiles may be either glazed or unglazed, but should wear well. What's more, it is vital that the tile you select be approved by its manufacturer for outdoor use.

A large number of ceramic tiles qualify, but quarry tiles are among the most popular. Quarry tiles are available in a variety of earth tones and come in 6-by-6- and 12-by-12-inch squares, as well as in rectangular brick shapes.

In tile work, the tiles are set in a mortar bed, and the joints are filled with a similar but thinner mixture called grout. The materials are very similar. For tile work, the best bet is to buy both in commercially prepared mixtures.

Laying a Brick Patio

Laying a brick patio in mortar is much like laying flagstones, with a few differences. First of all, unlike much flagging, paving bricks are regular units, so they can be laid in patterns. Of the many types of bricks, be sure to specify Class SX brick for patio use. Most brick patterns require a brick in which two brick widths plus one mortar joint equal one brick length. To see whether the bricks you've chosen will work, lay out a three- or four-brick section of the pattern while you're still at the brick yard.

Brick joints are usually ½-inch wide. Pieces of ½-inch plywood can be used as spacers between the bricks while laying them. Stretch a string or place a board along the edge of your work to make sure you're laying the bricks in a straight line with consistent spacing between courses.

If they're dry, bricks should be dampened so they bond well with the underlying mortar. They may be set either in 1:4 portland cement to sand or in Type M mortar—1 part masonry cement and 6 parts mortar sand. (Common prepackaged Type S mortar can be enriched to make Type M by adding 1 part portland cement to 2 parts of Type S mix.) While it's a good idea to tap each brick into the mortar, do it lightly. The units are small.

For increased adhesion between the bricks and their base, you can mix the mortar with a concrete bonder. Follow the directions on the container.

Brick lends itself to a trick that professionals use to keep mortar from sticking to the brick faces. After the bricks are firm in their mortar bed, apply clear sealer to the faces only, without any excess sealer that could run down the sides. A short-nap paint roller should do the job. When that dries, apply mortar between the bricks.

Mortar stains can be cleaned from bricks with chemical cleaners. Ask your dealer for a brick cleaner that's safe to use, and follow the label's directions.

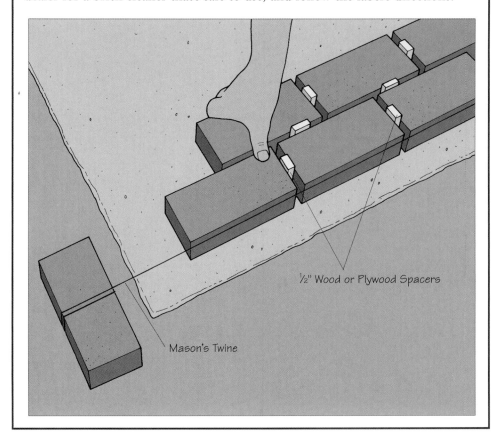

½" Wood or Plywood Spacers

Mason's Twine

The most practical method for laying patio tiles is called the thin-set method. In it, either dry-set mortar or latex portland-cement mortar is applied to the concrete slab and combed with a proper notched trowel to bed the tiles. A thin-set bed can be less than ⅛ inch and is ideal if you're tiling over an existing patio and you're concerned about raising the surface too much.

To raise a slab or to correct one with the wrong slope, apply a thicker bed, made with portland cement and sand, mixed 1:5. Lay a hefty 1¼-inch mortar bed on the slab. This method is useful for bridging irregularities or when you need to reshape a surface to improve drainage.

All three mortars are available commercially prepared. Adding a latex or acrylic additive to the mortar and grout when you mix them allows the mortar to cure without it having to be constantly damp. Follow the directions on the additive package when mixing it into your mortar.

If you're using an existing slab, it should be structurally sound and free

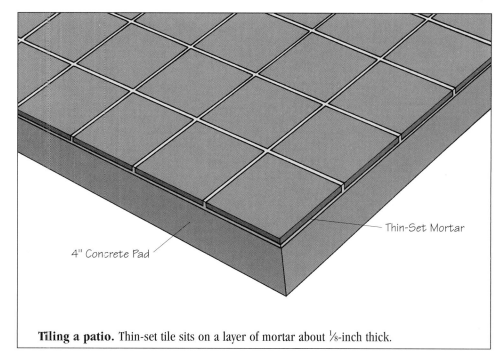

Tiling a patio. Thin-set tile sits on a layer of mortar about ⅛-inch thick.

4" Concrete Pad

Thin-Set Mortar

of oil and waxy films and foreign matter. No form oil, curing compounds, or powdery efflorescence should be present. Clean the slab with muriatic acid as described in "Covering an Existing Concrete Patio," page 182. The slab should be properly sloped, well-drained, suitably flat, and not subject to dampness from beneath. If the surface has been troweled, be sure to coat it with a concrete bonder.

If you're pouring a new bed, follow the directions in "Making a Concrete Patio," page 176, and give it a broomed surface.

With all ceramic tiling, any cracks in the base must coincide with joints between tiles. Fill these joints with a silicone rubber caulk.

1. Spread the mortar. To tile over a concrete slab following the thin-set method, first dampen the concrete

Cutting Tile

For cutting tile, you'll need a snap cutter. Most snap cutters consist of a metal frame that holds the tile in position, a carbide-tipped blade or wheel that scores the tile, and a device that snaps the tile once it's scored. Position the tile, draw the carbide cutter across the tile to score it, then press down on the handle until the tile snaps. Rent this tile-cutting tool from a masonry supplier.

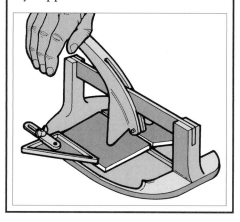

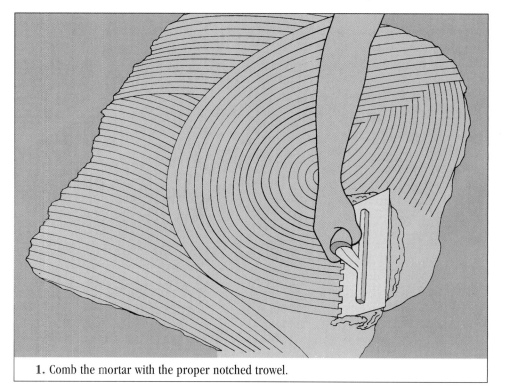

1. Comb the mortar with the proper notched trowel.

slab. Dry-set mortar should be mixed to a smooth-paste consistency, according to label's instructions. Then use the flat side of a notched trowel to spread mortar out over the slab, aiming for about a ½-inch layer. Comb the mortar with the notched side of the trowel, holding it at a 45-degree angle to the slab. Although the drying time varies from mortar to mortar, it's usually not very long: 10 to 15 minutes. Don't spread more mortar than can be covered in that time. Do not use mortar once it has skinned over.

2. Set the tiles. When setting individual ceramic tiles, you must allow space between them for the grout joints. To ensure uniform joints, buy molded plastic spacers from the tile dealer. These small plastic crosses come in various sizes; ½ inch is the typical space between quarry tiles. Some spacers can be removed (before the adhesive cures) and reused. Others can be left in place and grouted over.

Set the tiles in the freshly combed mortar using tile spacers at the corners to get even joints. You can press the tiles down slightly, as long as the mortar comes up no more than one-third of the way into the joints. Minimum thin-set mortar thickness after the tiles are installed is ³⁄₃₂ inch.

Some tiles have a textured back. To ensure 100 percent mortar coverage with no voids to collect water and freeze, coat the back of such tiles with thin-set grout. You can test the coverage you're getting by pulling off several tiles that are already laid.

Before the mortar hardens, level the tiles with a piece of scrap 2x8 and a hammer. Place the scrap on the tiles, and tap gently, pressing the tiles into place and leveling them.

3. Grout the joints. The next day, pry out all tile spacers, if necessary. Lightly dampen the tiles, and spread properly mixed commercial tile grout over them. Work diagonally across the tiles, pushing the mortar into the joints with a rubber grout float. Let the grout set for about 15 minutes. Then wipe the tiles clean with a damp sponge. Let them dry for about

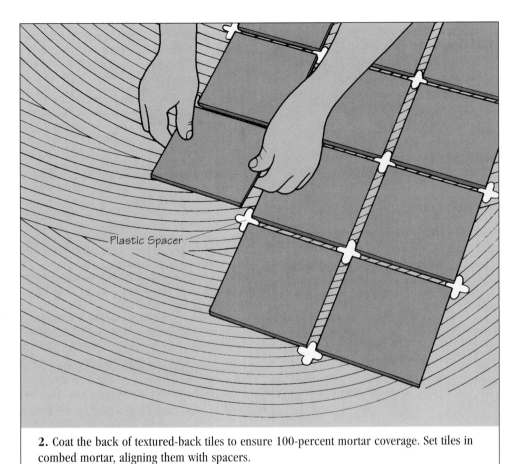

Plastic Spacer

2. Coat the back of textured-back tiles to ensure 100-percent mortar coverage. Set tiles in combed mortar, aligning them with spacers.

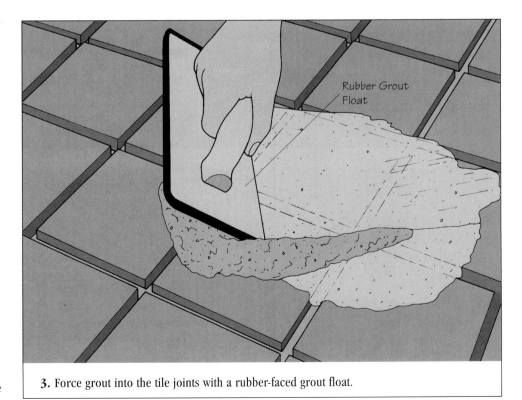

Rubber Grout Float

3. Force grout into the tile joints with a rubber-faced grout float.

40 minutes, until a haze forms and the grout firms. Polish off the haze with a soft, clean cloth. If you used a latex additive in the mortar and grout, damp curing of tiles is unnecessary. Otherwise, cover the tiles with 6-mil plastic and keep them damp for three to seven days; the longer the better.

Actual dimensions The measured dimensions of a masonry unit.

Aggregate Crushed stone, gravel, or other material added to cement to make concrete or mortar. Gravel and crushed stone are considered course aggregate; sand is considered fine aggregate.

Backfill Sand, gravel, pea stone, crushed stone, slag, or cinders used for filling around foundations or piping. In general, to back fill is to replace earth in a trench or around a foundation.

Bat A brick that is cut in half lengthwise.

Bed joint Horizontal masonry joint, opposed to a vertical masonry joint (head Joint). Also called beds.

Brick Clay that is molded to shape and fired at high temperatures in a large kiln or oven. The color of the natural clay determines the color of the brick.

Broom finish The texture created when a concrete surface is stroked with a stiff broom while the concrete is still curing.

Buttering Placing mortar on a masonry unit using a trowel.

Collar joint The vertical joint between wythes.

Concave joint A masonry joint that is recessed and formed in mortar. A curved steel jointing tool is used to make a concave joint.

Concrete Fresh concrete is a semifluid mixture of portland cement, sand (fine aggregate), gravel, or crushed stone.

Concrete block A masonry unit that consists of an outside shell with a hollow center that is divided by two or three vertical webs. The ends of the unit may have flanges that accept mortar and join with adjacent blocks, or they may have smooth ends for corners and the ends of walls.

Concrete pavers Commonly used for patios and walks, concrete pavers come in a number of shapes and colors and are designed to be laid in a sand base without mortar; some interlock to form repeating patterns.

Control joints Special joints, also called contraction joints, that are tooled into the surface and make concrete crack in straight lines at planned locations.

Curing The process by which concrete becomes solid and develops strength. Proper moisture reduces cracking and shrinkage.

Darby A long tool used for smoothing the surface of a concrete slab.

Edging joints The rounded edges of a pour that are resistant to cracking.

Excavation To dig out earth or soil so that a slab will be supported by a subgrade that is hard, uniformly graded, and well drained.

Expansion joint A planned break in the continuous surface of a patio into which a compressible material has been placed to absorb pressure when the surface expands when heated. This joint prevents buckling or crumbling of the surface. Expansion joints are required wherever dissimilar materials adjoin because they will expand and contract at different rates.

Face brick A type of brick used when consistency in appearance is required. A batch of face brick will be quite uniform in color, size, texture, and face structure.

Flagstone pattern "Carving" a design into concrete to create a pattern.

Floating The process of smoothing the surface of a pour with a float made of steel, aluminum, magnesium, or wood. This action drives large aggregate below the surface.

Footing Support for garden walls of brick, block, or stone. Generally made of concrete, footings are also used for stairs and are usually located below the local frost line to avoid problems from frost heave.

Formwork The forms or molds that contain and shape wet concrete. Forms are usually built from lumber; plywood is used for curved sections.

Frost heave Shifting or upheaval of the ground resulting from alternate freezing and thawing of water in the soil.

Frost line The maximum depth to which soil freezes in the winter. The local building department can provide information of the frost-line depth in your area.

Header The brick position in a wall in which the brick is rotated 90° from the stretcher position so that the end is facing out.

Hydration The process of cement particles chemically reacting with water. When this happens the concrete hardens into a durable material.

Mason's line A length of twine that is held at each end by an L-shaped block. The line can be stretched tight and is used as a straightedge guide, permitting the mason to check the evenness of the course being laid.

Mortar A mixture of cementitious materials, fine aggregate, and water. Mortar is used to bond bricks or blocks.

Nominal dimensions The dimensions of a masonry unit plus one mortar joint.

Portland cement A mixture of burned lime, iron, silica, and alumina. This mixture is put through a kiln, then ground into a fine powder and packaged for sale. The cement is the same color as the gray limestone quarried near Portland, England.

Prepackaged concrete mix A mix that combines cement, sand, and gravel in the correct proportions and requires only the addition of water to create fresh concrete.

Ready-mix concrete Wet concrete that is transported from a concrete supplier. The concrete is ready to pour.

Rebar Reinforcing bar (called rebar for short), is used for concrete that will carry a heavy load, such as footings, foundation walls, columns, and pilasters.

Reinforcing mesh Steel wires woven or welded into a grid of 6 or 10 inch squares. The mesh is primarily used in flatwork, such as walks and patios.

Retaining walls A wall built to hold back a slope of ground.

Rowlock A brick laid on its face edge horizontally so that the face is visible in the wall.

Sailor A brick laid on its end vertically so that the end is visible in the wall.

Screeding Using a straight 2x4 moved from one end of a concrete pour to the other to strike off excess concrete.

Segregation A condition that results when the concrete is overworked—such as when trying to remove air bubbles—and the water separates and rises to the top.

Soap A brick that is halved in width.

Soldier A brick standing upright with the edge facing out.

Split A brick that is halved in height.

Steel reinforcement Reinforcing mesh or rebar that is used to strengthen concrete.

Stretcher A brick that is laid lengthwise in the course.

Troweling Finishing the concrete after it has been screeded. This finishing step is for interior concrete applications and concrete without air-entrainment.

Weephole A hole in a retaining wall that allows water to seep through.

Wythe The vertical section of a wall that is equal to the width of the masonry unit.

INDEX

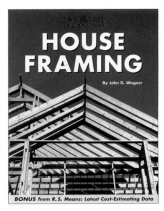
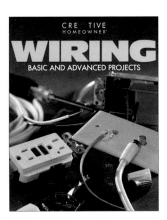

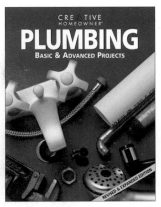

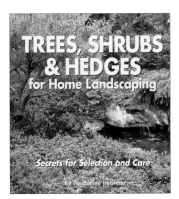
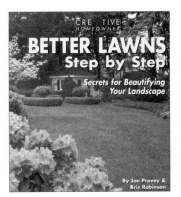